Withdrawn

The Relationship Between
Social and Cognitive Development

The Jean Piaget Symposium Series
Available from LEA

SIGEL, I. E., BRODZINSKY, D. M., & GOLINKOFF, R. M. (Eds.) • New Directions in Piagetian Theory and Practice

OVERTON, W. F. (Ed.) • Relationships Between Social and Cognitive Development

LIBEN, L. S. (Ed.) • Piaget and the Foundations of Knowledge

SCHOLNICK, E. K. (Ed.) • New Trends in Conceptual Representation: Challenges to Piaget's Theory?

The Relationship Between Social and Cognitive Development

Edited by
Willis F. Overton
Temple University

LEA LAWRENCE ERLBAUM ASSOCIATES, PUBLISHERS
1983   Hillsdale, New Jersey   London

Lawrence Erlbaum Associates, Inc., Publishers
365 Broadway
Hillsdale, New Jersey 07642

Library of Congress Cataloging in Publication Data
Main entry under title:

The Relationship between social and cognitive development.

(The Jean Piaget Symposium series ; 2)
Based on papers presented at the 10th Annual
Symposium of the Jean Piaget Society, held May 31–June 2,
1979, in Philadelphia, Pa.
Includes bibliographical references and indexes.
Contents: Empathy, guilt, and social cognition /
Martin L. Hoffman—Domains and categories in social-
cognitive development / Elliot Turiel—Cognition of
physical and social events / Frank B. Murray—[etc.]
1. Social perception in children—Congresses.
2. Social interaction in children—Congresses. 3. Piaget,
Jean, 1896– —Congresses. I. Overton, Willis F.
II. Jean Piaget Society. Symposium (10th : 1979 :
Philadelphia, Pa.) III. Jean Piaget Society. IV. Series.
[DNLM: 1. Cognition—In infancy and childhood—
Congresses. 2. Social perception—In infancy and child-
hood—Congresses. WS 105.5.C7 R382 1980]
BF723.S6R44 1983   155.4'13   83-5678
ISBN 0-89859-249-6

BF
723
S6
R44
1983

Printed in the United States of America
10   9   8   7   6   5   4   3   2   1

Contents

Preface

The primary purpose of this volume is to stimulate further thinking and research on the interrelationships between social, emotional, and cognitive development. The chapters in the volume were initially presented at the 10th Annual Symposium of the Jean Piaget Society and later modified in the light of various discussions that took place at the symposium itself.

In choosing a theme for the symposium, the Board of Directors of the Jean Piaget Society sought a topic area of both contemporary and long-range significance to the field of developmental psychology. As the field of social cognition emerged in the late 1960s it was primarily dominated by attempts to apply Piaget's cognitive theory to the developing child's reasoning about social phenomena such as the self, social roles, and relations between people. At the time both the conceptual issues and research methods appeared relatively clearly defined.

As investigations in this field continued into the middle and late 1970s however, it became increasingly evident that the relation between cognitive and social development was not as straightforward as originally suggested. New problems began to be posed, such as the issue of whether special processes are required for the understanding of social events as distinct from those required for the understanding of physical events. With these problems came also critiques of the adequacy of early research methods, and proposals for new methods, such as those involving contextual analyses of social phenomena. Finally, it became more obvious that any adequate treatment of the relations between cognitive and social development must include considerations of the role played by affective or emotional processes.

It was within this historical context that the Piaget Society chose to focus on interrelationships between social, emotional, and cognitive development as its theme for the 10th Annual Symposium. This theme, which is broader than, but includes the traditional area of social cognition, is clearly of contemporary significance in the early 1980s and it promises to be of deepening future importance for understanding of the general processes of development.

Having established the theme, leading investigators in areas related to it were invited to present their current positions with respect to conceptual and research issues and to confront each other in discussions across the course of the symposium. Other experts in the field were invited to present formal critiques and elaborations of the position papers and to join in the general discussions.

The present volume is the result of these presentations and discussions. As anticipated, a number of the chapters focus on contemporary issues, problems, and research related to the way the developing child comes to understand its social world. The importance of the inclusion of affective processes in any analysis of social cognition is emphasized by Hoffman in chapter 1. Hoffman describes a theoretical model of empathy and maintains that the development of empathy represents an affective-cognitive synthesis. Further, Hoffman stresses that social cognition and social-cognitive development are best understood as "abstractions from what is essentially a matrix of interacting cognitive and affective process (p. 47)."

The role of emotions is considered from a different perspective by Harter in Chapter 6. Beginning from a therapeutic orientation with the problem posed by the young child's difficulty in acknowledging opposing feelings, Harter explores the research question of how a cognitive developmental approach illuminates changes in the child's understanding of emotional concepts.

In Chapter 7, Zimiles, in turn, explores the question of whether the basic problem is the child's understanding of emotional concepts, or the inability to express and feel forbidden emotions.

In Chapter 2 Turiel emphasizes the need to carefully consider the specific nature of social domains in approaching an understanding of social-cognitive development. Turiel critiques earlier research in this area and presents a model of social cognition and that integrates both structural and contextual components.

In Chapter 3, Murray notes that an important issue raised by Turiel and others (See also Damon, Chapter 4) concerns the question of the distinction between the cognition of social and physical events. Murray argues that various physical domains have the same distinctness and independence that Turiel claims for the social domains. Further, in both domains a major developmental problem concerns the establishment of the idea of necessity.

Although in earlier works Damon has argued for the distinctness of physical and social cognition, in Chapter 4 he addresses several general controversies and considers similarities between the two domains. A major point that he shares with others (See also chapters 2,3,7,8) is that knowledge develops out of social interactions.

In Chapter 5, Bearison discusses a general trend among investigations of social cognition (See chapters 2,4,7). This is a movement towards a contextual analysis with less concern for the formalization of underlying structures. Bearison cautions that this approach faces the danger of losing the developmental dimension because contexts are not developmentally ordered.

In Chapter 8, Youniss discusses the history and implications of a traditional model in which social existance and social functioning have been explained on the basis of the organism's individual character. As an alternative he offers a model and supporting evidence for the view that social relating is the starting point and individuation a later product.

In Chapter 9, Sutton-Smith considers several theoretical and research issues concerning both social and cognitive features of play. In Chapter 10, Forman goes on to consider some of these issues in the context of recent Piagetian formulations.

Special thanks are expressed to the members of the Board of Directors of the Jean Piaget Society for their support throughout the preparation of this volume and to Mr. Shawn Ward for his editorial assistance.

Willis F. Overton

The Relationship Between
Social and Cognitive Development

1 Empathy, Guilt, and Social Cognition

Martin L. Hoffman
University of Michigan

For several years I have been putting together a theoretical model of empathy, especially the empathic response to another person's pain or distress, and guilt, which are two of the major social affects. There is empirical as well as theoretical justification for thinking of empathy and guilt as prosocial affects, as the research—whether anecdotal, correlational, or experimental—indicates that arousing empathic distress or guilt predisposes a person to help others. What seems appropriate in view of the theme of this volume, is first to summarize the latest version of my theory of empathic development, making more explicit than in the past the rationale and connection between affective and cognitive processes. Secondly, I discuss a type of guilt that relates to empathy and highlights the interaction between affect and cognition and present a speculative account of how it develops. Finally, I discuss the implications of empathic affect for social cognition. The motivational aspect of empathy and guilt—the fact that they both include a disposition to act altruistically or morally to others—which has been heavily researched and is reviewed elsewhere (Hoffman, 1982b), is mentioned here only in passing.

EMPATHY

Empathy has been defined over the years in many ways, most of which reduce to two basic categories: empathy as *cognitive awareness* of another person's inner states (thoughts, feelings, perceptions, intentions); and empathy as a vicarious *affective* response to others, that is, an affective response that is more appropriate to someone else's situation than one's own. My primary interest is in the second

1

definition, empathy as vicarious affect, although, as will be made clear, cognition cannot be ignored.

There is general agreement among the few writers on the topic that affective empathy is largely involuntary. Consider the following response made by one of Bandura and Rosenthal's (1966) subjects, who was given a strong dose of epinephrine before observing someone being administered a series of electric shocks:

> After the first three or four shocks, I thought about the amount of pain for the other guy. Then I began to think, to minimize my own discomfort. I recall looking at my watch, looking out the window, and checking things about the room. I recall that the victim received a shock when I was thinking about the seminar, and that I didn't seem to notice the discomfort as much in this instance.

This quotation illustrates the involuntary dimension of empathic arousal. It also illustrates the empathic discomfort produced in the observer and the use of defensive strategies that serve to reduce the discomfort. In general, people find it difficult to avoid empathizing, especially with someone in pain or discomfort, unless they engage in perceptual or cognitive strategies like turning away from the victim or thinking about other things. If one pays attention to the victim, one will ordinarily respond empathically. The reason for this is that very simple, primitive psychological mechanisms appear to underlie empathy. Let me now describe these mechanisms.

Vicarious Affect Arousal

There appear to be at least five distinct modes of empathic arousal, which vary in degree of perceptual and cognitive involvement, type of eliciting stimulus (e.g., facial, situational, symbolic), and amount and kind of past experience required. They are here presented roughly in order of their appearance developmentally.

1. Primary Circular Reaction and the Reactive Newborn Cry.   It has long been known that infants cry to the sound of someone else's cry. The first controlled study of this reactive cry was done by Simner (1971), who found it in 2- and 3-day-olds. He also established that the cry was not simply a response to a noxious physical stimulus, as the infants did not cry as much to equally loud and intense nonhuman sounds. There thus appears to be something especially unpleasant about the sound of the human cry. Simner's findings have been replicated in 1-day-olds by Sagi and Hoffman (1976), who report in addition that the subject's cry is not a simple imitative vocal response lacking an affective component. Rather, it is vigorous, intense, and indistinguishable from the spontaneous cry of an infant who is in actual distress. No one yet knows the reason for this reactive cry, although I can see three possible explanations: (a) it is innate; (b) it is a primary circular reaction: Because the infant cannot tell the difference between the sound of its own cry and the sound of someone else's cry, the sound of someone else's cry produces a cry response in the infant. The infant then cries to the sound of its own cry, and so on; (c) the sound of the infant's cry is associated with its own past distress—perhaps at birth. Consequently, the sound of the infant's cry serves as a conditioned stimulus for its own cry response. Because of the confusion between its own and someone else's cry, the sound of someone else's cry may also serve as a conditioned stimulus for the infant's cry response.

Regardless of which explanation is correct, the fact remains that infants respond to a cue of distress in others by experiencing distress themselves. This reactive cry therefore must be considered as a possible early, rudimentary precursor of empathy, though not a full empathic response, because it lacks any awareness of what is happening. It is also possible that the reactive cry may actually contribute to empathic distress later on because the co-occurence of distress cues in others and actual distress in self may lead to an expectation of distress in self when one perceives distress cues in others. This leads to the next mode.

2. Classical Conditioning.   The second mode requires more perceptual discrimination capability and therefore appears a bit later developmentally than the reactive newborn cry. It is a type of direct classical conditioning of empathy that results from the experience of observing the distress of another person at the same time that one is having a direct experience of distress. The result is that distress cues from others become conditioned stimuli that evoke feelings of distress in the self. Aronfreed and Paskal (1966) created the necessary co-occurrence of distress in the child and distress cues from someone else by subjecting the child to an aversive sound at the same time that the experimenter (who presumably heard an even more aversive sound through earphones) showed a pained expression. This may seem like a contrived way to achieve the needed co-occurrence between distress in self and distress cues from another but it has a great deal in common with something that may often occur in real life, namely the bodily transfer of the caretaker's affective state to the infant through physical handling (Hoffman, 1978). For example, if the mother feels anxious or tense while holding the infant, the mother's body may stiffen and her distress is thus transferred to the infant. After that, the facial and verbal expressions accompanying the mother's distress may become conditioned stimuli that can evoke distress in the infant even when there is no physical contact between them. Furthermore, through stimulus generalization, when *other* people show similar facial and verbal expressions of distress, this may evoke a feeling of distress in the infant. In this way, cues of distress in others become conditioned stimuli for distress in the child. This mechanism may explain the behaviors fitting Sullivan's (1940) definition of empathy as a form of "nonverbal contagion and communion"

between mother and infant, in which the infant is viewed as automatically empathizing with the mother, feeling euphoric when she does and anxious when
she is.

3. Direct Association.   A more indirect type of empathic conditioning was
described some time ago by Humphrey (1922). It holds that when we observe
someone experiencing an emotion, his or her facial expression, voice, posture,
or any other cue in the situation that reminds us of past situations in which we
experienced that emotion may evoke a similar emotion in us. The usual example
cited is the boy who sees another child fall down or cut himself and cry. The
sight of the child falling, the sight of the blood, the sound of the cry, or any other
distress cue from the victim or the situation that reminds the boy of his own past
experiences of pain may evoke the unpleasant affect associated with that experience. This mode of empathic distress arousal is not limited to distress originating
in physically communicated tensions or confined to early infancy. Furthermore,
it does not require the co-occurence of distress in self and distress cues from
others. The only requirement is that the observer have *past* experiences of pain or
discomfort. The feelings of distress that accompany these experiences are then
evoked by distress cues from the victim that call up any of those earlier experiences. It is thus a far more general associative mechanism, one that may provide
the basis for a multiplicity of distress experiences with which children, and adults
as well, can empathize.

4. Mimicry.   A fourth mechanism of empathic arousal was described seventy years ago by Lipps (1906). For Lipps, empathy is an innate, isomorphic
response to another person's expression of emotion. There are two steps: (1) the
observer automatically imitates the other with slight movements in facial expression and posture (''motor mimicry''); (2) this then creates inner kinesthetic
cues in the observer that contribute (through afferent feedback) to the observer's
understanding and feeling the same emotion. This conception of empathy has
been neglected in the literature probably because it seemed too much like an
instinctive explanation. There is some recent research (reviewed by Hoffman,
1978), however, suggesting its plausibility.

5. Symbolic Association.   The fifth mode, like the third, is based on the
association between the victim's distress cues and the observer's past distress. In
this case, though, the victim's distress cues evoke empathic distress not because
of their physical or expressive properties but because they symbolically indicate
the victim's feelings. For example, one can respond empathically to someone as
a result of seeing a picture of that person in an emotional situation, reading a
letter from him or her, or hearing someone else describe what happened to him or
her. The empathy-eliciting cue can be an emotional label (''I'm scared'') or a
description of the event (''My father was taken to the hospital''). This is ob-

viously a relatively advanced mode of arousal as it requires the ability to interpret symbols and process information semantically. The semantic processing may put distance between the observer and the other. It may also reduce the involuntary component, though not totally because the symbols serve primarily as the medium by which the other's feeling is communicated; if one understands how the other feels, one can usually be expected to respond empathically.

6. *Role Taking.* In the sixth mode, which is clearly the most advanced developmentally, the person imagines how it would feel if he or she were in the other's place. The pertinent research has been done mainly by Stotland and his associates. In one study (Stotland, 1969), a group of subjects were instructed to imagine how they would feel and what sensations they would have in their hands if exposed to the same painful heat treatment that was being applied to another person. These subjects gave more evidence of empathic distress both physiologically and verbally, than (a) subjects instructed to attend closely to the other person's physical movements and (b) subjects instructed to imagine how the other person felt when he or she was undergoing the treatment. The first finding is not surprising. It suggests simply that imagining oneself in the other's place is more empathy arousing than observing the other's movements. The second finding, however, may tell us something about what is actually imagined. Specifically, it suggests that empathic affect is more likely to be generated when the direct focus of attention is not on the model's feelings but on the model's situation and on how one would feel in that situation, that is, when one imagines how one would feel if the stimuli impinging on the model were impinging on oneself. From a purely cognitive standpoint, the process may resemble that in which we imagine how we would feel in a hypothetical situation having nothing to do with another person. The difference of course is that when we know that we are responding to what is happening to someone else rather than to what might happen to us, we have the subjective experience of feeling what the other person is feeling—the feeling that we are empathizing.

These six modes of empathic arousal do not form a stage sequence in the sense of each one encompassing and replacing the preceding. The first mode typically drops out after infancy, owing to controls against crying, although even adults feel sad when they hear a cry and some adults even feel like crying themselves, though they usually control it. The sixth mode, being deliberate, may be relatively infrequent—used at times, for example, by parents and therapists who believe it is important to feel something of what the child or patient is feeling. The intermediate four modes, however, enter in at different points in development and may continue to operate through the life span.

Which of these arousal modes operates in a given situation presumably depends on the cues that are salient. If the expressive cues from the victim are salient, then mimicry may be the predominant mode. Conditioning and association are apt to predominate when situational cues are salient. Cues based on pictorial or verbal communication will of course require symbolic association. And, in any of these cases, the possibility exists for additional arousal if the observer gives thought to how he or she would feel in the other's situation. In other words, an arousal mode exists for whatever type of cue about the other's feelings may be present, and multiple cues may increase the level of arousal. This is important because it indicates that empathy may be an overdetermined response in humans. Empathy may also be a self-reinforcing response. For example, as already mentioned in connection with the newborn's reactive cry, every time we empathize with someone in distress the co-occurrence of our own distress and distress cues from another person may increase the strength of the connection between the cues of another's distress and our own empathic response, thus increasing the likelihood in the future that distress in others will be accompanied by empathic distress in ourselves. Another aspect of these arousal modes worth noting is that most of them require rather shallow levels of cognitive processing (e.g., sensory registration, simple pattern matching, conditioning) and are largely involuntary. With several such arousal modes in the human repertoire, the evidence that empathy may be a universal and largely involuntary response—if one attends to the relevant cues one responds empathically—that had survival value in human evolution should perhaps not be surprising (Hoffman, 1981a).

Development of a Cognitive Sense of Others

Before discussing the cognitive component of empathy I should note that cognition did enter into the discussion of arousal in several ways. First, imagining oneself in the other's place, as in the most advanced mode, illustrates the role of cognition in actually generating empathic affect. Second, even in the earlier arousal modes, perceptual discrimination and pattern recognition must often mediate between the facial and situational cues of the model and the affect aroused in the observer. The role of cognitive mediation is especially apparent when the observer responds to the symbolic meaning of stimuli rather than to their physical attributes, as in the fifth mode. What I mean by the cognitive component, however, is something more fundamental and unique to empathy.

Though empathy may usually be aroused by the predominantly simple, involuntary mechanisms just described, the subjective experience of empathy is rather complex. The literature on empathy often stops with the idea that the observer feels vicariously what the model feels through direct experience. This is the essential feature of empathy, to be sure, but mature adults who observe another person in pain, for example, know that their own distress feeling is due to a stimulus event impinging on someone else. They also have an idea of what the other person is feeling—an idea based on how they would feel in the other's situation, their general knowledge about how people feel in such a situation, or their specific knowledge about that other person. Young children who lack the distinction between self and other may have vicarious affect aroused without these cognitions. In other words, how people experience empathy depends on the level at which they cognize others. This suggests that empathy development must correspond at least partly to the development of a cognitive sense of others. The cognitive sense of others undergoes dramatic changes developmentally and thus provides a conceptual basis for a developmental scheme for empathy.

Although extensive work has been done on role taking, there is as yet no formal literature on a broader conception of a cognitive sense of the other. I have worked out such a conception, based on several different bodies of research, which will now be summarized.

Person Permanence.   Person permanence refers to the awareness of another's existence as a separate physical entity. The young infant apparently lacks this awareness; objects, events, and people are not experienced as distinct from the self. Not until about 6 months, according to Piaget (1954), does the infant organize the fleeting images making up his or her world into discrete objects and experience them as separate from his or her own biologically determined sensations. The main empirical evidence comes from studies of object displacement. If a desired object is hidden behind a screen before the infant's eyes, he or she loses interest in it as though it no longer existed. By 6 months, the infant removes the screen to get the object, which shows that he or she can then internally reproduce the image of an object and use the image as a guide to the object. The infant's sense of the object is still limited, however, as it is short-lived, and the screen's presence is necessary as a sign of the object. We know this because until about 18 months the infant does not seek the object if the experimenter first places it in a container that is then hidden behind a screen and brought out empty after releasing the object. By 18 months the child retrieves an object after a succession of such invisible displacements, indicating that he or she can then evoke an object's image even when there is nothing in sight to attest to its existence. Piaget sees this as the beginning of object permanence—a stable sense of the separate existence of physical objects even when outside the individual's immediate perceptual field. The research since Piaget (e.g., Bell, 1970), suggests that "person" permanence occurs several months earlier; that is, by 1 year children can retain a mental image of a person in that person's absence.

Although not stressed in the literature, there is evidence that the process of acquiring a sense of the object, hence person permanence, is gradual (Bell, 1970; Uzgiris & Hunt, 1966). I have already noted that at 6 months the child's image of an object is not only dependent on external cues but is also short-lived. And even at a year, all we know is that the child can hold an image of the mother long enough to find her (Bell, 1970). It seems likely, too, that the child will often regress to the level of self–other confusion when fatigued or emotionally aroused. I know a child who at 13 months typically responded to another's sad look by hugging and patting the victim. His father described an incident at 15 months, when he was very tired and responded to the same cues by running to his mother and putting his head in her lap. In short, the emerging image of the other (and perhaps the emerging image of the self as well) may be unstable. The child is only vaguely and momentarily aware of the other person as distinct from the self; and the image of the other, being transitory, may often slip in and out of focus with changes in the infant's state. Only later may self and other be sharply differentiated throughout the normal course of daily events. The gradual nature of the process may be significant in the early development of empathy, as discussed later.

Perspective Taking.   The child's sense of the separate existence of persons is for some time highly limited. Although aware of people's existence as physical entities, he or she does not yet know that they have inner states of their own and tends to attribute to them characteristics that belong to himself or herself. Piaget (1932) thought it was not until about 7 or 8 years that this egocentrism began to give way to the recognition that others have their own perspective. This view was based on Piaget's famous three-mountain landscape task, on which children below 6 years of age typically made the egocentric error of attributing their own viewpoint to a doll situated in various locations around the landscape. The research has since shown that certain aspects of Piaget's original task (e.g., the size and complexity of the objects displayed, their asymmetrical placement, the requirement of a verbal response) may have served to mask the role-taking competence of younger subjects. Three-year-olds, for example, make very few errors when the display contains discrete, easily differentiated objects (small toys) and a verbal response is not required; that is, the subject indicates the other's point of view by manipulating an exact duplicate of the display (Borke, 1975). Two-year-olds will turn a picture toward another person who asks to see it (Lempers, Flavell, & Flavell, 1977).

Recent research also suggests that with simple tasks, not only spatial but also cognitive role-taking competence appears much earlier than previously thought. For decades following Piaget's landmark study of moral judgment, for example, it was widely assumed that children do not take the actor's intentions into account until 8 or 9 years of age. Recent research has clarified the ambiguities in Piaget's original stories (e.g., whether the child reaching for the jam really had bad intentions) and has shown that even 5-year-olds can infer whether another's actions are intentional or accidental. Furthermore, children of that age weigh intentions heavily when making moral judgments, if the consequences of the intended act are as harmful as the consequences of the accidental act, rather than less harmful, as in Piaget's original stories (e.g., Imamoglu, 1975).

Research is also accumulating that indicates even 4-year-olds can take the perspective of others under certain conditions in which the cognitive demands of the task are minimal. For example, children this age who watched two short videotaped action sequences, accompanied by an explanatory audio portion, showed awareness that someone else would not understand the story when the sound was turned off (Mossler, Marvin, & Greenberg, 1976). Four-year-olds also chose appropriate birthday gifts for their mothers, rather than toys attractive to themselves (Marvin, 1974). This age group has also been found to take the listener's perspective into account in verbal communication tasks. They used simpler and more attention-getting language, for example, when talking to children much younger than themselves than when talking to peers or adults (Shatz & Gelman, 1973); they were more explicit verbally when giving instructions to someone who apparently could not see than to someone who could (Maratsos, 1973); and they modified their language appropriately when discussing an experience they had a week earlier, depending on whether the listner had shared that experience or knew nothing about it (Menig-Peterson, 1975).

It seems likely that even younger children are capable of role taking in highly motivating, natural settings. Here are two anecdotal examples. In the first, which I observed, Marcy, aged 20 months, was in the playroom of her home and wanted a toy that her sister was playing with. She asked for it but her sister refused vehemently. Marcy paused for a moment, as if reflecting on what to do, and then ran straight to her sister's favorite rocking horse—which her sister never allowed anyone to touch—climbed on it and began yelling "Nice horsey!" Nice horsey!", keeping her eye on her sister all the time. Her sister put down the toy and came running angrily, whereupon Marcy immediately climbed down, ran directly to the toy, and grabbed it.

It may be useful to speculate about what went on in Marcy's head. One possibility is that she engaged in a logical role-taking sequence in which she first realized that to get the toy she had to induce her sister to leave it, then figured out that this could be accomplished by arousing her sister's concern about something more important to her than the toy, and finally thought of climbing on the horse. Another, more egocentric though equally complex possibility is that Marcy thought about what she would do if she were in her sister's place, realized that she would give up the toy only if suitably distracted, assumed her sister would do the same, remembered how strongly her sister felt about the horse, and utilized this knowledge to lure her sister away from the toy. More likely, in view of her age, Marcy's thought process was less formal operational—based more on imagery and association, perhaps, than either of these. For example, she may have first noticed the horse, which triggered an image (or script) derived from past experiences in which she climbed on the horse and her sister came running and pushed her off, and then realized that getting on the horse was a way of getting her sister away from the toy. Whatever the precise cognitive operations involved, it seems safe to assume at the very least that Marcy realized that her sister would not give up the toy voluntarily, that to get the toy she had to lure her sister away from it, and that a way to lure her was to climb on her horse. In other words, though not yet 2 years old, this child showed awareness of another's inner states that differed from her own, even though she probably could not have understood the instructions in the simplest role-taking experiment.

In the second incident, Michael, aged 15 months, and his friend Paul were fighting over a toy and Paul started to cry. Michael appeared disturbed and let go, but Paul still cried. Michael paused, then brought his teddy bear to Paul but to no avail. Michael paused again, and then finally succeeded in stopping Paul's crying by fetching Paul's security blanket from an adjoining room. Several aspects of this incident deserve comment. First, it is clear that Michael initially assumed that his own teddy bear, which often comforts him, would also comfort Paul. Second, Paul's continued crying served as negative feedback that led Michael to consider alternatives. Third, Michael's final, successful act has several possible explanations: (a) He simply imitated what he had observed in the past; this is unlikely since his parents were certain he had never seen Paul being comforted with a blanket. (b) He may have remembered seeing another child soothed by a blanket, which reminded him of Paul's blanket (more complex than it first appears, since Paul's blanket was out of Michael's perceptual field at the time). (c) He was somehow able to reason by analogy that Paul would be comforted by something he loved in the same way that Michael loved his own teddy bear. Whatever the correct interpretation, this incident, as well as a strikingly similar one reported by Borke (1972), suggests that a child not yet 1 year and 6 months can, with the most general kind of feedback, assess the specific needs of another person which differed from his own.

If we may generalize tentatively from these two instances, they suggest that role-taking in familiar, highly motivating natural settings may precede laboratory role-taking by a year or two. That is, the rudiments of role-taking competence may be present in some children before 2 years of age, although performance undoubtedly varies with the setting and cognitive complexity of the particular task.

(That even animals can take roles is evident in Lawick-Goodall's description of the following incident, summarized briefly here [Lawick-Goodall, 1968, p. 107].) Figan, a young chimpanzee, spotted a banana that Goodall had hidden in a tree, but it was just over the head of Goliath, a dominant male. After no more than a quick glance from the fruit to Goliath, Figan moved away and sat on the other side of the tent so that he could no longer see the fruit. Fifteen minutes later, when Goliath got up and left, Figan, without a moment's hesitation, went over and took the banana. Lawick-Goodall suggests that he had somehow sized up the situation; if he had climbed for the fruit earlier, Goliath almost certainly would have snatched it away. If he had remained close to the banana he would probably have looked at it from time to time, and, as chimpanzees are quick to notice and interpret the eye movements of their fellows, Goliath would probably have seen the fruit himself. Figan had not only refrained from instantly gratifying his desire but had also gone away so that he could not "give the game away by looking at the banana." If Lawick-Goodall's interpretation is correct, it appears that chimpanzees are capable of a rather high order of role taking when the conditions are right and motivation is high).

Personal Identity.   The third broad step in the development of a sense of the other pertains to the view of the other as having a personal identity—his or her own life circumstances and internal states beyond the immediate situation. This developmental stage has been ignored in the literature. The closest to it is Erikson's (1950) conception of ego identity, which pertains in part to the individual's sense of his or her own sameness through time. In support of Erikson, it seems reasonable that at some point the child develops the cognitive capacity to integrate his or her own discrete inner experiences over time and to form a conception of himself or herself as having different feelings and thoughts in different situations but being the same continuous person with his or her own past, present, and anticipated future. There is little relevant research. Kohlberg (1966) suggests that during the preoperational period (2–7 years) children not only lack the concept of conservation with respect to mass, weight, and number (Piaget, 1954) but also with regard to qualitative attributes such as gender. He found, for example, that it is not until 6 or 7 years that children firmly assert that a girl could not be a boy even if she wanted to or even if she played boys' games or wore boys' haircuts or clothes, thus demonstrating a sense of stabilization and continuity regarding gender. There is also evidence that a firm sense of one's own racial identity may not be established until about 7 or 8 years (Proshansky, 1966). (Although younger children use racial terms and show racial preferences, their racial conception appears to reflect verbal fluency rather than a stable attainment of racial concepts.) Finally, in a developmental study by Guardo and Bohan (1971), 6- and 7-year-olds recognized their identity as humans and as males or females mainly in terms of their names, physical appearance, and behaviors—which is consistent with the gender and racial identity research. Their sense of self-continuity from past to future was hazy, however, until 8 or 9 years, when more covert and personalized differences in feelings and attitudes began to contribute to self-recognition, although even then their names and physical characteristics were the main anchorage points of identity.

It appears, then, that somewhere between 6 and 9 years marks the beginning of the child's emerging sense of his or her own continuing identity. By early adolescence, this may be expected to expand considerably. Furthermore, once the child can see that his or her own life has coherence and continuity despite the fact that he or she reacts differently in different situations, he or she should soon be able to perceive this in others. He or she can then not only take their role and assess their reactions in particular situations but also generalize from these and construct a concept of their general life experience. In sum, an awareness that others are coordinate with oneself expands to include the notion that they, like oneself, have their own personal identities that go beyond the immediate situation.

To summarize, the research suggests that for most of the first year children probably experience a fusion between self and other. By the end of the first year they attain person permanence and become aware of others as physical entities distinct from the self. By 2 years they acquire a rudimentary sense of others not only as physically distinct entities but also as having internal states that are independent of their own. This is the initial step in role-taking, and with further development they can discern other people's internal states in increasingly complex situations. By late childhood or early adolescence they become aware of others as having personal identities and life experiences beyond the immediate situation.

Development of Empathy: Affective–Cognitive Synthesis

As children pass through these four social–cognitive stages, the vicarious affect that is aroused is experienced differently. Aside from feeling what the other feels, there is an increasing awareness that the source of the affect lies in the other's situation and not one's own, and an increasingly veridical awareness of what the other is actually feeling. I now describe the four hypothetical levels of empathic response that result from this coalescence of empathic affect and the cognitive sense of the other, as exemplified by the empathic response to someone in distress.

   1. Global Empathy.   For most of the first year, before the child has acquired "person permanence," distress cues from others may elicit a global empathic distress response—presumably a fusion of unpleasant feelings and of stimuli that come from the infant's own body (through conditioning or mimicry), from the dimly perceived "other," and from the situation. Because infants cannot yet differentiate themselves from the other, they must often be unclear as to who is experiencing any distress that they witness, and they may at times behave as though what is happening to the other is happening to them. For example, a colleague's 11-month-old daughter who saw another child fall and cry responded as follows: She first stared at the victim, appearing as though she were about to cry herself, and then put her thumb in her mouth and buried her head in her mother's lap—her typical response when she had hurt herself and sought comfort. Kaplan (1977) describes a very similar response in a younger child:

> At nine months, Hope had already demonstrated strong (empathic) responses to other children's distress. Characteristically, she did not turn away from these distress scenes though they apparently touched off distress in herself. Hope would

stare intently, her eyes welling up with tears if another child fell, hurt themselves or cried. At that time, she was overwhelmed with her emotions. She would end up crying herself and crawling quickly to her mother for comfort. [p. 73]

and Zahn-Waxler, Radke-Yarrow and King (1979) found the pattern to be characteristic of 10- to 14-month-old infants.

This first stage of empathic distress may be described as a primitive, involuntary response based mainly on the "pull" of surface cues and requiring the shallowest level of cognitive processing. It is important, however, precisely because it shows that humans may involuntarily and forcefully experience others' emotional states rather than the emotional states pertinent to their own situation—that humans are built in such a way that their distress is often due to someone else's painful experience.

The transition to the second level occurs when the child approaches person permanence. With the emergence of a sense of the other as distinct from the self, the affective portion of the children's empathic distress is extended to the separate image-of-self and image-of-other that emerges. As suggested earlier, children are at first probably only vaguely and momentarily aware of the other person as distinct from the self; and the mental image of the other, being transitory, may often slip in and out of focus. Consequently, children at this intermediate stage probably react to another's distress as though the dimly perceived "self" and the dimly perceived "other" were somehow simultaneously, or alternately in distress.

2. "Egocentric" Empathy. The second level is clearly established when the child is fully aware of the distinction between self and other and thus able for the first time to experience empathic distress while also being aware that another person—and not the self—is the victim. The child is still limited, however. He or she cannot as yet distinguish between his or her own and the other person's inner states and is apt to mix them up, as illustrated by his or her efforts to help others, which consist chiefly of giving the other person what he or she finds most comforting. The response of a colleague's 20-month-old son is illustrative. When a visiting friend who was about to leave burst into tears, complaining that her parents were not home (they were away for 2 weeks), his immediate reaction was to look sad, but then he offered her his beloved teddy bear to take home. His parents reminded him that he would miss the teddy if he gave it away, but he insisted—possibly because his empathic distress was greater than the anticipated unpleasantness of not having the teddy, which would be indicative of the strong motivational potential of empathic distress. Other examples more illustrative of the child's cognitive limitations, if less poignant, are: a 13-month-old who responded with a distressed look to an adult who looked sad and then offered the adult his beloved doll; and another child who ran to fetch his own mother to comfort a crying friend, even though the friend's mother was equally available.

In labeling this level, quotations were used because it is not entirely egocentric. Although the child's behavior shows confusion between what comforts self and what comforts the other, his or her behavior and accompanying facial responses indicate that he or she is also responding with appropriate affect.

3. Empathy for Another's Feelings.   With the beginning of a role-taking capability, the child becomes aware that other people's feelings may sometimes differ from his or her own and that their perspectives are based on their own needs and interpretations of events. (Such children may still at times project their own feelings to others, especially in the absence of objective data about other's feelings, but adults often do this too). More importantly, because the child now knows that the real world and his or her perception of it are not the same thing, and that the feelings of others are independent of his or her own, he or she becomes more cautious and tentative in his or her inferences and more alert to cues about what the other is feeling. In short, the sense of what the other is feeling is based on more veridical processes. By 4 years, even in artificial laboratory situations, children can fairly accurately recognize happiness or sadness in others and respond with the appropriate affect; (Borke, 1971; Feshbach & Roe, 1968; Strayer, 1980). And, with the development of language, which enables children for the first time to derive meaning from symbolic cues of affect, not just its facial and other physical expressions, they can begin to empathize with a wide range of emotions, including complex emotions like disappointment and feelings of betrayal. Eventually, they become capable of empathizing with several, sometimes contradictory emotions at once. Thus, while empathizing with the victim's distress, one may also empathize with the victim's desire not to feel obligated or demeaned, or the victim's potential feelings of inadequacy and low self-esteem—hence the victim's desire *not* to be helped. And, finally, children can be aroused empathically by information pertinent to someone's feelings even in that person's absence. This leads to the fourth empathic level.

4. Empathy for Another's General Plight.   By late childhood, owing to the emerging conception of self and other as continuous persons with separate histories and identities, one becomes aware that others have feelings beyond the immediate situation. Consequently, though one may continue to be empathically aroused by another's immediate distress, one's empathic concern is intensified when one knows that the other's distress is not transitory but chronic. This fourth level, then, consists of empathically aroused affect combined with an image of another's general life condition (general level of distress or deprivation, opportunities available or denied, future prospects, etc.).

As an extension of the fourth level, with the ability to group people into categories children eventually can be empathically aroused by the plight of an entire group or class of people (e.g., poor, oppressed, outcast, retarded). Because of different backgrounds, one's specific distress experience may differ from theirs. All distress experiences probably have a common affective core, however, and this together with the individual's high cognitive level allows for a generalized empathic distress capability. The combination of empathic affect and the perceived plight of an unfortunate group may be the most developmentally advanced form of empathic distress. It may also provide a motive base, especially in adolescence, for the development of certain social and political ideologies centered around alleviation of the plight of unfortunate groups (Hoffman, 1980).

We can now elaborate on the definition of empathy as an affective response more appropriate to another person's situation than to one's own. First, empathy is a response to a network of information that includes any or all of the following: expressive cues from the other reflecting the other's affective state in the immediate situation, cues from the stimulus events producing that affect, and one's representations of aspects of the other's life condition presumed to bear on the other's general affective experience. Second, these different types of information may or may not be available in a given instance, and when they are available the ability to use them depends on one's developmental level. What may be defined as an empathic response for a very young child may involve relatively simple levels of processing of visual or auditory cues in the immediate situation, whereas mature empathizers may, in addition, respond in terms of symbolic meanings of stimuli and representations of events beyond the situation.

Empathy is thus defined in terms of the underlying processes involved, and the developmental level of the observer. It is also assumed that these processes result in, if not an exact match, at least a high degree of similarity between the observer's affect and the affect experienced by the model in the immediate situation, or in the model's general life experience. For the empathic process to result in a high degree of similarity requires that the observer and the model process information similarly. This means that empathy may be unlikely when the observer and the model are at different developmental levels, at different levels of sanity, or from different cultures. Empathy might be possible in these cases if the observer had the ''code'' for the model's processing. A mature adult, for example, might be able to empathize with a child, an insightful therapist with a psychotic patient, and an anthropologist with someone from another culture. Besides having the code, the observer must also have the particular affect in his or her own repertoire. One might not be able to empathize with a masochist's joyful response to being beaten even if one fully understood the basis of that response, if one were not masochistic oneself.

Just how much similarity must there be for the response to qualify as empathy? I have argued elsewhere against insisting on a high degree of similarity (Hoffman, 1982a). For present purposes I will only note that when one is reminded by another's situation of a similar event in one's own past, one is apt to feel as the other does because people tend to process events similarly (assuming similar backgrounds and developmental levels, as discussed above). There will always be an idiosyncratic component, however, for example, one's concerns about one's child have their own nuances which differ from the other's. This limits the degree of similarity possible but I would still call it an empathic response despite the idiosyncratic component if one remains aware that the other is having the direct experience and one's own response is vicarious, and if one's attention remains focused on the other's feelings.

To summarize, one can empathize with someone who processes information in the same way; or with someone who processes information differently if one has the code for that person's processing and the necessary affective range. And one's vicarious affective response qualifies as empathy, despite its idiosyncratic component, if one's attention is focused on the other and the other's situation rather than on oneself.

COGNITIVE TRANSFORMATION OF EMPATHY

Many affect theorists (e.g., Schachter & Singer, 1962) suggest that how a person labels or experiences an affect is heavily influenced by his or her cognitive appraisal of the situation. These writers are explaining how we distinguish among different affects (e.g., anger, fear, joy) aroused *directly*. Whether or not they are right—there are other theorists who say appraisal is not necessary for experiencing discrete affects (Izard, 1971)—appraisal appears to be so intrinsic to *empathically* aroused affect as to alter the quality of the observer's affective experience.

Person Permanence and Transformation of Empathic into Sympathic Distress

I suggested earlier how a child's cognitive sense of others may combine with his or her vicarious unpleasant affect and produce four developmental levels of empathic distress. The transition from the first to the second of these levels may involve an important qualitative shift in the child's feeling. More specifically, once people are aware of the other as distinct from the self, their own empathic distress, which is a parallel response—a more or less exact replication of the victim's presumed feeling of distress—may be transformed at least in part into a more reciprocal concern for the victim. That is, they may continue to respond in a purely empathic manner—to feel uncomfortable and highly distressed them- selves—but they also experience a feeling of compassion for the victim, along with a conscious desire to help because they feel sorry for the victim and not just to relieve their own empathic distress.

What developmental processes may account for this developmental shift? First, as already discussed, with the acquisition of object permanence the unpleasant affect experienced as part of the child's initial global, undifferentiated "self" is transferred to its emerging parts ("self" and "other"). Second, it seems reasonable to assume that the experience of any unpleasant affect includes a wish, not necessarily conscious, that it be terminated. Such a wish must therefore be included in the unpleasant affect transferred to the "other" (as well as to the "self"). There is thus a part of the child's affective response to another's distress that includes a wish to terminate the other's distress. I call this *sympathetic distress*. It is qualitatively different from the remaining, more "purely" empathic component of the response, that pertains to the unpleasant affect transferred to the "self."

This notion of the child's simultaneously experiencing empathic and sympathetic distress is highly abstract and may require examples to clarify it. I know a child whose typical response to his own distress, beginning late in the first year, was to suck his thumb with one hand and pull his ear with the other. He also tended to do this when he saw someone else in distress, an example of the first level of empathic functioning. Something new happened at 12 months. On seeing a sad look on his father's face, he proceeded to look sad and suck his thumb, while pulling on his father's ear! It is as though this child, with the beginning of self-other differentiation, was experiencing a dual emotion—a feeling of his own distress and the wish to alleviate it (empathic distress) along with a feeling of concern for his father and the wish to alleviate his father's distress (sympathetic distress). In a similar example, Zahn-Waxler et al. (1979) describe a child whose first positive overture to someone in distress occurred at 12 months when he alternated between gently touching the victim and gently touching himself.

As mentioned earlier, the process of self-other differentiation is gradual and there is probably an early period in which the child is only vaguely and momentarily aware of the other as distinct from the self. The emerging "self" and the emerging "other" may thus slip in and out of focus. It follows that the child may often respond to another's distress by feeling as though the dimly perceived "self" and the dimly perceived "other" were somehow simultaneously, or alternately, in distress. The child may thus frequently have the experience of wishing to alleviate or terminate distress in the self, in close association with a similar wish regarding distress in the other. As a result of this co-occurrence, the child may subsequently be expected to have a strengthened connection between distress in others and his or her empathic and sympathetic response.

An early period of subjectively overlapping concern such as this, in which the "self" and the "other" are experienced as "sharing" the distress, would seem to provide a basis for the positive attitude toward the emerging "other" indicated in the two examples cited above. The gradual nature of self-other differentiation may therefore be important because it gives the child the experience of simultaneously wishing to terminate the emerging other's distress as well as distress in the self. This experience may provide a necessary link between the initially quasi-egoistic empathic distress response (*quasi*-egoistic rather than egoistic because the self was then a fusion of self and other and there was no actual conflict between a self and an other) and the earliest traces of a true sympathetic distress. If the sense of the other were attained suddenly, the child would lack this experience; and when he discovers that the pain is someone else's, he might simply experience a feeling of relief (or even blame the other for his own empathic distress). The co-occurrence of distress in the emerging "self" and in the emerging "other" may thus be an important factor not only in the transition between the first two levels of empathic distress but also in the partial transformation of empathic into sympathetic distress.

To summarize, there are two significant aspects of the child's early response to another's distress that may account for the seemingly paradoxical notion that self-other differentiation, which might be expected to create a barrier between persons, and empathic distress, which is partially egoistic, combine to produce the developmental basis for sympathetic distress. These aspects are manifest in the earliest stages of self-other differentiation: (1) the transfer of the unpleasant affect associated with the initial global self to its emerging separate parts ("self" and "other") and (2) the subjective experience of "sharing" distress, which is due to the gradual attainment of a sense of the other and gives the child the experience of wishing the other's distress to end.

The hypothesis that empathic distress is transformed into sympathetic distress is difficult to test. As yet the evidence is circumstantial: As already noted, (1) children seem to progress developmentally from responding to someone's distress first by seeking comfort for the self, and later by trying to help the victim and not the self and (2) there appears to be an in-between stage, in which they feel sad and comfort both the victim and the self, which occurs at about the time they gain person permanence. Insofar as this transformation does occur, the four developmental levels previously described may be said to apply to sympathetic as well as empathic distress. I will continue to use the term empathic distress generically, however, to refer to both empathic and sympathetic distress.

Language, Semantic Processing and Empathic Experience

As noted earlier, empathy is often mediated in part by language. To highlight the processes involved, consider situations in which language provides the only cue about another's affective state, for example, one receives a letter describing the other's feelings and the surrounding circumstances. In these situations language might produce an empathic response because of the physical properties of the words used or because the words have become signals of a particular affect (e.g., the way the word "cancer" evokes fear). These cases reduce to a type of conditioning or association and are less interesting here. What is special about language are the cases in which the observer must engage in semantic processing, and the meaning obtained from the message mediates the link between the model's and the observer's affective state. The message may pertain to the model's feeling (I'm worried), the model's situation (My child was just taken to the hospital), or, more commonly, both. In any case empathic affect may be aroused through at least three distinct types of role-taking processes.

These processes, in all of which cognition is heavily implicated, turned up in a number of interviews I conducted with adults about their empathic responses to someone's distressing experience which was communicated to them by letter or by a third person.

1. Focus on other. On learning of the other's misfortune one may (a) simply imagine how the other is feeling and this may result in an empathic affective response. The empathic affect is apt to be enhanced if one also (b) visualizes the other person's behavioral response. One may use visual imagery and picture the other's facial expression, posture, and overt behavior, or auditory imagery and imagine the other expressing his or her feelings verbally, for example, with a sad voice or cry. Depending on how vivid the image is, one may then respond empathically to the image, more or less as one would if the other were physically present. In this way one may provide oneself with the nonverbal cues that are missing, and then respond to them as though the other were present.

2. Focus on self. On learning of the other's misfortune one may not imagine the other's feelings or actions but instead (a) picture oneself in the model's place and imagine how it would feel, that is, one may imagine that the stimuli impinging on the other are impinging on oneself. If one can do this vividly enough, one may experience some of the same affect experienced by the other. One's affective response may be enhanced considerably if one also (b) is reminded of similar events in one's own past in which one actually experienced the emotion. Because of the associative links, some of the earlier emotions may be evoked in the present. This is especially likely if one employs visual or auditory imagery. Even if one lacks the actual experience, one may be able to imagine how it would feel if one had the experience. This might be possible, for example, if one had previously thought or worried a lot about how one would feel if it did happen.

3. Combination. On learning of the other's misfortune one may shift back and forth between these ''other-focused'' and ''self-focused'' processes.

Empathic responses that are based primarily on self-focused processes are subject to an interesting vulnerability: The focus on the self may take control of one's entire response. The result may be that one becomes lost in one's own egoistic concerns and the image of the other and the other's condition fades away. Narcissistic observers may often drift into an egoistic mode like this, but so might anyone if the other's situation had enough personal significance. In any case, although the observer's response was initially triggered by information about another's affective state, it would no longer qualify as empathy (we might call it an "aborted" empathic response) unless the observer returned to a focus on the other.

Empathic responses that are mediated entirely by language are also subject to another, more general type of vulnerability: The observer's affect may not match the model's because of the necessary intervening encoding and decoding processes. Consider the encoding process by the model. Words, which are ways of categorizing experience, are typically more effective at portraying the general rather than specific aspects of feeling; putting a feeling into words transforms it in part into the more general class of which it is an instance. For example, words like sad, afraid, happy may capture what is general about a feeling, what different experiences of it have in common, but the nuances of how one feels at a particular moment may be lost. The verbal message, in other words, is at best a generalized approximation of the model's feeling. And this generalized approximation is all that is available to the observer.

In the process of decoding, the observer will often relate this input to his or her past experience, as discussed previously. Reversing the models' encoding sequence, the observer goes from the general to the specific, imagining, with varying degrees of vividness, past events in which he or she had the feeling in question, and, consequently, having the feeling. The observer's feeling may have a lot in common with the model's, owing to the normative, shared meaning of the terms used by the model to describe the feeling, but there will also be an "error" component due to the encoding and decoding. The error component may be reduced if the model is particularly good at putting feelings into words and if the observer is intimately related to the model, knows how the model feels in different situations, and perhaps imagines the model's facial expression and behavior in the situation.

Let us now return to the more usual situation, in which the model is present and language is not the only cue; direct expressive cues from the model are also available. These expressive cues, which are largely nonverbal, usually visual or auditory, may have triggered the observer's empathic response in the first place, with the verbal message adding further information that influenced the observer's empathic affect and understanding of the model's feeling. Alternatively, the message's semantic meaning may have led to the observer's initial empathic response and also directed the observer's attention to the model, which then enabled the models' expressive cues to trigger additional empathic affect. In either case, the empathic process may have been kept "alive" by the expressive cues because they are salient, often vivid, and can hold the observer's attention. As a result, the image of the model remains with the observer rather than fading away, and the observer does not drift into the egoistic, "self-focused" mode. Thus, although language may be an effective mediator of empathy because it can provide information about the other's internal state, the process of deriving meaning from the other's verbal message and connecting it with relevant events in one's past may sometimes weaken the hold of the empathic affect aroused. The presence of the model and of nonverbal expressive cues from the model may help keep the observer's attention focused on the model and thus maintain the empathic response.

Nonverbal expressive cues may also help keep the empathic observer on target in another way. Although it is likely that people's verbal descriptions of their feelings are usually expressed in accord with their actual feelings, discrepancies sometimes occur. When this happens, the other's nonverbal expression may give the observer cues about the other's feeling that contradict the other's words. This is due to the tendency for people to "leak" their feelings through changes in facial expression, posture, or tone of voice. (Changes in facial response may be less revealing in older children and adults than in younger children, because people are often socialized to mask their true feelings and this is best accomplished through controlling one's facial responses [Ekman & Friesen, 1974; Littlepage & Pineault, 1979].) Although these cues are not often precise, they may be an accurate enough reflection of the other's true feelings to make the observer uncomfortable and keep him or her from being misled by the verbal message.

Impact of Person Identity on Empathy

The highest empathic level discussed earlier consists of vicarious affect combined with one's concept or image of the other's affective state and life condition beyond the situation. To highlight the effect of person identity on empathy, consider the case in which there are no immediate cues of the other's affect, just information about his or her life condition. How does this information produce empathic affect? One possibility is that empathic affect is aroused because one is reminded of an event or a series of events in one's own past that resemble aspects of the other's life condition. Or, one may not relate the other's condition to oneself but focus directly on the other and try to imagine what the other is experiencing and feeling. In other words, the previous discussion of self- and other-focused processes in regard to the role of language in empathy may also apply here. This should not be surprising since our knowledge about other people's affective state beyond the situation is ordinarily obtained through language—someone gives us background information about the person—although we can also build up such knowledge through direct observations of the person over time.

Usually the information about the other's life condition is not all that is available to the observer. Cues about the other's affective state in the immediate situation are also available. As already noted, the observer is responding to a network of information—expressive cues from the other, immediate situational cues, knowledge of the other's life condition—utilizing perhaps several of the empathic affect arousal modes described earlier. The separate sources of information are ordinarily congruent. They may at times be contradictory, however, as when knowledge about the other's life condition conflicts with the immediate situational or expressive cues. When such conflict or disequilibrium occurs, the situational or expressive cues may lose much of their force for the observer who knows that they only reflect a transitory state.

Indeed, the image of the other's life condition may sometimes actually be more compelling than the immediate cues because it signifies that the model's affect in the situation is short-lived and suggests many past and possibly future instances in which the model experiences the opposite affect. The opposite affect may then seem more representative of the model's experience. Imagine a child who is having a good time playing and laughing but who does not know that he or she is mentally retarded or has a terminal illness. An observer who has attained the fourth empathic level may imagine the events in store for the child and the feelings probably associated with these events. Such an observer may feel sadness rather than joy, thus matching the child's presumed general rather than immediate feeling state, or a mingling of sadness and joy, or an alternation between sadness and joy. Still another possibility is that the observer may temporarily suspend sadness so as to appear to share the child's joy, as a parent or therapist might do. In any case the mature empathizer deals with the conflict between the situation and the other's life-condition. This is all in contrast to a less mature observer who might simply respond with joy.

In other words, I am hypothesizing that the mental image of the other's general life condition may to some extent override contradictory cues in the present. Responding empathically to this image, then, may involve a certain amount of distancing—responding partly to one's mental image of the other rather than to the stimulus immediately presented by the other. Indeed, once this level of empathy is attained one may never again respond totally in terms of the other's feelings in the situation, but always at least partly in terms of one's representation of the other's general condition and type of affective experience beyond the situation. If this is true, then we may expect a certain amount of distancing even when there is congruence between the expressive, situational, and life-condition cues.

Knowledge about the other's life condition may sometimes transform a direct affective response into an empathic one. An example is the situation in which one is angry because one has been harmed by another, and the anger is diminished when one discovers that there are extenuating circumstances. In a recent study (Pazer, Slackman & Hoffman, 1980), children were asked to state how "mad" they would be if someone acted in a harmful manner toward them (e.g., stole their cat). The experimental subjects were given background information about the culprit (e.g., his own cat had run away and his parents would not get him another one). The subjects in this group who were 8 years or older said they would be less mad than control subjects who were given equally wordy background information that was not extenuating. Empathy data were not collected but since the extenuating circumstances put the culprit in a sympathetic light it seems reasonable to assume that empathy was aroused and may have led to the decrease in anger.

Causal Attribution and the Shaping of Empathic Affect

I have not yet mentioned another major cognitive input that shapes empathic affect: causal attribution. The burgeoning research on attribution indicates that people of all ages make causal inferences about events. We may therefore expect a person who encounters someone in distress to make inferences about the cause of the victim's plight. The nature of the inference depends primarily on the cues relevant to causality and the inference may serve as a cognitive input, in addition to those already discussed, that helps determine the observer's affective experience.

The simplest type of situation is that in which one is first empathically aroused, through one or more of the mechanisms described earlier, and then receives information about causality. The question is, how does the resulting causal attribution alter the observer's empathic affect? Consider situations in which the cues indicate that the other person is to blame for his or her own plight. Blaming the other may be incompatible with an empathic response because the other may no longer appear to be a victim. This attribution should therefore operate to neutralize the observer's empathic distress, and the observer may end up feeling indifferent or even derogating the victim. One's empathic response may thus be cut short by the assignment of blame to the victim.

Suppose the cues indicate that a third person is to blame for the other's plight. In that case one's attention may be diverted from the victim to the third person and one may feel anger toward that person because one sympathizes with the victim or because one empathizes with the victim and feels attacked oneself. Or, one's affective response may alternate between empathic distress and anger. It is also possible that one's anger may crowd out one's empathy entirely. If, on the other hand, one discovers that the victim previously did something harmful to the third person, the situation may be transformed into the previous one in which the observer blames the victim. The observer in this case might even begin to empathize with the third person's anger or with the underlying feelings of hurt that presumably led him or her to engage in the aggressive act. Yet another possibility is that one discovers that the victim has a history of being mistreated in the relationship with the third person, in which case one may assume the victim had a choice (why else would he continue the relationship?) and one may then end up blaming the victim.

What happens when the observer has the necessary information and makes the causal attribution beforehand? If one blamed the victim before witnessing his or her distress, would one respond empathically? Are such prior causal attributional processes powerful enough to prevent empathy, for example, might they alter the direction of one's attention so that one does not attend to the expressive cues from the victim (e.g., does not see the victim's face)? Or would one of the more compelling arousal processes like mimicry and conditioning still operate to produce at least a momentary empathic response? And what about situations involving a third person? Would advance knowledge that a third person caused the victim's distress arouse more anger and less empathy than when this knowledge becomes available only after empathy has been aroused? The answers to these questions are unknown. There is some evidence in Stotland's research (1969) that a set to avoid empathizing (with someone being given a painful heat treatment) does *not* reduce empathic distress. But that was an artificial laboratory situation involving no counter-empathic causal attribution. There are some situations in which we might confidently expect causal attribution to interfere with empathy, at least empathy with the victim, for example the situation in which one has prior knowledge that the victim has been the aggressor in the past.

Finally, we may ask what happens in situations in which there are no clear cues as to who if anyone is responsible for the victim's plight. In these cases individual differences in personality may play a role. Some people, for example, may use perceptual or cognitive strategies such as blaming the victim precisely for the purpose of reducing the discomfort of empathic distress. There may also be a general human tendency to attribute the cause of another's action to that person's own dispositions (Jones & Nisbett, 1971) and more specifically to blame others for their own misfortune in order to support one's assumptions about a "just world" (Lerner & Simmons, 1966). If, however, we take seriously the research showing a widespread tendency for people to respond empathically to another's distress (Hoffman, 1981), we can only assume that a derogatory attitude is not necessarily incompatible with an empathic response.

Furthermore, my respondents indicate that thoughtful observers may not always settle for their initial causal attributions in ambiguous situations; they may consider alternatives. An adult male in my informal sample saw the driver of an expensive sports car being wheeled in a stretcher to the ambulance. He had not seen the accident, coming on the scene just after it happened. He reports that:

> I first assumed it was probably a rich, smart aleck kid driving while drunk or on dope and I did not feel for him. I then thought, this might be unfair, maybe he was rushing because of some emergency, suppose he was taking someone to the hospital, and then I felt for him. But then I thought, that was no excuse, he should have been more careful even if it was an emergency, and my feeling for him decreased. Then I realized the guy might be dying and I felt bad for him again.

This response nicely illustrates the shifts in causal attribution and feeling that may occur in ambiguous situations, and it also shows how derogating another may be compatible with empathizing. It also makes it appear that the causal attributions changed first and this led to appropriate changes in feeling. But, we may ask, what made the attributions change in the first place? I suggest that the observer, who is known as a generally empathic person, had an initial empathic distress response that was so aversive as to trigger a "defensive" derogation of the victim, thus making the situation more tolerable. The stark reality of the victim's condition remained in view, however, which not only continued to evoke empathic distress but also made it difficult to sustain the initial negative attribution. The conflict between the reality, the continuing empathic distress, and the negative attribution may have led to a series of revised causal attributions.

In other words, this may be an instance of a temporary defense against empathic overarousal (see Hoffman, 1978 for a general discussion of empathic overarousal). If one's initial empathic distress is highly aversive, one may distance oneself from the victim by making several causal attributions. These causal attributions may operate to transform some of the observer's empathic distress into a derogatory feeling. But quite apart from the content of the attributions, the sheer amount of cognitive work involved in making them may serve to divert one's attention from the reality of the victim's condition. When one is empathically overaroused, then, one may handle this by mobilizing one's cognitive resources, thus gaining time and control over one's feelings, so that one can return to one's initial empathic response, though in a more manageable fashion.

It may be that only when the cause of the other's plight is something like an illness or accident over which the victim clearly has no control (and perhaps sometimes when the cause is ambiguous) that the analysis of empathic distress outlined earlier including the four developmental levels and the transformation of empathic into sympathetic distress, may apply.

Thus far in my analysis, the observer is an innocent bystander. A special case of interest is that in which the cues indicate that the observer is the cause of the other's distress. It seems reasonable to assume that if a person feels empathic distress and the cues indicate that he or she has caused the victim's distress, then the observer's empathic distress will be transformed by the self-blame attribution into a feeling of guilt. That is, the temporal conjunction of an empathic response to someone in distress and the attribution of one's own personal responsibility for that distress will produce guilt.

GUILT

According to Freud, guilt is not the result of actually harming someone in the present but the remnant of earlier fears of punishment that resulted in repression of hostile and other impulses. What triggers guilt is the return of repressed impulses to consciousness. The developmental process, briefly, is as follows.

The child is subject to many frustrations, some due to parental controls and others not, such as illness and physical discomfort, all of which contribute to a buildup of hostility. Expressions of the hostility are usually punished. To avoid anxiety over punishment, especially loss of love or abandonment, children repress their hostile impulses. Furthermore, to maintain the repression, as well as elicit continuing expressions of parental love, children adopt, in relatively unmodified form, the rules and prohibitions emanating from the parent. They also develop a generalized motive to emulate the overt behaviors and adopt the internal states of the parent. Most importantly, for present purposes, they adopt the parents' capacity to punish themselves when they violate a prohibition or are tempted to do so—turning inward, in the course of doing this, the hostility that was originally directed toward the parent. This self-punishment is experienced as a guilt feeling, which is dreaded because of its intensity and resemblance to the earlier anxieties about punishment and abandonment. Children therefore try to avoid guilt by acting always in accordance with incorporated parental prohibitions and erecting various mechanisms of defense against the conscious awareness of impulses to act to the contrary. Because the parents' prohibitions generally reflect social norms, the experience of guilt serves to punish socially deviant behavior. Guilt thus serves as a fairly reliable internal agent promoting adherence to the norms, supplementing external agencies such as the law.

This continues to be the major theoretical account of guilt in the literature. Though Freud and his followers recognized it as a quasi-pathological view of guilt, they viewed it as the necessary price that people must pay in return for the benefits of civilized life. Some of them, Freud included, recognized the need for a true interpersonal guilt—the bad feeling a person has about himself or herself because of actually doing harm to another—but such a conception has not been integrated into the main body of psychoanalytic theory. I think the fact that the best known theory of guilt is a quasi-pathological one may explain why a major goal of psychotherapy is to remove guilt, and the concept has acquired a negative reputation among psychologists. It should not be surprising that a society like ours, bent on the pursuit of happiness, would regard guilt with cautious hostility and conclude that the less of it the better. Yet it seems intuitively obvious that people do feel guilty over their harmful actions toward others, and that society benefits from this. There is some empirical evidence for both these intuitions, in the story-completion responses I obtained some time ago and in recent findings by Zahn-Waxler et al. (1979). A summary follows.

Prevalence and Social Value of Guilt

The story-completion items, in which a basically well-meaning protagonist of the same age and sex as the subject commits a transgression under pressure, were these: (1) A child who is hurrying with a friend to an important sports event (or movie) encounters a small child who seems lost. He suggests they stop and help, but his friend talks him out of it. The next day he finds out that the small child, who had been left alone by an irresponsible babysitter, ran into the street and was killed by a car. The adult version was similar except that the victim was an elderly person who was looking for something in the snow. (2) A child is having an exciting time sledding down a hill, which was set aside for this purpose with signs warning nonsledders to keep away. Suddenly a small child appears. Despite the protagonist's desperate efforts, he runs into the child, who has to be rushed to the hospital. This story has no adult version. (3) A child who has lost many contests at a school picnic and wants desperately to win the underwater swimming race, wins by taking advantage of the muddy condition of the water, and swimming only halfway and back. In the adult version, the protagonist is an unsuccessful, discouraged writer who, unable to meet a contest deadline, recalls some stories previously written but never published by a dead relative. In desperation he selects the best one, impulsively signs his name, mails it, and wins the contest.

Though each story was designed to measure guilt there were reasons for not expecting many guilt responses to any of them. In the first story, the transgression was one of omission—not stopping to help. The protagonist actually *did* nothing wrong and there was no reason for him to anticipate the tragic consequences of inaction. Furthermore, there were other people to blame: the driver of the car, the friend who talked against stopping, the negligent baby sitter, and the parents who hired the sitter. In the second story, though the protagonist was the direct agent of harm, it was clearly an accident that he tried his best to avoid and, besides, it was the victim's fault. The third story involves a deliberate act of cheating, but the possibility of detection was ruled out. The protagonist could thus have gotten away with it and enjoyed the prize and social approbation.

Despite the reasons for expecting little if any guilt, most of the responses, especially to the "lost-person" and "sledding" stories indicated that the subjects (fifth and seventh graders, and their parents) would feel very guilty in similar situations. The responses to the cheating story are worth noting. Some subjects externalized the situation (e.g., one of the judges had "X-ray eyes"; the protagonist did poorly and was exposed in a subsequent contest), but most accepted the transgression as detection-proof and gave primarily internal guilt responses. The basis of the guilt was not often made explicit, but when it was, the basis was interpersonal: The guilt was due to having deceived one's friends or deprived the true winner of the prize he deserved. The guilt was also sometimes delayed, the fruits of cheating being enjoyed at first, and the guilt creeping up only gradually and experienced most sharply when the protagonist found himself alone, usually that night in bed. Overall, the story-completion findings suggest that at least middle-class Americans, from about 10 years of age and older, typically respond with guilt feelings when they believe they have harmed others.

What about younger children? There is an unfortunate gap in the data extending all the way down to infancy. In the research by Zahn-Waxler et al. (1979)

parents are trained to observe and record their children's behavior. These investigators described guiltlike behavior in a third of their sample of 15- to 18-month-old children in certain situations. Upon seeing their mother cry, for example, they would ask apologetically, "Did I make you sad?" or, "Sorry, I be nice." In another example, a child is arguing with his younger sibling. The sibling is accidentally hurt. The child then alternates between continuing his aggressive behavior and comforting the sibling. He says he's sorry, kisses the sibling's hand, and then hits his own head. These examples suggest an early rudimentary tendency to feel guilty over harming others, which is perhaps a precursor of the more fully developed guilt response that comes later.

The story-completion research also provides evidence for the positive social value of guilt. The finding of interest is that the guilt feelings attributed to the story characters were almost always followed by some sort of reparative behavior, which often functioned to reduce the guilt. In the sledding story, for example, the protagonist visited the injured child in the hospital, brought him toys and games, or spent time personally supervising the hill to prevent future accidents. When reparation to the victim was not possible (e.g., in the lost-child story), the protagonist often did something for the family, went out of his way to help someone in a similar situation that occurred subsequently, or expressed a deep sense of frustration because there was nothing that could be done. Possibly the most interesting response to this story, given mainly by the older children and adults, was one in which the protagonist engages in a process of self-examination (e.g., "How could I have been so selfish?") and reordering of his value priorities, along with a resolution to be more thoughtful of others in the future. This response is interesting because it suggests a mechanism of moral growth for which the experience of guilt may be a requisite.

These findings supplement numerous laboratory studies done mainly in the late 1960s and early 1970s (Regan, Williams & Sparling, 1972), in which adults who were led to believe that they had harmed someone showed a heightened willingness to help other people as well as the victim. These studies are limited because they did not include a direct measure of guilt arousal, they showed only short-run effects (the altruistic deed immediately followed the guilt manipulation), and the subjects were all college students. In the story-completion research, however, the evidence for guilt was explicit and, as noted, there was a suggestion of long-term effects. Though by no means conclusive, the findings as a whole suggest, somewhat paradoxically, that guilt, which is usually the result of immoral, or at least egoistic action, may subsequently operate as an altruistic or moral motive.

If guilt over harming others is so prevalent and socially beneficial, it seems unlikely that it is always as irrationally based as previous conceptions would suggest. The question is, what alternative reality-based motive is there? I have already suggested an answer: empathic distress. Empathic distress is an affect but it also has motive force, as indicated by the growing body of research showing that it includes a disposition to help others (see review by Hoffman, 1981a). Of course there is more to guilt than empathy; guilt has a self-critical or self-blaming component as well. Hence, my hypothesis that guilt is due to the conjunction of an empathic response to someone's distress and the awareness of being the cause of that distress. Before conjecturing about the development of guilt over harming others, I would like to discuss a type of guilt that requires neither impulse repression nor the awareness of harming others, and that may reflect a socially significant but neglected aspect of human nature, namely, a tendency to be made uncomfortable by nothing more than one's relative advantage over others.

Existential Guilt

People not only feel guilty over harming others, whether by actually behaving in a harmful way or by inaction (as in the lost-person story), but under certain conditions they also appear vulnerable to guilt over other people's misfortunes when totally innocent. The well-known phenomenon of survivor guilt in natural disasters and in war is a case in point. An example from the Vietnam War is the Navy pilot whose right arm had been partially crippled by shrapnel but who nevertheless said, on being released after 2 years as a war prisoner: "Getting released, you feel a tremendous amount of guilt. You developed a relationship with the other prisoners . . . and they're still there and you're going away. [Newsweek, 1972, p. 27]." This remark, as well as statements by the Hiroshima atomic-bomb survivors cited by Lifton (1968), suggests that despite one's own plight, one may feel guilty if one feels far better off than others.

More important for our purposes because of the possible developmental implications are the feelings reported by the affluent 1960s social activists studied by Keniston (1968). The essence of guilt over feeling relatively advantaged is conveyed when Keniston describes these activists as stressing: "their indignation when they 'really' understood that the benefits they had experienced had not been extended to others [pp. 131–132]." One of them, in discussing some poor Mexican children he had known years earlier, vividly described his realization of relative advantage in a way that also suggests its possible role in moral action:

> I was the one that lived in a place where there were fans and no flies, and they lived with the flies. And I was clearly destined for something, and they were destined for nothing. . . . Well, I sort of made a pact with these people that when I got to be powerful I might change some things. And I think I pursued that pact pretty consistently for a long time [p. 50].

Something between guilt over survival and guilt over affluence is exemplified by the black student at Harvard who wrote that he and others like him:

> have had to wrestle with the keen sense of guilt they feel being here while their families still struggle in Black ghettoes. . . . The one sure way of easing guilt was

(by demanding) 'relevance' from Harvard, which means, in effect instruction that can be directed toward improving the quality of life for Blacks as a whole in this country . . . (and) via building takeovers, strikes, and other kinds of demonstrations [Monroe, 1973].

Guilt over survival and over affluence differ in certain obvious respects. Survivors have shared in the other's distress and feel guilty over not continuing to suffer, or suffering less than the others; their own condition may be bad but the other's condition is much worse. Affluent youths typically have not shared in the other's distress and the contrast to which they react is between their own life condition, which is extremely good, and the other's condition, which is extremely bad. What the survivor and the affluent as well as the formerly disadvantaged person have in common, however, is that they feel guilty over the vast difference in well-being that they perceive between themselves and relevant others. This effect of a perceived disparity between self and other contrasts interestingly with "social comparison processes" (Festinger, 1954; Masters, 1972), which lead one to feel good about oneself when one outperforms others. The seeming contradiction is easily resolved when we consider the difference in context. In evaluating one's competence, one uses the most available yardstick—how one compares with others; if one compares favorably, one's self-esteem is raised. When one encounters someone in circumstances far more distressful than one's own, self-evaluation is not the issue and one is apt to feel distressed and guilty over one's advantage, rather than enhanced.

I call this reaction existential guilt, to distinguish it from the type of interpersonal guilt discussed earlier, because the persons described have done nothing wrong, but feel culpable because of circumstances of life beyond their control. Whereas interpersonal guilt may result from the combination of empathic distress and awareness of being the cause of the victim's distress, existential guilt may result from the combination of empathic distress and awareness of being in a relative advantaged position with respect to the victim.

Existential guilt may take on some of the qualities of true guilt, especially guilt over inaction. The activist youths in Keniston's sample, for example, appear to have concluded that their privileged position makes it possible for them to do something to alleviate the condition of less fortunate people; if they do nothing, they therefore become personally responsible for helping to perpetuate this condition. And for some, who believed that actions by their relatives or members of their social class contributed to the plight of the less advantaged people, existential guilt actually appeared to change into a feeling of guilt over commission (guilt by association). An example of this is the response given by a congressional intern to the question, Why are so many middle-class youth turned off by the very system that gave them so many advantages and opportunities?

They feel guilty because while they are enjoying this highest standard of living, American Indians are starving and black ghettoes are overrun by rats . . . This goes on while they eat steak every day. Their sense of moral indignation can't stand this; and they realize that the blame rests on the shoulders of their class [New Republic, November 28, 1970, p. 11].

These and other statements suggest that for existential guilt to be experienced, the circumstances of the other's life must be vividly imagined, because a keen sense of the other's plight is needed to create both the necessary feelings of empathic distress in the actor and the awareness of his or her relative advantage over the victim. Existential guilt may thus require that one be directly exposed to the day-to-day life experiences of the less fortunate, hence in the position of witnessing the discrepancy in well-being, as well as the basic human similarities that exist between the victim and the self. Such exposure may be gained through the kind of close contact that Civil Rights workers had in the 1960s, through books, travel, and even some liberal arts and social science courses. The mass media may also play a significant role.

Another cognitive requisite of existential guilt is that one must be aware of the absence of any justification for one's relatively advantaged position. Recent history has seen the breakdown of many former justifications of this kind. Perhaps the most significant contribution to this breakdown in the past century is the emergence and rising acceptance in most developed societies of equalitarian and social norms—all people have equal worth. The diminished hold of traditional religious doctrine, such as the Calvinist view of well-being as a sign of grace, is another contributing factor. Of more recent importance is the widespread acceptance of the scientific evidence against genetic inferiority and in favor of environmental determinism. Finally, one of the last remaining justifications in our society, the idea that one deserves what one earns, appears only now to be losing its effectiveness, owing to recent increases in the proportion of young people from affluent homes who depend on welfare aid as well as on loans and gifts from parents.

These views about existential guilt seem less applicable now than in the 1960s. Informal interviews with young people suggest the reason. They now place a higher value on success and, despite their parents' affluence, they do not feel relatively advantaged, because of their own concerns about finding desirable jobs and their belief that many of the formerly disadvantaged groups now enjoy a favored position in the job market. These remarks, which may contain elements of a backlash, suggest that although existential guilt may be a developmental phenomenon, it also may be heavily influenced by culture and most likely to appear in certain times and places.

Development of Guilt

It is too soon to advance a coherent theory but I would like to discuss the cognitive prerequisites of guilt and offer some preliminary speculations about the development of guilt and its parallels with empathy. The aim is to stimulate further research and theoretical discussion about this important, though neglected concept.

First, it must be noted that, like empathic distress, guilt has three components: affective, cognitive, and motivational. The affective dimension pertains to the painful feeling of disesteem for the self that results from the awareness of the harmful consequences of one's action; in the extreme, a sense of being a worthless person. The motivational dimension pertains to the fact that when one feels guilty one also feels the urge to undo the damage or to make some form of reparation. The cognitive dimension, though having a lot in common with empathy, is far more complex and requires further discussion.

Cognitive Dimension of Guilt

For a person to feel guilty requires an awareness of the harmful effects that one's behavior might have on others. One dimension of this awareness is the cognitive sense of others, that is also important for empathy. For example, a child who does not know that others have independent internal states may not feel guilty over hurting their feelings. And a child who is not yet aware of the self and the other as separate entities may even be uncertain as to who committed the harmful act—the victim or the self.

The cognitive dimension of guilt also includes the awareness that one has been the agent of the harm. This requires the ability to make causal inferences involving one's own actions, for example, the ability to infer from the temporal relation between one's act and a change in the other's state, that one's act was the cause of that change in state. Though research has been done on children's awareness of cause–effect relations in both the social and physical domains, there is very little research on cause–effect relations involving the child's own actions. What little research there is suggests that children may begin to be aware that their actions can have simple physical effects on the external world before 1 year of age. Keeping in mind both this and the social–cognitive levels discussed earlier, we can make some reasonable speculations about the kinds of behaviors that might make the child feel guilty. The simplest case is when the child commits a physically harmful act. This is minimally demanding cognitively because the consequences of the act are immediate and observable. Guilt over inaction, or omission, is more demanding cognitively because it requires the ability to imagine something that might have happened but did not, and to be aware of the consequences of that omission. That is, the observer witnesses the victim's distress, imagines what might have been done to prevent or alleviate it, and realizes that though he or she did not cause the distress, his or her inaction contributed to its continuation. Guilt over inaction therefore must be a later developmental acquisition. Perhaps even more demanding cognitively is guilt over contemplating a harmful act, or anticipatory guilt. Anticipatory guilt requires that one can not only establish connections between thoughts, intentions, and actions, but also that one can imagine both an act and its harmful social consequences when neither of these has yet occurred.

Another seemingly important cognitive dimension of guilt is the awareness that one has choice and control over one's behavior. Without this awareness there would appear to be no logical grounds for feeling guilty. Here, too, there is very little research. The recent moral judgment research does show that children as young as 3 or 4 years will judge another child as being naughtier if what he or she did was intentional rather than accidental (Imamoglu, 1975). Though the actions judged were not the child's own, the findings do suggest that 4-year-olds may be sensitive to choice and control. What about younger children? Psychoanalytic writers have long suggested that there is a period of "omnipotence" in early infancy, before the differentiation of self and others, before "person permanence" (See Mahler, Pine, & Bergman, 1975). This makes sense when we consider that at that age the infant's utterances of distress are typically acted upon fairly quickly by the mother. If the infant, as a result, feels that he or she controls the world, then he or she may also have a rudimentary sense of controlling himself or herself, as he is a part of that world. There is no evidence, however, that infants have any awareness of *choice*. The cry that controls the mother's behavior is very likely a natural response to discomfort, rather than an instrumental act of choice. It may not be until much later that children are aware of choice and act on the basis of choice.

If there is an early period of omnipotence that is linked to a nondifferentiated state, then it seems likely that as the infant becomes aware of his or her own separateness, he or she also becomes aware of the fact that other people's action are mediated by *their* desires, not his or her own, and also that his or her actions are to some extent subject to control by others. With this insight, the delusion of omnipotence can no longer be maintained and it may give way to a sense of helplessness and loss of control of his or her own behavior. This, in time, is presumably followed by a more realistic awareness of having partial control and choice. Until the necessary research is done, it seems plausible to assume tentatively that there is an early developmental progression from a sense of omnipotence, to a sense of helplessness, and finally to an awareness of having some but not total control over one's actions.

A final cognitive dimension of guilt may appear sometime later in development, at least in most societies. This includes the awareness that there exists a moral norm against harming others and that one's act, or contemplated act, is discrepant from that norm. To the extent that one has been socialized to view oneself as an upholder of the norm, this discrepancy may be a threat to one's self-image, and the resulting negative affect may add to the intensity of the empathically based guilt. The awareness of a norm against harming others thus may contribute affectively as well as cognitively to the guilt response.

Developmental Levels of Guilt

I do not present here a complete developmental model for guilt, as I did for empathy, but rather a brief preliminary scheme that utilizes the points made in the foregoing discussion. In this scheme the capacity for guilt develops in parallel with the levels of empathic distress described earlier.

First, a minimal requirement for feeling guilty over harming others is that one is psychologically separate from them. We may therefore not expect any signs of guilt until the child has the faint beginnings of awareness of others as separate physical entities from himself or herself, which is around the end of the first year. Furthermore, in the earliest instances of guilt we may expect to see the most primitive kind of causal schema, which, according to Heider (1958) is based on the simple contiguity of events. That is, the child may feel that he or she is to blame just because of the temporal or geographical association of his or her action with another person's signs of distress. Whether or not the child actually caused the distress is irrelevant. Though he or she may be confused about who is the causal agent, the child may nevertheless feel something like guilt, even if totally innocent. Consider the guiltlike responses of 15- 18-month-old infants in Zahn-Waxler et al's (1979) sample, mentioned earlier. These examples illustrate the young child's empathic distress and his or her confusion about causality. Perhaps more importantly, they also suggest a rudimentary sense of being responsible for an act, that predates some of the cognitive requisites of guilt mentioned earlier such as the sense of having choices. Why should the child feel that he is to blame? I suggest that he feels culpable because of his sense of omnipotence, which, together with his cognitive limitations, leads him to view all things associated with his actions as caused by them. To summarize, an early, nonveridical sense of being the causal agent may combine with empathic distress to produce a rudimentary feeling of guilt.

A note of caution before we proceed. The examples of early guiltlike behavior may reflect a primitive guilt feeling in the child, as suggested. It is also possible, however, that the child feels empathic distress and says ''I'm sorry,'' and yet the words do not reflect a feeling of culpability, but rather a simple parroting of what others have said in similar situations. A careful examination of the child's words, along with accompanying changes in his facial expression and any other behavioral indices of guilt, may be necessary to resolve this issue. The child's hitting himself on the head may be more convincing evidence for guilt feelings than conventional expressions like ''I'm sorry,'' although it is possible that the child has seen others engage in this behavior too.

In any case, sometime later in development when the child is aware of the impact of his or her actions, the stage may be set for the development of true interpersonal guilt. This development should proceed along lines corresponding roughly to the levels of social–cognitive development discussed earlier. Thus the earliest true guilt should occur when the child has engaged in some simple physical action that has harmed someone, such as knocking another child down, hitting him, or breaking his toy. The cues from the victim indicating that he is hurt, usually a cry or a pained look, will elicit a guilt feeling, though it may be fleeting. Instances of this abound in the nursery school. For example, a child takes a toy from another, who cries. The child who took the toy responds with a seemingly genuinely sad look on his face and returns the toy, sometimes with a comforting gesture. We do not know why he responds that way. It might be to avoid a scolding by the teacher, but the child's manner is often that of a contrite and sympathetic, not fearful child, and it seems plausible that he or she might feel guilty. Interesting instances of delayed reparation can also be found, which suggest guilt. An example is the child who offered to give a ride on a swing to someone he had accidentally knocked down 15 minutes earlier.

Once the child begins to be aware that others have their own internal states—by 2 or 3 years, as noted earlier—guilt over hurting people's feelings should become a possibility. At about the same time, the child may also begin to show evidence of having the cognitive requisites of guilt over inaction. Finally, when the child becomes aware that other people have their own existence and personal identity—in late childhood or early adolescence—he or she can begin to feel guilty over the harmful effects of his or her action or inaction beyond the immediate situation. In its earliest manifestation, such guilt may be felt when one imagines discrete instances of distress in the victim, although eventually it may also be felt when one is aware of the harmful effects that one's actions may have on the victim over time.

Relation Between Guilt and Empathic Distress

I now summarize this highly speculative developmental scheme for guilt, highlighting its parallels with empathic distress. First, before becoming aware of others as separate physical entities, the child responds to simple expressions of pain in others with empathic distress and also at times with a rudimentary guilt feeling even though he or she may lack a keen sense of being the causal agent. Once it is recognized that others are separate entities, he or she experiences empathic distress when observing someone who is physically hurt, and this empathic distress may be transformed into guilt if his or her own actions were responsible for the hurt. Similarly, once aware that others have internal states, the empathic distress one experiences in the presence of someone having painful or unhappy feelings may be transformed into guilt if one's actions were responsible for those feelings. Finally, once aware of the identity of others beyond the immediate situation, one's empathic response to their general plight may be transformed into guilt if one feels responsible for their plight, or if one's attention shifts from their plight to the contrast between it and one's own relatively advantaged position.

Although empathic distress is here viewed as a prerequisite for the development of guilt, it seems likely that guilt may eventually become largely independent of its empathic origin. In some situations, for example, those in which the victim is visibly sad or hurt, guilt may continue to be accompanied by empathic distress. In other situations, however, the victim and his or her hurt may be less salient than other things, for example, than the actor's behavior or motivation. In these cases, the actor may feel guilt without empathy. And, in most instances of anticipatory guilt, there may rarely be empathic arousal except in the unusual case in which one imagines the other's response to one's planned action especially vividly. In general, then, at some point in development the awareness of being the causal agent of another's misfortune may be enough to trigger guilt feelings without empathy. Thus although empathic distress may be a necessary factor in the *development* of guilt, it may not, subsequently, be an inevitable accompaniment of guilt.

It seems likely, moreover, that once the capacity for guilt is attained, especially guilt over omission or inaction, the weight of influence may be the other way around. That is, guilt may become a part of all subsequent responses to another's distress, at least in situations in which one might have helped but did not. From then on, even as an innocent bystander, one may rarely experience empathic distress without some guilt. The line between empathic distress and guilt thus becomes very fine, and being an innocent bystander is a matter of degree. To the degree that one realizes that one could have acted to help but did not, one may never feel totally innocent. Empathy and guilt may thus be the quintessential prosocial motives, for they may transform another's pain into one's own discomfort and make one feel partly responsible for the other's plight whether or not one has actually done anything to cause it.

Evidence for the connection between empathy and guilt is scanty and largely circumstantial. It includes the fact that children typically respond empathically to others in distress, taken together with the finding (discussed later) that discipline techniques that point up the victim's distress and the child's role in causing it appear to contribute to guilt development. There is also some experimental evidence (Thompson & Hoffman, 1980). The subjects—first, third, and fifth grade children—were shown stories on slides, which were also narrated by the experimenter, in which a story character does harm to another person. For example, a boy who accidentally bumps into another boy, scattering his newspapers, does not stop to help because he is in a hurry. After each story, two guilt measures were administered. One is simple: The subject is asked how one would feel if he or she were the story character who committed the transgression. The other is a projective item: The subject completes the story, and guilt scores are derived from the amount of guilt attributed to the culprit. Before administering the guilt measures, half the subjects were asked to tell how they think the *victim* in each story felt. The subjects in this empathy-arousal condition produced higher guilt scores than a control group who were not asked to think about the victim. These results do not bear directly on the origin of guilt but they suggest that guilt may at least be intensified by arousal of empathy for the victim of one's actions.

THE ROLE OF SOCIALIZATION

The discussion so far has dealt with the natural processes of empathy and guilt development assumed to occur under ordinary conditions in most cultures because of the tendency of humans to respond vicariously to others. People also have egoistic needs, however, which must not be overlooked, and socialization, which in part reflects the larger themes in society, may build upon the child's empathic or egoistic proclivities in varying degrees. I have suggested elsewhere (Hoffman, 1970) that there may be little conflict between empathic and egoistic socialization in early childhood, even in individualistic societies like ours. At some point in life the two may begin to clash, however, sometimes dramatically, as one becomes aware that the society's resources are limited and one's access to them is largely contingent on how well one competes with others. Parents know this, and it may affect their child-rearing goals. For this and other reasons (e.g., their patience with the child, their own personal needs, and the stresses under which they operate), wide variations in child-rearing practices, hence in children's capacity for empathy and guilt, can be expected. What follows are speculations about these socialization effects.

Empathy

There is little research on socialization and empathy but if we assume that helping another in distress reflects an empathic response—which seems reasonable in view of the findings relating empathy to helping—then we can find modest support for speculations based on our theoretical model.

First, we would expect a person to be more likely to empathize with someone else's emotion if he or she has had direct experience with that emotion. It follows that socialization that allows the child to experience a variety of emotions, rather than protecting him or her from them, will increase the likelihood of his or her being able to empathize with different emotions. That is, it will expand his or her empathic range. The only evidence to date for this hypothesis is that preschool children who cry a lot themselves appear to be more empathic than children who do not often cry (Lenrow, 1965). There is a theoretical limitation to this hypothesis: Certain extremely painful situations might be repressed, resulting in an inability to empathize with the emotions involved.

A second expectation can be derived from the idea that empathy is a largely involuntary response. By involuntary we mean that if a person pays attention to the victim, he or she usually will have an empathic response. It follows that socialization experiences that direct the child's attention to the internal states of other people should contribute to the development of empathy. We should therefore expect that in situations in which the child has harmed others, the parent's use of discipline techniques that call attention to the victim's pain or injury or encourage the child to imagine himself in the victim's place—inductive techniques—should help put the feelings of others into the child's consciousness and thus enhance his or her empathic potential. The positive correlation between inductive techniques and helping in older children has long been known (see review by Hoffman, 1977); and the same thing has recently been reported in children under 2 years (Zahn-Waxler et al., 1979).

We would expect role-taking opportunities to help sharpen the child's cognitive sense of others and increase the likelihood of paying attention to others, thus extending his or her empathic capability. We must remember, however, that role taking is affectively neutral—useful in manipulating as well as helping others. Role-taking opportunities in positive social contexts therefore should be a more reliable contributor to empathy and helping, than role taking in competitive or neutral contexts.

Finally, we would expect that giving the child a lot of affection would help keep him or her open to the needs of others and empathic, rather than absorbed in his or her own needs. And, we would also expect that exposing the child to models who act altruistically and express their sympathetic feelings would contribute to the child's acting empathically rather than making counterempathic attributions about the cause of people's distress. Both these expectations have been borne out by the research (Hoffman, 1982b)

It thus appears that empathy and helping may be fostered by relatively benign, nonpunitive socialization experiences. These experiences may be effective because empathy develops naturally, as I suggested, and is to some extent present at an early age. Empathy may thus serve as a potential ally to parents and others with prosocial child-rearing goals for the child—something to be encouraged and nurtured, rather than punished, as egoistic motives must sometimes be. Besides benefiting from the child's existing empathic tendencies, these same socialization experiences may also help enhance the empathic tendencies. In other words, there may be a mutually supportive interaction between naturally developing empathy and these socialization experiences.

Guilt

Socialization should be especially important in guilt development for the following reason. Guilt feelings are not only aversive, as is empathic distress, but they are also highly deprecatory and threatening to the child's emerging self-image. We may therefore expect children to be motivated to avoid guilt. And they can often succeed in this because most situations in which children harm others are ambiguous in one way or another in regard to who, if anyone, is to blame. That is, children rarely harm others intentionally and without provocation, in which case it would be easy to assign blame. The ambiguity is most apparent when one has harmed another accidentally—whether in rough play or in independent pursuit of one's own interests. But ambiguity also exists in fights and arguments, where it may seem as reasonable to assign blame to the other as to blame the self. In competitive situations one might conceivably feel guilty about wanting to be victorious over the other, about wanting the other to lose, but then one knows that the other is similarly motivated, and so there may be no grounds for guilt. Besides blaming others, or blaming no one, children can use perceptual guilt-avoiding strategies such as turning away from the victim. It seems to follow that even when children have the necessary cognitive and affective attributes for guilt, they often will not experience it unless an external agent is present who somehow compels them to attend to the harm done to the victim and to their own role in the victim's plight. This is exactly what parents often do when the child does harm to someone, and it seems reasonable to expect that the type of discipline used in these situations will have an effect on the development of a guilt disposition in children.

Indeed, the discipline research does show, fairly consistently, that parents who frequently use discipline techniques in which the salient component is induction, that is, techniques in which the parent points up the harmful effects of the child's behavior on others—combined with a lot of affection outside the discipline encounter—have children who tend to experience guilt feelings when they have harmed others (Hoffman, 1977). Parents who frequently use power assertion—which includes force, deprivation of material objects or privileges, or the threat of these—are apt to have children who tend to respond with fear of retaliation or punishment, rather than with guilt. The frequent use of love withdrawal, in which the parent simply gives direct but nonphysical expression to his or her anger or disapproval of the child for engaging in undesirable behavior, does not seem to relate to guilt although such a relationship might be expected from a psychoanalytic perspective.

My theoretical explanation of these findings, presented elsewhere (see especially Hoffman, in press), can be summarized briefly: *First,* though the research describes discipline techniques as fitting one or another category, when examined empirically most discipline techniques have power-assertive and love-withdrawing properties, and some also contain elements of induction. The first two comprise the motive-arousal component of discipline techniques, that may be necessary to get the child to stop what he or she is doing and attend to the parent. Having attended, the child will often be influenced cognitively and affectively by the information contained in the induction that may be present. *Second,* if there is too little arousal the child may ignore the parent; too much arousal, and the resulting fear, anxiety, or resentment may prevent effective processing of the inductive content, for example, it may direct the child's attention to the physical features rather than the semantic content of the induction (Mueller, 1979). It may also direct the child's attention to the consequences of his or her action for the self. Techniques having a salient inductive component ordinarily achieve the best arousal balance, and direct the child's attention to the consequences of his or her action for the victim. *Third,* the child may process the information in the inductive component and thus gain knowledge about the moral norm against harming others. More significantly, processing the information should often enlist the capacity for empathic distress, at whichever of the four developmental levels, discussed earlier, the child is capable of at the time. The child thus may feel badly due to the other's distress rather than, or in addition to anticipated punishment to the self. *Fourth,* inductions point up the fact that the child caused the victim's distress, which is especially important for young children who may not spontaneously see the causal connection between their action and another's state because of motivation, cognitive limitations, or ambiguities in the situation. Inductions may thus often result in the temporal conjunction of empathic distress, and the attribution of blame to the self that is needed to transform the empathic distress into guilt. (This analysis is most applicable to those instances in which the victim of the child's act exhibits clear signs of being sad and downcast, hurt, or otherwise distressed. If the victim is angry and retaliates, the child may feel anger or fear rather than empathic distress and guilt.)

These cognitive and affective processes may explain the origin of guilt feelings in the discipline encounter but we must also explain how guilt feelings become dissociated from their origin in the discipline encounter, generalized to situations in which the parent is absent, and experienced by the child as derived from within. That is, what makes the child feel guilty even when no one is present to point out the harm that he or she has done? Casting the problem in terms of certain memory concepts—notably Tulving's distinction between "episodic" and "semantic" memory and Craik and Lockhart's view about "depth of processing"—offers a possible solution. Namely, the cognitive products of the information processing that occurs in discipline encounters are hypothesized as being semantically organized and encoded in memory. They are then activated in future discipline encounters, modified, and cumulatively integrated with similar information provided by inductions in countless discipline encounters over time. The associated guilt feelings are also activated in these future situations. The source of the information—the discipline encounter settings, including the parent's behavior—is organized separately in a shallower, nonsemantic mode (Craik & Lockhart, 1972) or encoded in "episodic" memory (Tulving, 1972). Consequently, it interferes minimally with the semantic organization and it may be relatively soon forgotten. In addition to this selective memory, the child's active role in processing the information in inductions is important because it contributes to the child's experience of the moral cognitions and guilt feelings generated in discipline encounters as originating from within.

It seems likely that once guilt feelings are aroused in discipline encounters the ideas about the harmful consequences of one's actions that gave rise to them may be suffused with guilty affect and become emotionally charged or "hot" cognitions whose affective and cognitive features are inseparable. These emotionally charged cognitions may then be encoded in memory and eventually experienced in future temptation situations or moral encounters as an affective-cognitive unity. Another interesting possibility is that although the guilt feelings derive from the ideas about harmful consequences, they may be encoded separately, through a special process or channel reserved for affects. If so, then in later temptation situations the guilt feelings may be evoked without any conscious awareness of the ideas about conscquences that gave rise to them. (This may sound like the Freudian notion of free-floating guilt but it is not based on repression.)

Stated most generally, this theory suggests that it is (a) the appropriate mix of parental power, love, and information; (b) the child's processing of the information in discipline encounters and afterwards; and (c) the cognitive and affective products of that processing that determine the extent to which the child feels guilty when he or she has harmed another, contemplates acting in a way that might harm another, or does not help another when it is appropriate to do so. Thus the child's empathic and cognitive capabilities that I described earlier may be mobilized for the first time in discipline encounters, with guilt feelings as the result, and the newly gained guilt capability may then be generalized to other situations.

EMPATHY AND SOCIAL COGNITION

Though my aim has been to throw light on affective empathy and the contribution of affective empathy to guilt, I have thus far stressed the importance of cognition. I try now to redress the balance. First, as noted earlier, though empathy may be aroused by the highly cognitive process of imagining oneself in the other's place, in most instances empathic affect is aroused by more primitive, relatively noncognitive mechanisms such as conditioning, association, and mimicry. These mechanisms let us know that the other person is emotionally aroused and, as noted later, they also provide initial information about what affect that person is experiencing. The primary role of cognition is to help us know that the affect aroused in us is a response to someone else's situation and to give us a more exact idea of just what the other's affect is. In short, cognition may serve largely to fine tune our subjective experience of empathic affect, the raw material for which is produced by minimally cognitive arousal mechanisms. Empathy may thus be as illustrative of the impact of affect on cognition, as the reverse.

I would now like to place this discussion in the context of the larger issue of the difference between social cognition and cognition in the physical domain (See Hoffman, 1981b for a fuller discussion). It has traditionally been assumed that cognition is a unitary process and that the cognitive processes in these domains are the same. According to Piaget (1963), for example, ''The reaction of intelligence . . . to the social environment is exactly parallel to its reaction to the physical environment [p. 60].'' Recent writers question this. Glick (1978) views the two domains as substantially different. Thus whereas the movement of things is predictable from a knowledge of the physical forces acting upon them, people can move themselves. People are also sensitive to subtle variations in context, and their behavior is only loosely predictable from the social forces acting upon them. Consequently, social cognition must operate under different rules. It is based less on logic and more on probability, shared cultural belief systems, cultural stereotypes and scripts. These bases of social cognition, moreover, are often nonveridical because they tend to override immediately available data. For example, when we use stereotypes we often overlook the idiosyncratic properties of a particular person.

Gelman and Spelke (1981) point to a number of distinctions that adults make between people and things. Besides those mentioned by Glick, they note that although people and things both change over time, only people reproduce and act to sustain themselves and their offspring. Things may change (e.g., ice melts) but they cannot do this by themselves. Only people can know, perceive, emote, learn, think, and mentally represent. Gelman and Spelke also note that apart from differences in their properties, people and things are perceived differently. Though both may have a definite size and shape, for example, it is only when perceiving a thing that one focuses exclusively on physical properties. When perceiving a person one may note his or her physical properties, but one's focus is often on his or her internal states, which are more indeterminate and deceptive. And although both people and things may be acted on in similar ways (e.g., pushed), the response of people is far less predictable.

There are several other factors contributing to the complexity, hence the difficulties involved in social cognition. These factors derive from the interactional context within which social cognition usually operates. First, people are not only acted upon but they act back. Furthermore, how they react is not a simple function of how one acted toward them but is mediated by internal states which are unobservable such as how they interpreted one's act and what they hope to accomplish by their response. Second, the people one encounters behave differently and the meaning of their action differs depending on the nature of one's relationship to them (e.g., relationships based on kinship, friendship, power, contract, chance encounters). Furthermore, one's relationship with a person may change dramatically over time. Finally, there are a variety of emotions associated with different relationships. The emotions aroused in interacting with objects are far less varied, revolving, for example, around such matters as whether one succeeded or failed on tasks involving the objects. The emotions aroused in social interactions are also apt to be more intense, and this may operate against cognitive processes such as deriving meaning from verbal cues (Kahneman, 1973).

For all these reasons people are more complex to deal with than objects and their responses would appear to be less predictable. We might reasonably conclude, therefore, that social cognitive development must lag behind the development of physical cognition. Yet the evidence, weak as it is, seems to point in the opposite direction. As noted earlier, children appear capable of carrying an internal representation of a person, in the person's absence, long before they can do the same with physical objects. It is true that the measures of object- and person-permanence used in the research are not comparable, and there is evidence that if size, animation, and familiarity were controlled the difference might disappear (Jackson, Campos, & Fischer, 1978). The research does appear to be ecologically valid, however, because persons *are* animated in the real world and most persons with whom the child interacts are apt to be larger and more familiar than the objects with which he or she deals. Indeed, these may be among the main reasons why person permanence precedes object permanence.

Person permanence may also precede object permanence because infants normally have a far greater emotional investment in the persons in their lives than in the objects they encounter. Permanence involves representing an object, divorcing the representation from the immediate stimulus, and remembering the representation. These capabilities may be mobilized for the first time in relation to objects in which the infant has a strong emotional investment.

There is as yet no evidence for this but there is evidence that positive emotion may aid memory (Isen, Shalker, Clark, & Karp, 1978). This suggests that the infant's involvement with persons may contribute to his or her ability to keep them in mind even in their absence. It would be interesting to see if the permanence of "transitional objects," objects invested with emotion that help tide the child over in the parent's absence (Winnicott, 1960), precedes the permanence of other objects.

In a study by Fein (1972) subjects of five age groups were asked to judge the causality or noncausality of physical and social picture sequences. Young children tended to perceive all sequences as causal, this tendency decreasing with age. Accurate discrimination between social causal and noncausal sequences was established by age 7, but for the physical sequences this skill was not fully established until age 11. Fein's explanation is that social rules are learned early, and the child is exposed to violations of them and can therefore discriminate between instances of social causation and violations of social causation. The child does not observe violations of physical laws, and the ability to discriminate between laws and violations in the physical domain may thus be hampered. I would add that the child has not only observed but also experienced instances of social causality, that is, he or she has acted in certain ways and been rewarded, and has acted in other ways and been punished. In other words, the child's direct experience of how people respond to his or her own actions may promote an understanding of how people respond to the actions of others. And, because a child's observations of how people respond to his or her own actions has an affective as well as well as a cognitive dimension, emotion may contribute further to the ability to distinguish between causal and noncausal social sequences.

There are two other findings that I mention here briefly. First, children can apparently recognize two independent, simultaneous causes of a person's action somewhat earlier in life than they can do the same with regard to the action of an object (Erwin & Kuhn, 1979; Kuhn & Ho, 1977). Second, children appear to be adept at backward temporal ordering of social events before they can conserve length or quality (Van der Lee & Oppenheimer, 1979). The latter finding suggests that reversibility in the conservation of the attributes of things is not, as previously thought, a prerequisite for reversibility in the social domain.

Thus far I have been talking about social cognitive competencies that have a parallel in the physical domain. There are social–cognitive competencies that have no such parallel, such as the ability to assess other people's internal states. As already noted, humans are more apt to attend to the internal states of people than of things. There is also a more fundamental difference, namely, whereas knowledge or ignorance of the inner workings of a class of things predicts to knowledge or ignorance of any item in that class (if you know how steam engines work, you know what is happening inside any steam engine you encounter), this is not true of people. Until recently it was generally assumed that children had to be capable of concrete operations before they could assess another person's internal states. This view fit well with Piaget's assertion that children below 7 or 8 years of age are egocentric but it does not fit the evidence, especially the anecdotal evidence cited earlier that children as young as two years are capable of role-taking in certain situations. If we may generalize tentatively from that evidence, it would appear that some kind of rapid processing of information about other people's feelings, at least in familiar, highly motivating natural settings, is possible in children who are still in the sensorimotor period as regards the physical domain.

I mention these comparisons not because my argument requires that social cognition precedes physical cognition. It does not. The comparisons are not definitive in any case because in none of them were the tasks strictly comparable. The comparisons do point out, however, that social cognitive development may not lag behind development of cognition in the physical domain. How is this possible in view of the high degree of complexity and unpredictability of people relative to things, discussed earlier?

In connection with permanence I have already suggested certain qualities of people that may facilitate social cognition (e.g., they are animated, and objects of emotional investment). Are there other human qualities that serve to facilitate social cognition? One possible answer is the interactional context in which social cognition often takes place. Although the context may contribute to the complexity of social cognition, it may also compensate for this because it presents the child with occasional discrepancies from the behavior expected of others. These discrepancies give the child continuous corrective feedback about the interpretations he or she makes of the other's behavior and internal states, and they motivate the child to attempt a reassessment. The example of 15-month-old Michael and his friend Paul, cited earlier, illustrates how this process may work.

Furthermore, as I have noted elsewhere (Hoffman, 1975), the observer and the model are both humans—with the same nervous system and a shared background of similar experiences, especially during the long period of socialization. Given this similarity in organizational structure, and the developmental and cultural similarities discussed earlier in this paper, the observer and the model are apt to respond to stimuli in similar ways. Thus, if the observer relies only on social scripts and shared belief systems, and attributes his own interpretation of events to the model, he will generally be correct. Furthermore, when this is done, he or she can act more quickly than if he or she considers all the currently available data, and acting quickly may often be adaptive in the social world because one often has little time for cognitive appraisal and reflection.

Although the role-taking research has stressed the ability to assess another's view when it *differs* from one's own, egocentric and normatively based attributions in real life are more apt to be right than wrong. The process may thus not be based on reality testing, but it may usually be effective. It will not be effective when others behave contrary to the norm, deviate from the script, or attempt to deceive by acting in ways that differ from their stated intentions. In these cases, being flexible and able to use all the available data, such as information about the model's personality and past behavior, would be more adaptive. But these types of unexpected behavior by others are apt to be less frequent than behavior that fits the norm. In the course of most people's lives, therefore, behavior based on hurriedly made "egocentric" attributions, shared belief systems, and scripts generally may lead to accurate predictions and in most instances may be adaptive.

Concerning the observer's understanding of the model's feelings, if one responds vicariously through involuntary, minimally cognitive mechanisms, as suggested earlier, then the affect aroused may provide nonverbal, kinesthetic cues from the viscera and the somatic musculature. These cues are linked to the actor's own past experience and thus provide information about the affect experienced by the model. The actor's visceral arousal may not provide *distinctive* cues about the model's feelings (it has long been known that visceral arousal does not reflect discrete emotions), but the visceral cues do serve to inform the observer that the model is emotionally aroused.

Furthermore, recent research suggests that distinctive cues about the other's affect may be provided by feedback from the actor's somatic musculature. Thus the different emotions appear to be accompanied by different degrees of tone in the skeletal muscles (e.g., the loss in muscle tone that accompanies sadness is associated with characteristic postures that are diametrically opposed to those seen in a happy mood) and by different patterns of facial muscle activity (Gelhorn, 1964; Izard, 1971). There is evidence also that cues from one's facial musculature may contribute to the actual experience of an emotion (Laird, Wagener, Halal, & Szegda, 1982).

We may tentatively conclude that the observer's visceral and somatic responses indicate that another person is affectively aroused and they provide rough cues about the particular affect the other is experiencing. This may put a new light on Michael's act, in the example cited earlier, of bringing his own teddy bear to comfort his friend. Although Michael's act was seemingly egocentric it showed that he had received the basically correct emotional message that his friend was sad and needed comforting. Although he was probably incapable of cognitively assessing the other's state, he was able, perhaps through empathic arousal and feedback mechanisms, to know something important about the other's feeling. It may be true that people in general become aware of the harmful or beneficial effects of their actions partly through nonverbal cues from others that both reflect the other's internal state and produce empathic responses in oneself.

Empathy may thus alert one to someone's affective response and it may provide initial information about what the affect is. In this way empathy provides cues about one of the major sources of people's unpredictability, namely, their feelings. As noted earlier, a person's empathic response may at times offer cues about the other's feelings that contradict the other's words, because people's feelings are often "leaked" through changes in their facial response, posture, or tone of voice. Social cognition may thus gain valuable assistance from empathy, and this may compensate for the complexity and relative unpredictability of its subject matter.

There are developmental implications of this argument. In my theoretical model of empathy the subjective experience of one's vicarious affective response is expanded as one develops a cognitive sense of others and can understand the causes of the other's state. The present discussion suggests that, because of simple empathic arousal mechanisms, the ability to be aroused vicariously may contribute to the social cognitive development, by alerting the child to affect in others, providing initial cues of what the affect is, and mobilizing his or her cognitive processes. The role of social cognition, then, may be to help one know that the affect one is experiencing is a response to someone else's situation, to give one a more precise idea of what the affect is, and to provide causal information that may further shape one's affective response. In short, social cognition may help fine tune one's assessment of what the other is feeling, although the initial cues of the other's feeling may often be affective.

Social cognition may also at times initiate the empathic process, as in the most advanced empathy-arousal mode in which the resulting vicarious affective response provides cues that give additional meaning to the observer's initial cognitive assessment of the other's feeling. In general, then, the empathic, hence also the nonverbal communication process under discussion may originate either through (a) simple mechanisms like conditioning, association, and mimicry that arouse affect, followed by cognitive elaboration or (b) through a more deliberate social–cognitive process that in turn triggers a vicarious affective reaction. Either way, the cues of the model's affective state or situation serve as stimuli for arousing a similar affective state in the observer, which in turn provides the observer with information about the model's affective state.

Social cognition, then, operates not alone but in the context of a complex, mutually facilitating give and take between affective and cognitive processes. In social interactions one is constantly making attributions about the other's thoughts and feelings that are based on one's own internal states and on cultural norms and scripts. Although limited, these attributions generally lead to expectations about others that are sufficiently correct for most purposes due to the similarity in organizational structure between actor and model. At the same time, one is also responding with empathic affect, which allows for a sensitivity to nonverbal cues and may thus help alert one to the affective states of others. When one acts on the basis of incorrect attributions there is often corrective feedback. This stimulates one to readjust one's attributions and helps one identify the other's affect with more precision.

Social cognition and social–cognitive development are thus abstractions from what is essentially a matrix of interacting cognitive and affective processes. To return to our initial question, social objects may seem unpredictable from the standpoint of the detached observer who confines his or her analysis to the cognitive processes involved. From the standpoint of an adult or child actually engaged in social interaction and subject to the affective–cognitive interplay, however, other people may seem quite predictable and understandable—certainly to a greater degree than a piece of machinery that provides few if any cues about its principles of operation.

I now summarize the argument. Because people are more complex than things, one would expect a developmental lag in social cognition. There appears to be no such lag and I have suggested several reasons for this. First, people compensate for their complexity by providing feedback that allows one to reassess and correct one's interpretations of their behavior and internal states. Second, people have similar organizational structures and are therefore apt to respond to events in similar ways. Consequently, even in the absence of feedback, when action is based on hurriedly made egocentric attributions, shared belief systems, and scripts, it will generally be adaptive.

Third, there appears to be a natural tendency in humans to respond vicariously or empathically through involuntary, minimally cognitive mechanisms like conditioning and mimicry. The resulting empathic affect provides nonverbal, physiologically based cues, linked to the actor's own past experiences, that alert him or her to the fact that the model is experiencing an affect and may also provide initial information as to what the affect is. Social cognition's role may be to fine tune the actor's assessment of the other's feeling. Social cognition may thus gain a valuable assist from empathy which may compensate for the complexity of its subject matter.

An obvious conclusion is that social cognition cannot be divorced from affect. Piaget and others have always acknowledged that affect is crucial in human behavior, indeed that it is the driving force behind cognitive activity, but they have also assumed that once cognitive processes are set in motion they can be studied without recourse to affect. That may be true of cognition in the physical domain but apparently not in the social domain in which affect appears to be not only the driving force but also a source of crucial information.

REFERENCES

Aderman, D., Brehm, S. S., & Katz, L. B. Empathic observation of an innocent victim: The just world revisited. *Journal of Personality and Social Psychology,* 1974, *29,* 342–347.

Aronfreed, J., & Paskal, V. *Altruism, empathy, and the conditioning of positive affect.* Unpublished manuscript, University of Pennsylvania, 1966.

Bandura, H., & Rosenthal, L. Vicarious classical conditioning as a function of arousal level. *Journal of Personality and Social Psychology,* 1966, *3,* 54–62.

Bell, S. M. The development of the concept of the object as related to infant–mother attachment. *Child Development,* 1970, *41,* 291–311.

Borke, H. Interpersonal perception of young children: Ego-centrism or empathy? *Developmental Psychology,* 1971, *5,* 263–269.

Borke, H. Chandler and Greenspan's "Ersatz ego-centrism": A rejoinder. *Developmental Psychology,* 1972, *7,* 107–109.

Borke, H. Piaget's mountains revisited: Changes in the egocentric landscape. *Developmental Psychology,* 1975, *11,* 240–243.

Cialdini, R. B., Darby, B. L., & Vincent, J. E. Transgression and altruism: A case for hedonism. *Journal of Experimental Social Psychology,* 1973, *9,* 502–516.

Craik, F. I. M., & Lockhart, R. S. Levels of processing: A framework for memory research. *Journal of Verbal Learning and Verbal Behavior,* 1972, *11,* 671–684.

Ekman, P., & Friesen, W. V. Detecting deception from the body or face. *Journal of Personality and Social Psychology,* 1974, *29,* 188–198.

Erikson, E. H. *Childhood and society.* New York: Norton, 1950.

Erwin, J., & Kuhn, D. Development of children's understanding of the multiple determination underlying human behavior. *Developmental Psychology,* 1979, *15,* 352–353.

Fein, D. A. Judgment of causality to physical and social picture sequences. *Developmental Psychology,* 1972, *8,* 147.

Feshbach, N. D., & Roe, K. Empathy in six- and seven-year olds. *Child Development,* 1968, *39,* 133–145.

Festinger, L. A theory of social comparison processes. *Human Relations,* 1954, *7,* 117–140.

Gelhorn, E. Motion and emotion: The role of proprioception in the physiology and pathology of the emotions. *Psychological Review,* 1964, *71,* 457–472.

Gelman, R., & Spelke, E. The development of thoughts about animate and inanimate objects. In J. Flavell & L. Ross (Eds.), *Social cognitive development.* New York: Cambridge University Press, 1981.

Glick, J. Cognition and social cognition: An introduction. In J. Glick & K. A. Clarke-Steward (Eds.), *The development of social understanding.* New York: Gardner Press, 1978.

Guardo, C. J., & Bohan, J. B. Development of a sense of self-identity in children. *Child Development*, 1971, *42*, 1909–1921.

Heider, F. *The psychology of interpersonal relations.* New York, Wiley, 1958.

Hoffman, M. L. Conscience, personality, and socialization techniques. *Human Development*, 1970, *13*, 90–126.

Hoffman, M. L. Developmental synthesis of affect and cognition and its implications for altruistic motivation. *Developmental Psychology*, 1975, *11*, 607–622.

Hoffman, M. L. Moral internalization: Current theory and research. In L. Berkowitz (Ed.), *Advances in experimental social psychology* (Vol. 10). New York: Academic Press, 1977

Hoffman, M. L. Empathy, its development and prosocial implications. In C. B. Keasey (Ed.), *Nebraska Symposium on Motivation* (Vol. 25). Lincoln: University of Nebraska Press, 1978.

Hoffman, M. L. Adolescent morality in development perspective. In J. Adelson (Ed.), *Handbook of adolescent psychology.* New York: Wiley Interscience, 1980.

Hoffman, M. L. Is altruism part of human nature? *Journal of Personality and Social Psychology*, 1981, *40*, 121–137. (a)

Hoffman, M. L. Perspectives on the difference between understanding people and understanding things: The role of affect. In J. Flavell & L. Ross (Eds.), *Social Cognitive Development.* New York: Cambridge University Press, 1981. (b)

Hoffman, M. L. Measurement of empathy. In C. Izard (Ed.), *Measurement of emotions in infants and children.* New York: Cambridge University Press, 1982. (a)

Hoffman, M. L. Development of prosocial motivation: Empathy and guilt. In N. Eisenberg (Ed.), *Development of prosocial behavior.* New York: Academic Press, 1982. (b)

Hoffman, M. L. Affective and cognitive processes in moral internalization: An information processing approach. In E. T. Higgins, D. Ruble, & S. W. Hartup (Eds.), *Advances in social cognitive development.* New York: Cambridge University Press, in press.

Humphrey, G. The conditioned reflex and the elementary social reaction. *Journal of Abnormal and Social Psychology*, 1922, *17*, 113–119.

Imamoglu, E. O. Children's awareness and usage of intention cues. *Child Development*, 1975, *46*, 39–45.

Isen, A. M., Shalker, T. E., Clark, M., & Karp, L. Affect, accessibility of material in memory, and behavior: A cognitive loop? *Journal of Personality and Social Psychology*, 1978, *36*, 1–12.

Izard, C. E. *The face of emotion.* New York: Appleton–Century–Crofts, 1971.

Jackson, E., Campos, J. J., & Fischer, K. W. The question of decalage between object permanence and person permanence. *Developmental Psychology*, 1978, *14*, 1–10.

Jones, E. E., & Nisbett, R. E. The actor and the observer. Divergent perceptions of the causes of behavior. In E. E. Jones, et al. (Eds.), *Attribution: Perceiving the causes of behavior.* Morristown, N.J.: General Learning Press, 1971).

Kahneman, D. *Attention and effort.* Englewood Cliffs, N.J.: Prentice–Hall, Inc., 1973.

Kaplan, L. J. The basic dialogue and the capacity for empathy. In N. Freedman & S. Grand (Eds.), *Communicative structures and psychic structures.* New York: Plenum, 1977.

Keniston, K. *Young radicals.* New York: Harcourt, 1968.

Kohlberg, L. A cognitive developmental analysis of children's sex-role concepts and attitudes. In E. Maccoby (Ed.), *The development of sex differences.* Stanford, Calif.: Stanford University Press, 1966.

Kuhn, D., & Ho, V. The development of schemes for recognizing additive and alternative effects in a "natural experiment" context. *Developmental Psychology*, 1977, *13*, 515–516.

Laird, J. D. Remembering what you feel: Effects of emotion on memory. *Journal of Personality and Social Psychology*, 1982, *42*, 646–657.

Lawick-Goodall, J. *The behavior of free-living chimpanzees in the Gambe Stream Reserve.* London: Baillière, Tindall & Cassell, 1968.

Lempers, J. D., Flavell, E. R., & Flavell, J. H. The development in very young children of tacit knowledge concerning visual perception. *Genetic Psychology Monographs*, 1977, *95*, 3–53.

Lenrow, P. B. Studies in sympathy. In S. S. Tomkins & C. E. Izard (Eds.), *Affect, cognition and personality*. New York: Springer 1965.

Lerner, M. J., & Simmons, C. Observer's reaction to the innocent victim: Compassion or rejection? *Journal of Personality and Social Psychology*, 1966, *4*, 203–210.

Lifton, P. Death in life: Survivors of Hiroshima. New York: Random House, 1968.

Lipps, T. Das Wissen von Fremden Ichen. *Psychologische Untersuchungen*, 1906, *1*, 694–722.

Littlepage, G. E., & Pineault, M. H. Detection of deceptive factual statements from the body and the face. *Personality and Social Psychology Bulletin*, 1979, *5*, 325–328.

MacLean, P. D. A triune concept of the brain and behavior. Toronto: University of Toronto Press, 1973.

Mahler, M. S., Pine, F., & Bergman, A. *The psychological birth of the human infant*. New York: Basic Books, 1975.

Maratsos, M. P. Nonegocentric communication abilities in preschool children. *Child Development*, 1973, *44*, 697–700.

Marvin, R. S. *Aspects of the pre-school child's changing conception of his mother*. Unpublished manuwcript, University of Virginia, 1974.

Masters, J. C. Social comparison by young children. In W. W. Hartup (Ed.), *The young child* (Vol. 2). Washington, D.C.: National Association for the Education of Young Children, 1972.

Menig-Peterson, C. L. The modification of communicative behavior in preschool aged children as a function of the listener's perspective. *Child Development*, 1975, *46*, 1015–18.

Monroe, S. Guest in a strange house. *Saturday Review of Books*. February 1973, pp. 45–48.

Mueller, J. H. Anxiety and encoding processing in memory. *Personality and Social Psychology Bulletin*, 1979, *5*, 288–294.

Mossler, D. G., Marvin, R. S., & Greenberg, M. T. Conceptual perspective taking in 2- to 6-year-old children. *Developmental Psychology*, 1976, *12*, 85–86.

Pazer, S., Slackman, E., & Hoffman, M. Age and sex differences in the effect of information on anger. Unpublished paper, Psychology Department, Graduate School, City University of New York, 1980.

New Republic, November 28, 1970, p. 11.

Newsweek. October 9, 1972, p. 27.

Piaget, J. *The moral judgment of the child*. New York: Harcourt, 1932.

Piaget, J. *The construction of reality in the child*. New York: Basic Books, 1954.

Piaget, J. *The psychology of intelligence*. New York: International Universities Press, 1963.

Proshansky, H. M. The development of intergroup attitudes. In M. L. Hoffman & L. W. Hoffman (Eds.), *Review of Child Development Research (Volume 2)*. New York: Russell Sage Foundation, 1966.

Regan, D. T., Williams, M., & Sparling, S. Voluntary expiation of guilt: A field experiment. *Journal of Personality and Social Psychology*, 1972, 24–42.

Rosenham, D. Some origins of concer for others. In P. H. Mussen, J. Langer, & M. Covington (Eds.), *Trends and issues in developmental psychology*. New York: Holt, Rinehart, & Winston, 1969.

Sagi, A., & Hoffman, M. L. Empathic distress in newborns. *Developmental Psychology*, 1976, *12*, 175–1976.

Schachter, S., & Singer, J. E. Cognitive, social and physiological determinants of emotional state. *Psychological Review*, 1962, *69*, 379–399.

Shatz, M., & Gelman, R. The development of communication skills. Modifications in speech of young children as a function of a listener. *Monographs of the Society for Research in Child Development*, 1973, *38*(5, Serial No. 152).

Simmer, M. L. Newborn's response to the cry of another infant. *Developmental Psychology*, 1971, *5*, 136–150.

Stotland, E. Exploratory investigations of empathy. In L. Berkowitz (Ed.), *Advances in experimental social psychology* (Vol. 4). New York: Academic Press, 1969.

Strayer, J. *Empathy, emotions, and egocentrism.* Presented at meetings of the International Congress of Psychology, Leipzig, Germany, July 1980.

Sullivan, H. S. *Conceptions of modern psychiatry.* London: Tavistock Press, 1940.

Thompson, R., & Hoffman, M. L. Empathy and the arousal of guilt in children. *Developmental Psychology,* 1980, *15,* 155–156.

Tulving, E. Episodic and semantic memory. In E. Tulving & W. Donaldson (Eds.), *Organization of memory.* New York: Academic Press, 1972.

Uzgiris, I., & Hunt, J. McV. *Ordinal scales of infant development.* Paper presented at the 18th International Congress of Psychology, Moscow, August 1966.

Van der Lee, H., & Oppenheimer, L. *Development of temporal ordering of social events.* Unpublished manuscript. Psychologisch Laboratorium, Universiteit van Nijmegen, 1979.

Watson, J. S., & Ramey, C. T. Reactions to responsive contingent stimulation in early infancy. *Merrill–Palmer Quarterly,* 1972, *18,* 219–227.

Winnicott, D. W. Theory of the parent–infant relationship: International Journal of Psychoanalysis, 1960, *41,* 585–595.

Zahn-Waxler, C., Radke-Yarrow, M., & King, R. A. Childrearing and children's prosocial initiations toward victims of distress. *Child Development,* 1979, *50,* 319–330.

Zajonc, R. B. Feeling and thinking: Preferences need no inferences. *American Psychologist,* 1980, *35,* 151–175.

2 Domains and Categories in Social–Cognitive Development

Elliot Turiel
University of California, Berkeley

The study of children's social judgments cannot be restricted to analyses of developmental processes. To deal adequately with the question of development or acquisition it is necessary to study also the nature of the domain in which the development occurs. As Noam Chomsky (1979) has aptly put it: "No discipline can concern itself in a productive way with the acquisition or utilization of a form of knowledge, without being concerned with the *nature* of that system of knowledge [p. 43]." Chomsky's comments came in the context of a discussion of the relations between linguistics and psychology. He maintained that the study of language should not be separated from psychology, as the study of the acquisition or utilization of language. A similar point can be made regarding the study of social–cognitive development. Concern with the development of understandings of the social world or with social behavior requires a concomitant concern with the classification and definition of social domains.

Traditionally, study of the nature of social domains, specifically of society and culture, has been mainly the province of sociologists and anthropologists rather than psychologists. It is said, for instance, that the discipline of anthropology, itself, arose around the concept of culture (Geertz, 1973). Students of culture have identified for investigation a variety of elements related to systems of social interaction and regulation, including tradition, taboo, custom, convention, ethics, rules, law, as well as religious, economic, and political systems. By no means, it should be added, is there unanimity within the discipline over the most adequate way to explain these elements of culture. The disagreements about

53

culture are as major as the disagreements within psychology about development. Some anthropologists hold that all cultures, including small communities, are characterized by diversity and elements not necessarily integrated with each other (Geertz, 1973; Schwartz, 1978; Shweder, 1979a, 1979b), whereas others maintain that cultures are homogeneous, integrated wholes (Benedict, 1934, 1946; Whiting & Child, 1953.) In both these approaches, however, there is only a limited coordination of explanations of culture and social domains with the developmental question of how individuals come to be functioning members of the culture. For the most part, implicit (and untested) assumptions are made about how the individual acquires culture, becomes part of society, and is guided by social rules. Culture is taken to be primary, and the assumption stated most generally is that the individual, starting early in life, accommodates to the patterns or elements of the social system and thereby comes to reflect them in his or her personality, thinking, and behavior (Benedict, 1934, 1946; Geertz, 1973; Whiting & Child, 1953; Whiting & Whiting, 1975).

The assumption that development is accommodation, stems from an acceptance of the idea that there is a close correspondence between what is in the culture and how individuals behave. It should not go unnoticed, however, that much disagreement exists over "what is in the culture." Even more importantly, assumptions are made about development that are not based on systematic investigations of developmental processes. It is psychologists, as would be expected, who have explicitly and extensively investigated the development of the individual's social judgments and actions. The other side of the coin is, however, that research on psychological mechanisms of development has not been based on systematic examination of categories of social interaction or social knowledge. This has certainly been true of those (such as social learning and psychoanalytic theorists) taking a noncognitive approach to social development (cf. Turiel, 1978a). This has also been true of those who have studied social–cognitive development; such study has not been sufficiently informed by considerations regarding the nature of forms of social knowledge. A system of classification of social interactions is essential to an understanding of social thinking. In other words, the nature or domain of a social interaction has a significant bearing on how an individual thinks about it and on how it influences a child's development. It makes a difference to psychological explanation, as well as to an understanding of the social development of individuals, whether we are dealing with economic, political, religious, moral, or conventional systems. In sum, there is a need to coordinate the domains of investigation with the explanation of thought and behavior.

The idea that the study of cognitive development should be coordinated with considerations of the systems of knowledge under investigation is, of course, not new to developmental psychology. It has been one of the salient, though often insufficiently appreciated characteristics of Piaget's genetic epistemology (1970a, 1970c). Piaget (1970c) put it as follows:

The first rule of genetic epistemology is therefore one of collaboration. Since its problem is to study how knowledge grows, it is a matter then, in each particular question, of having the cooperation of psychologists who study the development as such, of logicians who formalize the stages or states of momentary equilibrium of this development, and of scientific specialists who show interest in the domain in question. Naturally we must add mathematicians, who assure the connection between logic and the field in question, and cyberneticians, who assure the connection between psychology and logic. It is then in function, but in function only, of this collaboration that the requirements of fact and validity can both be respected [p. 8].

Toward the general aim of defining and formulating a system of classification of domains and forms of knowledge Piaget and his collaborators have: (1) distinguished between logical–mathematical knowledge and physical (empirical) knowledge (Piaget, 1970b, 1970c), dealing with domains such as classification, seriation, number, space, and time; (2) distinguished between operative activities and the figurative activities of imagery (Piaget & Inhelder, 1971), imitation (Piaget, 1951/1962), perception (Piaget, 1969), and memory (Piaget & Inhelder, 1972); and (3) distinguished between reversible and irreversible operations (Piaget, 1974; Piaget & Inhelder, 1975).

Although recent research on social–cognitive development has been greatly influenced by Piaget's theories and innovative methods, his concerns with the classification of systems of knowledge has not been carried over. Two aspects of Piaget's work have had the most influence. One is his early work (of the 1920s and the beginning of the 1930s) on egocentricism and on moral judgments. The second is the ideas of structure and restructurization in development. In research on social–cognitive development the predominant view of structure has been an integrative global one; it is assumed that the structure of the individual's thinking forms a coherent system. That is, different aspects of social judgment are presumed to be linked with each other, as well as with thinking in nonsocial domains. An alternative interpretation, however, is that there are partial structures encompassing delimited domains of knowledge (Turiel, 1975). In this regard Piaget (1967) has stated:

We shall define structures in the broadest possible sense as a system which presents the laws or properties of a totality seen as a system. These laws of totality are different from the laws or properties of the elements which comprise the system. I must emphasize the fact that these systems are merely partial systems with respect to the whole organism or mind. The concept of structure does not imply just any kind of totality and does not mean that everything is attached to everything else [p. 143].

As a consequence of reliance on Piaget's early work and as a consequence of the global interpretation of structure, adequate distinctions are not always made in the social domains and in social cognitive functions. One of the aims of the present chapter is to illustrate how this is the case through an examination of the antecedents of the recent research on social cognitive development. A working model of social cognition is then presented that combines (a) a view of structural development as a constructive process stemming from individual–environment reciprocal interactions, with (b) the view that the individual's social judgments do not form a unified system. The model is then elaborated through discussion of research that provides supporting evidence.

A Brief History

Much of the research since the late 1950s on the development of role taking and moral judgments has its roots in the research conducted by Piaget in the 1920s. One thrust of Piaget's theorizing in his earliest writings dealt with the proposition that children progress from an egocentric to a perspectivistic state. He proposed that children younger than 6 or 7 years of age do not clearly differentiate between self and others or between thoughts (the psychological) and external events. A consequence of the failure to differentiate the self from others is that the child is unable to take the perspective of another person. For instance, in communicating with others the child is unable to take into account the requirements of the listener (Piaget, 1923). A consequence of the failure to differentiate thoughts from external events is that the child attributes an objective reality to internal mental events such as dreams (Piaget, 1929). A major developmental transition was posited to occur when the child shifts from an egocentric state to one in which the self is differentiated from others and there is the ability to take another's perspective.

However, the most extensive research in a social domain undertaken by Piaget during this early period dealt with children's moral judgments. Those were also the only studies on moral development to be done by Piaget. Three specific aspects of Piaget's moral development theory had a substantial influence on later research. One was the characterization of moral development as a process of differentiating moral from nonmoral judgments. The second was the proposed interrelations between "general" cognitive orientations and moral judgments. And the third was the proposed relations between changes in perspective-taking abilities and changes in moral judgments.

Piaget proposed that children progress through two moral judgment levels (following an early premoral phase), the first being labeled *heteronomous* (generally corresponding to ages 3 to 8 years) and the second labeled *autonomous*. In the heteronomous level, the child has unilateral respect for adults (regarded as authority) and morality is, therefore, based on conformity. The right or good is seen by the child as adherence to externally determined and fixed rules and commands. The young child's morality of conformity and unilateral respect becomes transformed into a morality of cooperation and mutual respect. The basis for the autonomous level is the emergence of concepts of reciprocity and equality. At this level, rules are viewed as products of mutual agreement, serving the aims of cooperation, and thus are regarded as changeable.

In formulating the levels of heteronomy and autonomy, Piaget studied children's judgments about several specific issues, including rules, punishment, intentionality, lying, stealing, and distributive justice. A brief description of the levels can be provided by considering some of the studies of children's thinking about rules and about intentionality in situations involving property damage, deceit, and theft. The definitions of the moral levels were derived, in part, from the way Piaget had framed children's general cognitive capacities. Two presumed characteristics regarding the increasing differentiations that occur with development were relevant. One proposed characteristic was the child's egocentricism, the failure to clearly distinguish the self's perspective from that of others. A second relevant feature was the young child's failure to differentiate the physical world from social and mental phenomena; young children confuse the subjective and objective aspects of their experience.

According to Piaget, one concrete manifestation of young children's inability to differentiate perspectives and to differentiate the physical from the social is their attitudes toward social rules. It was proposed that children at the heteronomous level view all social rules as absolute. The inability to take the perspective of others leads the child to assume that everyone adheres to the same rules. There is a failure to comprehend the possibility that rules may be relative to the social context or to an individual's perspective. In turn, there is an inability to clearly distinguish physical from social phenomena that leads to a confusion of social regularities with physical regularities, such that social rules are seen as fixed in much the same way as are physical regularities. For instance, Piaget maintained that children regard rules of games as unchangeable; they believe it would be wrong to modify the rules of a game even if they were changed by general consensus.

Another manifestation of the young child's cognitive confusions is that judgments of right and wrong are based on the material consequences of actions, rather than the actor's intentions or motives. Piaget examined the relative importance that children attribute to intentions and consequences in situations involving material damage, lying, and stealing. Younger children, it was found, attribute greater importance, in judging culpability, to amount of damage (e.g., breaking the 15 cups accidentally is worse than breaking one cup intentionally), whereas older children attribute more importance to the intentions of the actor. Similarly, younger children assess the wrongness of lying or stealing, not by the motives of the actor, but by their quantitative deviation from the truth or the amount stolen. In judgments about theft, for instance, children judging by consequences would say that stealing a larger amount to give to a very poor friend is worse than stealing a lesser amount for oneself.

In contrast with the heteronomous level, at the autonomous level respect is no longer unilateral, rules are not viewed as absolute or fixed, and judgments are based on intentions. Piaget proposed that these changes are stimulated by the

increasing interactions with peers (such as in school) and the decreasing orientation to relations with adult authority that usually occurs during late childhood.
Relations with authorities (parents, teachers, etc.), he maintained, are likely to
lead to conformity and an attitude of unilateral respect on the part of the young
child. That is, the child feels that the authorities are superior and that their
dictates are right by virtue of their superior status. In order for the shift from a
heteronomous to an autonomous orientation to occur the child must more clearly
differentiate the self from others and, thereby, be able to take the perspective of
others. Relations with adult authorities who impose external rules upon the child
are likely to reinforce a heteronomous orientation, whereas relations with peers
are more likely to stimulate attempts to take the perspectives of others. Therefore, through increasing interactions with those he or she can relate to on an
equal footing, the child is stimulated to view his or her own perspective as one
among many different perspectives. In the process, mutual respect replaces
unilateral respect for authority and the bases of a sense of justice—reciprocity,
equality, and cooperation—emerge. Rules are then regarded as social constructions, based on agreement, that serve functions shared by the participants of
social interactions. The increasing awareness of others' perspectives and subjective intentions leads to judgments that are based on intentionality rather than
consequences.

In addition to the connections to general cognitive capacities, Piaget's characterization of moral judgments was a global one in that development was defined as
entailing a progressive differentiation of principles of justice (ought) from the
habitual, customary, and conventional (is). In essence, the claim was that concepts of justice do not emerge until the autonomous stage (see Piaget, 1932/1948,
p. 350). Thus, the heteronomous morality of constraint and unilateral respect is a
morality of custom, convention and tradition, while autonomous morality of
mutual respect and cooperation prevails over custom and convention. Prior to the
development of concepts of justice, therefore, the child must progress through the
"simpler," conformity-based conventional orientation (see Piaget, 1932/1948,
pp. 64–66).

In sum, Piaget proposed a model of development as the differentiation of
domains of knowledge. Only at more advanced stages are moral judgments and
knowledge of the social order (or even morality and physical law) distinguished.
It is precisely on this basis that Piaget thought it was methodologically valid to
examine children's concepts of rules of marble games as a means to understanding their moral reasoning.

The Impact of Piaget's Early Formulations

From the time that Piaget published his reports of research on social development, until around 1960, little was done on social–cognitive development. However, during the same period (and continuing until the present) a good deal of

progress occurred in the theorizing and research of Piaget and his colleagues in nonsocial domains. The global characterization of development as entailing general differentiations (between self–other, internal–external, physical–social, moral–societal) was replaced by: (1) more specific analyses of the structure and development of logical–mathematical and physical concepts; (2) analyses of imagery, imitation, perception, and memory (the figurative activities); and (3) elaborations of equilibration as the process governing developmental transitions.

Around 1960 there began a period of burgeoning research on just those topics that Piaget had originally researched: morality and role taking. The initial impetus for the moral judgment work came from Kohlberg (1958, 1963a, 1963b) and for the role-taking work from Feffer (1959; Feffer & Gourevitch, 1960). The influence of Piaget's early notions was by no means limited to the content of the topics studied: It went more deeply than that! Most importantly, the globality of the early Piagetian analyses was accepted. A structural view, it was assumed, is one that asserts that all aspects of thought are interrelated: Moral judgments are integrally related to the types of thinking used in nonsocial domains; all aspects of thought follow the principles of structure and transformation; all development proceeds from a state of global undifferentiation to states of greater differentiation.

In Kohlberg's theory of moral judgments, like that of Piaget, it is proposed that the developmental process is one in which morality (principles of justice) emerges out of its differentiation from nonmoral judgments (including prudence and convention). On the basis of studies that included older age groups (up to about 20 years) than those in Piaget's studies, Kohlberg presented a modified and extended version of the moral stage sequence. The sequence contains six stages, grouped into three general levels. The major modifications of Piaget's moral stage scheme made in the stages formulated by Kohlberg are: that at the earliest stages (Stages 1 and 2) moral judgments are based not on respect for authority and rules, but on a confusion of morality with power and punishment; that adolescence is characterized by a level of conventional morality (Stages 3 and 4); and that autonomous morality (Stages 5 and 6) is seen as developing during late adolescence or early adulthood. According to Kohlberg, therefore, the emergence of concepts of justice comes even later than had been proposed by Piaget. Nevertheless, Kohlberg's formulation is similar to Piaget's in that development is defined as a process of differentiating the moral from the nonmoral.

The range of the applicability of the proposed moral judgment stages is wide (Kohlberg, 1971, pp. 215–216). The differentiation thesis is that stages below those of autonomous morality (Stages 5 and 6) are applicable to a variety of judgments (punishment, prudence, authority, convention, aesthetics). The extensiveness of the formulation goes even further. On the basis of a definition of mental structure as encompassing the mind as a whole and that "everything is attached to everything else," Kohlberg hypothesized that the stages of moral judgment are related to what are presumed to be more basic aspects of (nonsocial) cognitive development (i.e., those identified by Piaget as sensorimotor, preoperations, concrete operations, and formal operations). It was proposed (Kohlberg, 1969, 1971) that development through an invariant sequence of moral judgment stages is partially dependent on development in the "cognitive" stages; cognitive development is necessary but not sufficient for moral development. Specifically the prior emergence of certain stages of cognitive development are necessary for, but do not guarantee (thus are not sufficient), the emergence of certain moral judgment stages (see also Keasey, 1975; Kuhn, Langer, Kohlberg, & Haan, 1977; Selman, 1976a; Tomlinson-Keasey & Keasey, 1974).

At the same time that Kohlberg was extending Piaget's theory of moral development (see also Kramer, 1968; Rest, 1973; Turiel, 1966, 1969), Feffer began further research on Piaget's early notion regarding the shift from egocentricism to perspectivism (Feffer, 1959; Feffer & Gourevitch, 1960). (The work of Piaget and Inhelder (1948/1956) on children's concepts of spatial perspectives also provided an impetus to research on social role taking). Further research on role taking was later undertaken by Flavell (1968), DeVries (1970), Selman and Byrne (1974), Selman (1976b), and others.

The procedure used by Feffer and Gourevitch was to ask children to tell stories about ambiguous situations as it would appear from the viewpoint of different actors in the situation. They proposed five ordered and age-related categories that describe increasingly systematic ways of accounting for perspectives of different actors in a story (Feffer & Gourevitch, 1960, pp. 386–387). A few years later Flavell (1968) conducted a series of studies of children's abilities to take the perspectives of others in communication tasks, spatial tasks, in recounting stories, and in guessing games (also used by DeVries). For each task a series of age-related strategies, levels, and stages were reported.

Even more recently, Selman and Byrne have, in an explicit way, combined the egocentricism–role-taking dimensions with the stage and sequence constructs. They maintained that "social role taking can be conceptually defined in structural terms" (Selman & Byrne, 1974, pp. 806–807). A sequence of five stages was proposed that ranged from: (1) an egocentric state in which the child is unable to differentiate the points of view of others; to (2) an awareness of different perspectives, without the ability to coordinate perspectives simultaneously; to (3) self-reflective role taking, in which there is an awareness that others are aware of the self's perspectives; to (4) mutual role taking, in which there is an awareness that self and other can simultaneously and mutually take each other's perspectives; to (5) an ability to take the perspective of generalized others or the social system.

In keeping with the global definition of structure, proposals of further domain interrelationships have emerged from the role-taking research. It was hypothesized that stages of role taking and moral judgment are in a partially dependent relation with each other (Selman & Damon, 1975; Kohlberg, 1971; Selman,

1971). Moreover, a compounded set of structural dependencies has been proposed: Development in stages of cognitive development is necessary, but not sufficient, for development in stages of moral judgment (Kohlberg, 1976, Selman, 1976a).

Additional Formulations

In recent years increased attention has been given to the development of social cognition. The moral judgment stages proposed by both Piaget and Kohlberg provided one basis for a good deal of this research (see Keasey, 1979 for a review of recent research dealing with the Piaget moral judgment stages). Role taking has also been the subject of many investigations (see Shantz, 1975 for a review). At the same time, however, several other content areas of social concepts have been studied by researchers taking a structural perspective. A list containing most of the content areas studied is presented in Table 2.1. A perusal of Table 2.1 shows that the scope of topics considered by various researchers to be part of social–cognitive development has been expanded beyond Piaget's concerns with morality and role taking.[2]

Table 2.1 is divided into two parts that represent the two general theoretical strategies used. The first part contains a list of those studies in which a social domain was analyzed through the application of a stage-sequence formulation from another domain. The strategy in this group of studies is to explain subjects' responses in a given domain of thought by applying extant stage descriptions from some other domain. One of the first examples was the proposition (Kohlberg, 1966) that children's sex-role concepts are determined by their stages of cognitive development (as described by Piaget). Kohlberg attempted to trace sex-role concepts to the formulation of the concept of an invariant gender identity. He maintained that the child's understanding that gender identity is invariant does not come about until the stage of concrete operations. The cognitive operations resulting in the concept of conservation of number, substance, or weight were presumed to result in the concept of the invariance of gender identity. A similar analysis of the concept of generic identity was provided by DeVries (1969). She proposed that when confronted with superficial transformations (e.g., putting a mask of a dog's face on a cat) the preoperational (nonconserving) child believes that the identity of an animal is changed.

A similar strategy has been used by Scarlett, Press, and Crockett (1971), Bigner (1974) and Montemayor and Eisen (1977) in their studies of children's concepts of other persons and the self. Subjects' descriptions of peers and siblings were analyzed in accordance with Werner's (1957) orthogenetic principle. These studies thus represent additional examples of the approach that views development as entailing the differentiation of domains of knowledge. The

---

[2]The list in Table 2.1 contains studies up to 1979.

TABLE 2.1
Topics of Social Judgment Studied

I. Studies in which prior developmental analyses have been directly applied to a social domain

A. Application of Piaget's stage formulations (logical–mathematical and physical concepts).

Topic	Reference
Sex role	Kohlberg (1966)
	Emmerich, Goldman, Kirch, & Sharabany (1977)
	Marcus & Overton (1978)
Generic identity	DeVries (1969)
Altruism	Bar-Tal, Raviv, & Sharabany (1977)
Death	White, Elson, & Prawat (1978)

B. Application of Werner's orthogenetic principle.

Topic	Reference
Description of persons: Peers	Scarlett, Press, & Crockett (1971)
Description of persons: Siblings	Bigner (1974)
Self	Montemayer & Eisen (1977)

C. Application of Kohlberg's moral judgment stages.

Topic	Reference
Sexuality	Gilligan, Kohlberg, Lerner, & Belenky (1970)
	Stein (1973)
Politics	Lockwood (1976)
Altruism	Krebs (1978)

II. Direct analysis of the domain

Topic	Reference
Moral judgment	Kohlberg (1963b)[a]
Role (Perspective) taking	Feffer & Gourevitch (1960)
	Flavell (1968)
	Selman & Byrne (1974)[a]
	Selman (1976a)[a]
Distributive justice (Morality)	Damon (1977)
Social convention (Social organization)	Turiel (1978a)
Groups	Neiderman (1978)
Social institutions	Furth (1978)[a]
Authority	Damon (1977)
Sex role	Ullian (1976a, 1976b)
Social roles	Watson (1979)
Friendship (Interpersonal relations)	Bigelow (1977)
	Selman & Cooney (1978)[a]
	Youniss & Volpe (1978)
Kindness (Interpersonal relations)	Youniss (1975)

(continued)

TABLE 2.1   (*Continued*)

Mind	Broughton (1978)[a]
Self/identity	Broughton (1978)[a]
	Lemke (1973)
	Nucci (1977)
	Wolfson (1972)[b]
Person	Barenboim (1977)
	Pratt (1975)
Deviance and disorder	Coie & Pennington (1976)
Origins of babies	Bernstein & Cowan (1975)[b]

[a]Studies proposing that development in the given social domain is partially dependent on development in nonsocial cognitive domains.

[b]Studies entailing a partial application of Piaget's stage formulations and partially entailing a direct analysis of the domain.

orthogenetic principle states that development proceeds from a global undifferentiated state to states of increasing differentiation and integration. The very general dimensions of egocentric–nonegocentric and concrete–abstract were used in these studies to explain the development of children's concepts of persons.

Although the studies mentioned thus far entailed the application of general developmental principles (Werner) or nonsocial cognitive stages (Piaget) to social domains, in some cases social domains have been analyzed through the application of a stage-sequence formulation from a different social domain. Implicit, if not explicit, in such endeavors is the assumption that a form of social judgment (e.g., morality) is used by individuals in a wide variety of social situations. Examples of this approach can be seen in studies of judgments about sexuality (Gilligan, Kohlberg, Lerner, & Belenky, 1970; Stein, 1973). In these studies responses made by adolescent subjects to questions dealing with sexuality were simply assumed to be codeable on the basis of the moral judgment stages formulated by Kohlberg.

In contrast with the studies listed in the first part of Table 2.1, the studies listed on the second part of the table are ones in which direct analyses have been made of the content area. In most cases the method used in choosing the topic for investigation is "ad hoc empirical" (as opposed to basing the choice on a systematic classification of social domains). By this is meant that researchers choose issues that are considered important and/or interesting in social life, such as morality, friendship, or deviance, and then obtain responses regarding the issue from subjects of different ages. All the topics listed in the table have been subjected to a stage (or level) sequence analysis. Children's thinking about the issue is described as undergoing age-related qualitative changes through an invariant sequence. Thus, developmental changes in thinking about these issues are presumed to entail reorganizations of thought. Moreover, in some cases (see table footnotes) it is hypothesized that development through the proposed stages is partially dependent on development in other domains of structural development.

Recent Approaches to Social Cognitive Development

It was stated earlier that researchers of social–cognitive development have relied on Piaget's early work and thereby failed to make adequate distinctions among different social domains and among different types of cognitive functions. In addition, the review of recent research has shown that aspects of Piaget's later formulations have been juxtaposed upon the analyses of social cognition. In particular, two ideas have been juxtaposed: the idea that development entails structural transformations and a global interpretation of structure. Four predominant theoretical–empirical strategies and/or hypotheses (they are not necessarily mutually exclusive) can be identified from the foregoing discussion.

1. Reliance on Earlier Research.   In the first place, there has been a tendency to define the field of social cognition through those topics that have a prior history of research activity. This has been particularly true for the topics of role taking and moral judgment. The obvious advantage of such an approach is that one may build on previous advances. However, as already stated, rather than building on the previous work, there has been a dependence on it. Piaget's choice of role taking as a topic of investigation was based on his initial assumptions regarding the global developmental shift from egocentricism to perspectivism and not on an analysis of its place in social knowledge. Most likely, the choice of morality as a topic of study did have an epistemological basis. Piaget recognized (see Chapter 4 of Piaget, 1932/1948) both the importance of morality for social life and its long-standing status as a topic of great philosophical and social scientific concern. Nevertheless, Piaget did not attempt to relate the development of moral judgment to a more general analysis of the nature of social knowledge. Consequently, the subsequent reliance upon Piaget's early work has resulted in a perpetuation of global analyses and a lack of concern with a system of classifying forms of social knowledge.

2. Direct Applications from One Domain to Another.   In some cases there has been a direct application of existing descriptions of developmental changes in one domain to another domain. Typically, it is assumed that there are core cognitive stages used in a variety of social domains. This is the rationale for the application of stages of logical–mathematical and physical cognition to sex-role concepts or gender identity (see Table 2.1). Such an approach is reductionistic; sex-role concepts, as an example, are treated as the application of physical concepts to persons. Similarly, existing descriptions of developmental changes within a social domain have been applied to another social domain. Table 2.1

shows, for instance, that in some studies judgments about sexuality have been coded for moral judgment stage (Gilligan et al., 1970; Stein, 1973). As discussed elsewhere (Turiel, 1978a, pp. 65–66), the results of those studies actually point to the inappropriateness of such a procedure in that they have indicated that adolescent judgments about sexuality are nonmoral ones. In general, there is a great susceptibility to error inherent in the application of existing stage descriptions from one domain to another because it is unlikely that independent analyses will be made of the new domain.

The reductionistic features of applying a preestablished system to a new domain can be illustrated by considering the findings of recent research on the development of sex-role concepts (Marcus & Overton, 1978; Ullian, 1976a, 1976b). Kohlberg (1966) first proposed that the formation of gender identity is a primary factor in sex-role development. The formation of sex-role concepts requires a conceptualization of a stable gender identity, as well as associated categorizations of self and others. It had been found that children do not form an understanding of the invariance of gender identity until 5 or 6 years of age. Younger children do not maintain the constancy of gender identity in the face of superficial transformations in the person (e.g., in hairstyle or dress). Given the correspondence in age between the shift in conceptualization of gender identity and the shift from the preoperational to the concrete operational stage (as defined by Piaget), it was proposed that the child's understanding of gender constancy is based on the attainment of what was regarded as the more basic concrete operational concepts of conservation of mass, number, and length. Indeed, subsequent research (De Vries, 1969; Emmerich, Goldman, Kirsch, & Sharabany, 1977; Marcus & Overton, 1978) found that the attainment of gender constancy is correlated with conservation concepts.

The sex-role development formulation initiated by Kohlberg served the important function of reconceptualizing the problem in cognitive terms. Kohlberg has convincingly pointed out that sex-role development entails the formation of concepts of identity and is not merely the manifestation of biologically determined dispositions or culturally learned behavioral traits. Children's concepts of sex-role identity are based on the ways in which they order the perceived differences and similarities between males and females. As already stated, however, the direct application of nonsocial cognitive stages to sex-role concepts falls short of an adequate analysis of their social–cognitive dimensions.

First, consider the idea that knowledge of the invariance of gender identity is related to the development of concepts of conservation. The rationale for relating these two concepts is that they both entail knowledge of invariants. There is, however, an important difference between conservation and gender constancy; conservation is a quantitative notion, whereas gender constancy is based on knowledge about social identities. In fact, it is necessary to distinguish between the child's concepts of a stable identity of physical objects and the conservation of quantities (Piaget, 1968). Children develop concepts of physical identity (e.g., they recognize that it is the same water after it is poured from one beaker to the next) prior to the development of concepts of conservation (e.g., the recognition that it is the same amount of water after the transformation). Correspondingly, children develop stable concepts of generic identity (De Vries, 1969) and personal identity (Lemke, 1973) prior to the development of the concept of gender constancy.

Knowledge of the invariance of gender constancy is a form of *qualitative* identity that does not require *quantitative* notions and, therefore, would not be dependent on the attainment of concepts of conservation. Sex-role concepts entail a system of social categorization, including a classification of types of persons (male or female) and concepts of what it means to be masculine or feminine. One basis for the classification rests on differences in the physical–biological characteristics of males and females. More significantly, sex-role categorizations are based on psychological attributes and knowledge of social–conventional behavioral uniformities (Carter & Patterson, in press). The use of psychological and social attributes in the formation of sex-role identity does not presuppose an understanding of its invariance. A study by Marcus and Overton (1978) showed that young children (4- to 5-year-olds) who did not yet maintain gender constancy, nevertheless, displayed same-sex preferences. Thus, children form sex-role concepts based on behavioral traits, even in the absence of an understanding of the biology of gender identity. On the physical–biological dimension, it is likely that their classification of male–female differences is also based on observable physical characteristics (e.g., hairstyle, clothing).

By the ages of 6 or 7 years children form an understanding of the biological meaning of gender identity, such that it is judged to be invariant in spite of variances in observable physical characteristics. However, the psychological and social definitions of gender identity contain potential empirically variable features, as well. Research by Ullian (1976a, 1976b) has shown that there are age-related changes in concepts of masculinity and femininity from childhood through adolescence. Although this is not the place to describe the levels formulated by Ullian, it should be noted that concepts of masculinity and femininty include descriptive judgments of biological and psychological attributes, as well as prescriptive judgments of conventionally necessary behavior for males and females. These qualitative notions apparent in concepts of masculinity and feminininity would have not been uncovered if the analyses had solely entailed an application of nonsocial cognitive stages to the domain. It is in this sense that the strategy of applying stage descriptions from one domain to another can be reductionistic.

3. The Necessary but Not Sufficient Hypothesis.   In the approach just discussed one domain is treated as content for what is regarded as a more basic domain. However, a more commonly held idea, as can be seen in Table 2.1, is that social domains are partially dependent on what is considered to be a core cognitive structure (the necessary but not sufficient hypothesis). Elsewhere it was maintained (Turiel, 1978a, 1978b) that the research evidence is inconclusive because the hypothesis has been addressed solely through correlational studies. Correlations between different measures of developmental level do not provide an adequate means of testing the hypothesis of structural relations. At best, correlations provide an assessment of the degree of correspondence in (and patterns of) the rates of change of the two measures used; measures of two structurally unrelated aspects of development could produce high correlation coefficients if there were a correspondence in their individual rates of change. This was demonstrated by Fischer (1977), who reported a high correlation (.88) between a developmental sequence of classification skills in 2- to 7-year-old children and their shoe sizes.

More fundamentally, however, there is a contradiction in the hypothesis that development in one system of an invariant sequence of stages is necessary but not sufficient for development in another system of an invariant sequence of stages. This is explicated in some detail because the hypothesis is frequently posed (it has even been reified in some of our textbooks) and because it is deeply rooted in the integrative global definition of structure. The general thesis, it should be reiterated, is that: (1) each system of thought forms an invariant sequence of stages; and (2) development in one system (call it System A) is a necessary but not sufficient condition for development in the other system (call it System B). However, it is assumed that stage change can occur in System A without a concomittant change in System B. Thus, there is not a one-to-one correspondence between the two systems. Taken together, these propositions are contradictory; there would not be sequential invariance in both systems because one is dependent on the other. That is, if it were the case that development in System A is a prerequisite for development in System B, then the stages in System B would not form an invariant sequence.

Consider some hypothetical examples. Let us assume that development in System A proceeds through Stages 1, 2, 3, and 4, while development in System B proceeds through Stages a, b, c, and d. Further assume that Stage 2 is necessary but not sufficient for Stage b, that Stage 3 is necessary but not sufficient for Stage c, and that Stage 4 is necessary but not sufficient for Stage d. Given the assumptions of the prerequisite hypothesis, consider two possibilities for subjects who are initially at Stage 1 and Stage a.

The first example is as follows:

(1a) The subject then progresses to Stage 2. This change allows for progress to Stage b, but does not guarantee it (the not sufficient aspect of the hypothesis).

(1b) Next, the subject progresses to Stage b.

(1c) Then the subject progresses from Stage 2 to Stage 3. This, in turn, allows for progress to Stage c.

In the foregoing example, the subject would progress through the two sequences in the prescribed order.

Now consider a second example (also a subject who is initially at Stage 1 and at Stage a):

(2a) The subject then progresses to Stage 2. This allows for progress to Stage b, but does not guarantee it.

(2b) The subject remains at Stage a, but eventually moves to Stage 3.

(2c) The subject then progresses within System B.

The System-B sequence reflected in (1a) to (1c) would be different from that of (2a) to (2c). In the first case a *combination of Stage 2 plus Stage a* produces Stage b; and a combination of Stage 3 and Stage b produces Stage c. In the second case the combinations are different. The System-B change in (2c) would be a function of the *combination of Stage 3 plus Stage a*. The resulting change is therefore likely to be some alternative, and unspecified type that would reflect the Stage 3 and Stage a combination.

The purpose of presenting these hypothetical combinations and sequences is to show that if (a) one system of stages is prerequisite for another system of stages, then (b) the stages in the second system would not form an invariant sequence. An invariant sequence of development exists when each stage is generated from the previous stage in the same system, through interactions with the environment. Insofar as one system is dependent on another, then there may be variability in the sequence of the dependent system (unless there is a one-to-one correspondence between the two systems). The theoretical tasks entailed in explicating a prerequisite relation between domains are to determine: (1) the precise relations of intersection between the two domains; (2) why change in one system is a necessary condition for change in the other; and (3) the potential *variant* sequences of development in the dependent system. The proposition of an invariant sequence of stages, therefore, implies that it represents an independent structural domain.

4. The Ad Hoc Empirical Approach   A prevalent strategy in the recent research on social cognition has been to choose topics in an ad hoc empirical fashion, which are then analyzed in accordance with the stage-sequence model. The main advantage of such issue-oriented empirical explorations is that they sometimes do uncover information regarding children's social judgments. There are pitfalls, however, when these studies are not tied to a more general analysis of the nature of the domain and its relation to other types of social judgments.

In the first place, the ad hoc empirical approach often fails to consider the all important question of whether or not a topic is a well-formulated one for an investigation that deals with the individual's knowledge systems. There is the always difficult problem of making an assessment of the degree of importance or triviality (epistemologically not practically) of the topic. In addition, because the aim of the investigation is to describe ways in which children construct knowledge about the topic, it is of some importance that the topic actually be a sufficiently rich object of thought and knowledge.

From an epistemological viewpoint, problematic examples of topics that have been studied can be found in Table 2.1. A case in point is the study of children's concepts of friendship, a topic that has received a fair amount of attention recently. Friendships are among the significant relationships that individuals have with each other. Through their friendships individuals engage in social interactions, upon which various issues are brought to bear (e.g., morality, regulations, conventions, understanding of persons). It must be asked, however, whether individuals form a system of knowledge about friendship that, in itself, is not part of the other domains to which relations with friends pertain. An analogy can be drawn to the study of concepts of social rules. As discussed later, the research findings show that individuals do not form a unitary concept of social rules; the meaning attributed to social rules varies in accordance with the domain to which the rules pertains. Similarly, it may be that concepts of friendship can be subsumed under other topics. In such a case, the meaning attributed to friendship would be dependent on the different aspects of those social interactions. Answers to these questions are yet unavailable because of the prevelance of an ad hoc empirical approach in the study of concepts of friendship. It is especially necessary that the type of knowledge entailed in concepts of friendship be specified because the topic has not traditionally been part of philosophical–epistemological concern. Friendship has no branch in philosophy, as there is of moral philosophy or of the philosophy of logic. The study of friendship has been tied to the study of interpersonal relations (Selman & Cooney, 1978; Youniss & Volpe, 1978), which does have a tradition within psychology (particularly in the clinical branches). Nevertheless, it is necessary to elucidate the role of knowledge about interpersonal relations within social knowledge.

Part of the process of elucidating the nature of a topic like friendship, or any of the others listed in Table 2.1, is to determine whether or not it forms an organized system of thought that undergoes structural transformations in ontogenesis. Indeed, one of the major pitfalls of the ad hoc empirical approach is that the application of a stage analysis to a given topic may be inappropriate. Inappropriate application of a stage analysis occurs when it is imposed on a cognitive function that does not form an organized transformational system (Turiel, 1979). It was maintained elsewhere (Turiel, 1979) that role taking is just such a topic; role taking does not form an organized system of thought and, therefore, its development does not follow a stage model.

It is necessary, therefore, to provide theoretical and empirical bases for distinguishing social cognitive functions that form organized systems of thought from those that do not. The systems of organization constitute the means by which objects and events are *transformed,* are comprehended, interpreted, and manipulated (Piaget, 1970b; Turiel, 1979). At the same time, individuals also utilize what is referred to as *methods* for gathering information or data from the social environment (Turiel, 1979). The individual extracts and reproduces information about people, about interactions between people, and about systems of social organization. Under the general category of social information may be included knowledge about the behaviors and existing psychological states (thoughts and feelings) of specific persons, the composition of individuals within social groups, the rules, laws, and regulations of social systems, the institutions existing within specific societies, and so on. These forms of social information are extracted and reproduced through the use of methods, which include such activities as observation, communication, imitation, and symbolically taking the perspective of another (role taking). As methods of information gathering, these activities serve as means for representing social information, without directly producing conceptual transformations; through the use of methods the individual attempts to reproduce what is given in the external environment. The methods, therefore, do not form organized systems and do not undergo structural changes. With increasing age there may be *quantitative* changes in the methods, such as increments in their accuracy and scope.

The contention that *role taking* does not follow a stage model is based both on considerations regarding the type of functions served by role taking and on previous research findings. The hypothesis is that the activity of role taking does not serve to transform events; rather, it produces information about the states of others. It enables one to ascertain what another person is thinking, feeling, or seeing when such information is unavailable through other more direct means (e.g., through direct communications with the person). As a method, role taking is defined as the activity of symbolically putting oneself in the place of another person. The function of attempting to put oneself in the place of another is to reproduce unobservable internal states. The attempt at placing oneself in the perspective of another person is unnecessary when knowledge of another's internal state is available through other means. For instance, if the other communicates (assuming honesty and completeness) about his or her internal state (e.g., thoughts, feelings, perceptions), then the sought-after information would be directly available. In the absence of such communications, however, the individual seeking the information may use a more indirect means of obtaining it by symbolically placing himself or herself in the position of the other.

Role taking, therefore, provides data in context; it is a way of obtaining information about a particular person in a given situation. The method of role taking is analytically separable from conceptual systems, but not unrelated to them. Role taking can be related to concepts in two respects. First, the information that one derives about persons through role taking (or other methods) may be put to conceptual uses. As examples, information about others may be used in making a moral judgment that attempts to reconcile conflicting interests or needs; the same information can also be used for the very different purpose of swindling other people. Another example of the type of use to which information about persons is put is the construction of a psychological explanation of that person or of persons in general. Keep in mind, however, that the role-taking activities or the information derived through such acts do not in themselves constitute concepts of the person, although they are influenced by existing conceptual structures (this issue is discussed further in a later section).

The activity of role taking is also influenced by the individual's conceptual systems in the following sense: A situation that calls for taking the perspective of another person involves conceptualizations on the part of the actor that are independent of the role-taking activity. The extent to which the actor understands the concepts involved, assuming a role-taking competence on his or her part, will determine the accuracy and scope of the role taking in the situation. This can be illustrated through a hypothetical example. Suppose we were to design the following "role-taking" task. The subjects are between 3 and 4 years of age. Each subject observes another child who is 10 years old being asked to solve a task dealing with the conservation of continuous quantities. After the liquid is poured from one beaker to the other and before the 10-year-old responds, the subject is asked to predict the 10-year-old's response to the standard conservation question (which has more or are they the same). Although this experiment has not been done, it is quite likely that most 3- and 4-year-old subjects would incorrectly predict that the 10-year-old will say that one beaker has more liquid than the other. Obviously, such an experiment would not provide information regarding the subjects' role-taking abilities. Regardless of role-taking ability, their performance would be based on their level of conceptualization of the conservation task. In addition, their performance would be influenced by their knowledge about how children respond to such tasks. Thus, it could also be asked if a 10-year-old would be able to "role take" accurately the response of a 4-year-old to the conservation task. It is likely that 10-year-olds (and many adults) would not display accurate role taking, as most of them have little understanding of how 4-year-old children respond to conservation tasks.

In this hypothetical experiment the assessment of a child's role taking would be confounded with the level of conceptualization of conservation required by the task, as well as by the child's psychological knowledge. It is essentially this type of confounded paradigm that is used in role-taking studies; role taking has not been studied in a pure or absolute form. There is a reason, however, that the role-taking studies have used a confounded paradigm. Namely, that role taking, as a method, is necessarily used in the context of conceptual domains (and the method is used in relation to various conceptual domains). The tasks devised by researchers to study role taking typically have involved concepts of space, probabilistic notions (e.g., in guessing-game tasks) and concepts of inner psychological states (strategies, thoughts, knowledge, and feelings). Role taking has also been studied in communication contexts and story-telling situations. As in the conservation example, in any of these studies a child with the competence to engage in role taking would be unable to do so on a task that calls for a conceptual level not yet attained. Accordingly, on a different task requiring a conceptual level attained by the child, he or she will display his or her role-taking competence. (Thus, the different conceptual contexts for role taking should not be regarded as different types of role taking.)

The findings from role-taking studies clearly show: (1) that role-taking competence emerges at around the ages of 3 or 4 years (because it is a symbolic activity, the development of representational thought is a prerequisite for the emergence of role taking); and (2) that role-taking performance varies according to the level of competence in the associated conceptual domain of the task (Turiel, 1979). For the present purposes, a brief review of some of the studies will suffice to demonstrate that the presence or absence of similar types of role-taking responses, in subjects as young as 3 or 4 years and as old as 12 to 13 years, vary according to the type of task and experimental method used.

First consider the findings from role-taking tasks in the context of spatial concepts. Flavell (1968) was among the first to administer a battery of role-taking tasks to subjects of a wide age range. A clear finding in the studies was the variability from task to task in the average ages at which role-taking responses were displayed. On some spatial perception tasks children as young as 3 or 4 years were able to take the perspective of others, whereas on the other spatial perception tasks they were unable to do so until 12 or 13 years of age. Furthermore, the specific method used to present a form of the Piaget and Inhelder (1948/1956) "three mountain" spatial task resulted in non-role-taking responses on the part of subjects as old as 16 years; in the original Piaget and Inhelder version of this task the average age of attainment is 8 or 9 years. The variability found by Flavell in the ages at which role taking occurs is characteristic of research on spatial perception. In some studies systematic attempts were made to determine the youngest ages at which children can produce role-taking responses. Those studies have shown that role-taking responses are displayed by children as young as 3 and 4 years of age (as summarized by Flavell, 1979; also see Fishbein, Lewis, & Keiffer, 1972; Shantz, 1975; Shantz & Watson, 1970). These observed wide-ranging age discrepancies in performance are consistent with the distinction between the conceptual demands of the task and role taking as a method of information gathering. Inasmuch as the tasks entail *both* role-taking activities and conceptual activities on the part of the subject, role-taking performance is determined by whether or not the child has attained the level of spatial conceptualization required by the task.

The pattern of findings on role-taking tasks in the context of spatial concepts is paralleled by findings in guessing-game (entailing probabilistic and psychological concepts), communication, and story-telling tasks. In some tasks used by Flavell (1968) requiring the subject to guess another's strategies in a game context, role-taking responses generally were not displayed until 10 or 11 years of age. In contrast, a simpler form of the guessing-game task (De Vries, 1970) resulted in role-taking responses on the part of 5-year-old children. In communication tasks used by Flavell (1968), children did not take the perspective of the other until the ages of 5 or 6 years, but in other studies (also designed to determine the youngest ages at which children can produce role-taking responses) it was shown that 3- and 4-year-olds are able to take another's perspective in the context of communication tasks (Maratsos, 1973; Menig-Peterson, 1975; Shatz & Gelman, 1973). Similar age variability is found when the subject's task is to relate a story to a person who has less information about it (compare Flavell, 1968, and Chandler & Greenspan, 1972, with Mossler, Marvin, & Greenberg, 1976).

In summary, the findings of role-taking research show that it is a skill formed early in childhood. The use of role taking in a given situation is dependent on the individual's level of conceptual knowledge in the domain with which the role-taking activity is associated. Moreover, the findings *do not* support the proposition that development progresses from egocentricism to perspectivism through structural reorganizations. Role taking, therefore, provides an example of a topic for which the application of a stage analysis is inappropriate. Consequently, it should not be assumed that any topic of investigation can be analyzed through a stage-sequence model. Rather, a rationale is needed to make appropriate distinctions among different types of social–cognitive functions.

As stated at the outset, a central feature of Piaget's research on nonsocial cognition is the attempt to coordinate the study of development with formulations of the nature of the domains of knowledge. However, it could be maintained, in a seemingly contradictory way, that in the body of research on social cognition reviewed, structural developmental theory has been both *overapplied* and *underutilized*. On the one hand, the theory has been overapplied in the sense that what is commonly regarded as its most characteristic feature—that development progresses through stages—is imposed on a variety of social domains, without concern for drawing a distinction between those functions that form organized systems and those that do not. On the other hand, the theory has been underutilized in the sense that the emphasis has been on one proposition, that of stages, in what is actually a much broader and differentiated theory.

In this light, a working model is now considered that is designed to deal with the coordination of research on children's understanding of the social world with systematic classification of social domains. Although it is a model partially based on previous findings, it is also meant to provide a framework for further theory and research.

The Development of Social Knowledge: Methods and Domains

As we have seen, there are two manifestations of a global definition of structure. The first, that development entails general differentiations of domains, has not been supported by the research on role taking. In the second type of global definition it is posited that different systems of thought are structurally interrelated. In the previous section it was pointed out that there are contradictions in the integrative global view of structure that leads to the necessary but not sufficient hypothesis. Those contradictions could be resolved in two alternative ways. One would be consistent with a global interpretation of structure. It could be maintained that the social domains are content for logical–mathematical reasoning and physical concepts, and, therefore, do not form sequential systems of structural reorganization. The second way of resolving the contradictions is in the direction of a domain-specific interpretation of structure. Such an interpretation is that there are domains of social knowledge that are not dependent on nonsocial cognitive structures and that are constructed through the individual's interactions with the social environment. Moreover, social knowledge can also be divided into distinct domains. That is, there is not one central system of social cognition, as has sometimes been implied for morality or for role taking. It is proposed, therefore, that the individual's social judgments do not form a general unified system. Two broad distinctions are made. One is a distinction between the methods of information gathering and the transformational organized systems of thought. Not all cognitive functions form organized systems and not all development entails qualitative changes. The second is the distinctions among domains of thought.

The distinction between methods of information gathering (identified as activities such as observation, communication, imitation, and role taking) and transformational systems has already been outlined. The proposed characteristics of the methods are illustrated in the features of role-taking activities: (1) first, the methods are means for producing information about, for instance, the states of others, elements of social groups, and the content of social institutions; (2) the methods do not form an autonomous system of knowledge; rather, they are skills used in conjunction with conceptual systems, such that the use of the method is dependent on the level of conceptual attainment in a given task. The conceptual systems may set limits to, influence, or even determine the method used; (3) accordingly, age-related changes in the use of the methods are quantitative, rather than qualitative. There may be increments in the accuracy of a method based on changes in conceptual knowledge. The hypothetical example of a role-taking task in the context of a conservation problem can be used once again to illustrate this point. With changes in the child's concepts of conservation and in his or her knowledge about how people respond to such tasks, the subject would be able to predict more accurately the other person's response to a conservation problem.

Within the general category of social–cognitive functions it is necessary to draw distinctions among domains of thought. As stressed earlier, the concept of structure requires a narrower definition than the one that asserts that all aspects of thought are interrelated. Cognitive structures are partial in that they encompass delimited domains of knowledge. Another way of putting this is that individuals have theories about the world that form integrated systems. The coherence of such theories, however, is tied to specific domains (as in the distinction Piaget has drawn between logical–mathematical knowledge and knowledge about the physical world). In the course of ontogenesis, therefore, individuals develop distinctly different forms of social knowledge, reflected in structural systems that parallel each other; parallel developmental sequences may progress at similar or varying rates. Moreover, the assumption of separate developmental sequences implies that relations between them are of an informational nature, rather than ones of interdependence.

The partial structure hypothesis is related to an explanation of developmental processes (Turiel, 1974, 1975). A fundamental and generally accepted premise of the structural approach is that thought is organized and that it is constructed out of the child's interactions with the environment. Thought and knowledge are neither given in the biological makeup of the individual nor do they stem directly from the environment. The source of the construction of thought is the child's actions upon, and interactions with objects, events, and persons. One basis for the proposition that concepts are organized within domains rests upon the idea that they are constructed out of the individual's interactions with the environment. Because conceptual knowledge is constructed through an interactive process, the nature of conceptual constructions, though not determined by the environment, would be influenced by it. Therefore, individual–environment interactions with fundamentally different types of objects and events should result in the formation of distinct concepts. Consequently, to understand the concepts constructed out of the child's interactions, it is necessary to distinguish among the different types of events experienced.

The proposition that thought is organized within domains is in contradiction with the global characterization of development as the process of cognitive differentiation. In the global characterizations discussed earlier, development of a form of thinking (e.g., moral judgments) was explained as originating in its fusion with other types of judgments (e.g., the physical–social, morality–society fusions). The differentiation model actually proposes that a type of thinking, say moral judgments, is absent in young children because it is fused with other types of judgments, say nonmoral judgments. It is said, for instance, that the emergence of moral judgments comes relatively late in development, when they are differentiated from (and displace) other forms of judgment. In the contrasting domain-specific view of the organizations of thought, it is proposed that the absence of domain differentiations neither adequately characterizes the child's thinking nor explains the origins of a domain of thought. Rather, it is proposed that children do make domain differentiations, forming judgments about specific domains. The precursors of developmentally advanced concepts have their origins in concepts within a given domain and not in a global fusion of various domains.

The tasks, then, are to identify those social domains that form organized systems of thought, to trace their respective sequences of development, and to determine the types of individual–environment interactions from which they stem. The identification of social–cognitive domains can be informed by an a priori classification, as well as by previous research findings. Furthermore, once domains are identified it is necessary to demonstrate that they are distinct from each other and that they form organized systems of thought.

The social world is comprised of persons and of interactions or relations between persons. In turn, there are two central aspects of knowledge about social relations: the systems of social relations, and prescriptions regarding how social interactions ought to occur. Accordingly, three general categories can be identified (Turiel, 1979) as forming the basis of the child's structuring of the social world: the *psychological* (knowledge of persons), the *societal or social organizational* (knowledge of systems of social relations), and the *moral*. These three categories, which correspond to traditional disciplines (psychology, sociology/anthropology, and moral philosophy), subsume many of the topics listed in Table 2.1. The first category refers to the individual's concepts of people as psychological systems. Studies that have examined children's concepts of the person, personality, the self, and identity would fall under this category. The second category includes the individual's concepts regarding how people interact with, or relate to, each other in systematic ways. Studies of children's concepts within the societal domain—of concepts of systems of social interactions or culture—include those dealing with social convention, social systems, groups, social institutions, authority, and social roles. The third category refers to prescriptive moral judgments regarding how people ought to behave toward one another. This domain is defined by individuals' concepts of justice.

Given the present state of our knowledge, the identification of the three categories should be regarded as a working hypothesis that provides general parameters for grouping investigations of the development of social concepts. An analysis of how some of the research findings on the development of social concepts lend themselves to groupings in accordance with the three categories is presented in a later section. First, however, it is necessary to show how domains form distinct developmental systems. Two types of studies bear upon this question. One proposition is that domain distinctions are related to the interactional process of development. Thus, an identification of domains needs to be coordinated with the study of development, such that connections are drawn between the child's different forms of social experience and the construction of distinct conceptual domains. It is also necessary to provide evidence that children of varying ages do indeed discriminate among domains.

Social Interactions and Social Cognitive Domains

In a set of studies on morality and social convention an attempt was made to coordinate study of development with study of the nature of social domains. The studies have been aimed at identifying the parameters of the two domains

(Turiel, 1978a, 1979), at determining the experiential bases of development within each domain (Much & Shweder, 1978; Nucci & Nucci, 1982; Nucci & Turiel, 1978), and at ascertaining if and how the domains are distinguished by children and adolescents (Turiel, 1978b; Weston & Turiel, 1979).

Social conventions are being classified as part of the societal domain because they are behavioral uniformities that coordinate interactions of individuals within social systems (Turiel, 1978b, 1979). Individual members of the society have shared knowledge about conventions; this characteristic of shared knowledge is what makes them conventional. Consequently, conventions (e.g., modes of greeting, forms of address) provide people with means of knowing what to expect of each other and thereby serve to coordinate interactions between people. The coordination of interactions, however, cannot be said to be synonomous with convention. There are ways in which people coordinate their interactions without necessarily involving conventions. For example, two people working together on a recipe, when it cannot be accomplished by one person, will coordinate their activities in order to achieve their goal. Conventions involve coordinations at the level of social organization; they are uniformities that coordinate the stable interactions of individuals functioning within a social system and the ends are social organizational.

Social–conventional acts are symbolic of elements of social organization. As such, the acts in themselves are arbitrary, and alternative courses of action can serve similar functions. That is, by virtue of their shared knowledge, a given conventional uniformity in one social system may serve the same symbolic function as a different uniformity in another social system. The arbitrary nature of acts in the conventional domain has implications for what constitutes a transgression. Namely, it is not the intrinsic nature of the act that leads one to regard an act as a transgression, but rather its deviation from the uniformity. For an individual to perceive a given act as a transgression, he or she would have to know something about the status of the act as a societally determined uniformity. The other side of the coin is that conventions are validated by consensus and, therefore, are relative to the societal context. In addition to the variability of conventions from one social system to another, they may be altered by consensus or general usage within a social system.

The individual's concepts of social convention are, therefore, closely related to his or her concepts of social organization. In contrast with convention, moral prescriptions are not perceived to be alterable by consensus. This is not to say that morality is fixed and unalterable. We know, for instance, that historical changes have occurred with regard to such matters as slavery. However, the bases for those changes are not perceived as shifts in the general consensus or in social organization, but on the intrinsic merits, from the moral point of view, of one type of action over another. Again in contrast with convention, in the moral domain actions are not arbitrary, and though moral prescriptions form part of social organization, they are not defined by social organization nor is their rationale based on their status as implicit or explicit regulations. The individual's moral prescriptions (e.g., regarding killing and the value of life) are determined by factors inherent to social relationships, as opposed to a particular form of social organization. An individual's perception of an act such as the taking of a life as a transgression is not contingent on the presence of a rule, but rather stems from factors intrinsic to the event (e.g., from the perception of the consequences to the victim). This means that moral issues are not perceived as relative to the societal context. The moral theories formed by individuals are based on concepts regarding the welfare of persons, the rights of persons, and justice, in the sense of comparative treatment of individuals and means of distribution.

Social Experiences and the Development of Social Concepts

Earlier it was proposed that the precursors of developmentally advanced concepts have their origins in concepts within a domain, and that experiences stimulating development differ according to domain. That is, the types of experiences stimulating moral development can be distinguished from those stimulating concepts of social convention. As examples, consider the following two events, each entailing prescriptions and prohibitions, that could very well be experienced by young children in a nursery school setting.

Event A

A number of nursery school children are playing outdoors. There are some swings in the yard, all of which are being used. One of the children decides that he now wants to use a swing. Seeing that they are all occupied, he goes to one of the swings, where he pushes the other child off, at the same time hitting him. The child who has been pushed is hurt and begins to cry.

Event B

Children are greeting a teacher who has just come into the nursery school. A number of children go up to her and say "Good morning, Mrs. Jones." One of the children says "Good morning, Mary."

Both events are social in nature and each may constitute a breach of explicit regulations or norms. That is, the school may have regulations that prohibit children from hitting others and from addressing teachers by their first names. Moreover, adults may transmit instructions regarding behavior in these situations. However, the transmission of such instructions does not, by any means, completely account for the influences of social events on children's development. Children's interpretations of the events, including features of the interactions that occur between people, also influence development.

From the child's cognitive perspective, the foregoing events, in spite of some similarities, differ from each other in significant ways. First consider Event A as an example of a moral transgression. Such experiences are related to the formation of a child's moral judgments. However, for children to regard the act in

Event A as wrong or as a transgression, direct instructions from others are not necessary. Children can generate prescriptions through abstractions from the experience itself (either as observers or participants). Primary in the perception of such an event would be the pain experienced by the victim and the reason for the offender's act. By coordinating those different notions with each other, the child can generate prescriptions regarding the event. For instance, the child will connect his own experience of pain (an undesirable experience) to the observed experience of the victim. Accordingly, moral judgments, though not directly given in experiences, are inferences stemming from those experiences. Moral considerations stem from factors intrinsic to actions, such as harm inflicted upon persons, that are independent of social regulations or the expectations and directives of authorities (e.g., parents and teachers). The type of interactions among people described in Event A, with their inherent features, can (and likely do) occur in any social system.

For Event B to be considered a transgression, in contrast to Event A, the child would have to view the act as a violation of an implicit uniformity or an explicit regulation within the social system (the school or the more general social system). There is no intrinsic prescriptive basis for a requirement in a school that children refer to teachers by their titles. Uniformity or regulations regarding forms of address (or other conventions) are determined by the social system and their functions are related to the way the system is organized. Conventions are understood in relation to their social context.

Three observational studies document that children's social interactions within the context of moral and social-conventional events differ from each other. Two of the studies (Nucci & Turiel, 1978; Nucci & Nucci, 1982), were aimed at obtaining information about the types of social interactions engaged in by children and in testing the proposition that patterns of social interaction in the context of moral events (such as Event A) differ from those in the context of social conventions (such as Event B). This was accomplished through systematic observations of social behaviors in preschools and higher grade classrooms (second, fifth, and seventh grades). The study focused on interactions revolving around moral and conventional transgressions, thereby examining social environments as created by children's transgressions and responses to transgressions. Naturally occurring moral and social-conventional transgressions were observed and the responses of both children and adults (teachers) to each transgression were recorded. It was found that children at all grades responded to moral transgressions to an equal extent as the adults. Younger children, however, were less likely to respond to conventional transgressions than the older children or the adults.

The main finding of these studies was that two distinct forms of interactions occurred in responses to each type of transgression. The interactions related to moral events took a form that differed from the interactions related to social conventions. As expected, responses to moral transgressions focused on the intrinsic consequences of actions, while responses to transgressions of conventions focused on features of social organization. For instance, responses to moral transgressions included statements regarding the pain or injury experienced by a victim. Responses to conventional transgressions included statements about social order, rules and sanctions.

These findings are paralleled by those from a study by Much and Shweder (1978). Much and Shweder conducted linguistic analyses of naturally occurring verbal interactions, among nursery school children and kindergarteners, in the context of transgressions of school regulations, conventions, and moral precepts. In this study, too, it was found that children's dialogues varied by domain. Discussions emerging from transgressions in the conventional domain dealt primarily with the social context and rules. The discussions about moral transgressions dealt primarily with the actions themselves.

The observational studies, therefore, provide evidence for one aspect of the partial-structure hypothesis: that the nature of social interactions experienced by children differs according to domain. However, the observations of social interactions do not provide direct evidence for a second aspect of the partial-structure hypothesis: that children discriminate between morality and social convention. Evidence for this proposition comes from additional findings of the Nucci and Turiel and Nucci and Nucci studies. One of the procedures used in those studies was to interview children about the transgressions just after they had occurred. The children were asked whether or not the act would be wrong if there were no rule in the school pertaining to the act. The child's interpretation of the event was classified as moral if it was stated that the action was wrong regardless of the presence or absence of a rule and as social-conventional if it was stated that the action was wrong only if a rule pertaining to the act existed in the school. When questioned about social-conventional events most of the children (81% in the preschools, 87% in the grade schools) stated that the act would be right if no rule existed in the school. When questioned about moral events, most of the children (86% in the preschools and 87% in the grade schools) stated that the act would not be right even if no rule existed.

Thus, it appears that children from 4 or 5 years up to 12 years of age discriminate between rules in moral situations and rules in non-moral situations. Other studies with subjects ranging from 6 to 19 years of age provide further evidence that the distinction between morality and social convention is not age related. In one study (Nucci, 1977), children and adolescents (from 7 to 19 years) were presented with a series of statements depicting actors engaging in moral transgressions (e.g., lying, stealing) or transgressions of social convention (e.g., a boy using the girls' bathroom; eating with one's hands). They were then given the task of selecting statements depicting actions they considered wrong regardless of the presence or absence of a rule. Virtually all the children and adolescents in each age group considered the moral transgressions to be wrong, regardless of the presence or absence of a social regulation. In contrast, judgments about the social-conventional acts were deemed to be contingent on social regulations by virtually everyone in each age group.

Essentially the same results were obtained in another study (Turiel, 1978b), which showed that children and adolescents regard conventional rules to be part of social organization and therefore relative to the social context. Moreover, they regard moral rules to have intrinsic validity and therefore are not dependent on group consensus for their jurisdiction. Subjects between 6 and 17 years of age were interviewed about a variety of moral and social-conventional rules. One type of question dealt with the relativity of rules. For example, it was asked whether they would approve or disapprove of the lack of any rules, in another country, prohibiting theft.

With regard to moral issues, such as stealing, the majority of subjects at all ages did not accept the validity of establishing a social system that had no rules controlling the activity. That is, subjects stated both that it would be wrong not to have the rule and that it would be wrong to steal even in the absence of the rule. In contrast with this, most stated that rules pertaining to conventional issues could vary legitimately from one social setting to another. It should be noted that the most clear-cut example of a rule type judged to be relative to its context and determined by consensus is that of game rules. Almost everyone stated that it would be valid to change game rules by agreement. For the most part, children maintained that rule changes merely alter the nature of the game. These findings directly contradict Piaget's (1982/1948) contention that children do not discriminate between game rules and moral rules, a contention used by him to support the idea that children fail to differentiate domains of knowledge.

These studies, therefore, provide evidence that young children distinguish between morality and social convention and that the distinction is maintained with increasing age. The results of these studies (see also Weston & Turiel, 1980) serve to illustrate a point made earlier regarding the problems in the ad hoc empirical approach to choosing topics for developmental investigation. The findings on social rules provide a clear example of a topic that, in itself, cannot be adequately treated as one about which individuals form organized systems of knowledge. As we have just seen, the individual's understanding of rules is related to more than one domain. Judgments about rules involve an interaction between the rule itself and the domain of the action to which the rule pertains; thus, the meaning attributed to a given rule will vary in accordance with the conceptual systems to which the rule is related (e.g., moral or conventional). By studying social rules in the context of a more general analysis of social domains it was possible to show that concepts of rules do not form an organized system and, therefore, are not appropriate for a stage analysis.

Development Within Domains

The emphasis of much of the discussion up to this point has been on aspects of social cognition that are *not* age related. It was maintained that the methods of information gathering, which includes role taking, do not undergo qualitative transformations in ontogenesis. It was just claimed that children's concepts of social rules do not form an independent structural system. And research findings were reviewed showing that the distinction between morality and social convention appears at an early age (by 4 or 5 years) and is maintained across a wide age range. However, these assertions should not be taken to mean that that cognitive development does not undergo age-related structural changes. Rather, it is being proposed that: (1) social–cognitive development should not be analyzed in a global fashion; (2) the individual's social judgments do not form a unified system; (3) there are non-age-related distinctions between domains; (4) distinctions should be drawn between functions that do and do not form organized systems; and (5) the place to look for structural age-related changes is within delimited domains of knowledge.

Indeed, the claim is that developmental patterns can be more clearly analyzed if they are separated from nondevelopmental phenomena. In addition, an adequate analysis of development requires that domains of knowledge first be identified. The expectation is, therefore, that structural changes occur within the moral, societal, and psychological domains. As noted earlier, several of the studies listed in Table 2.1 have focused on topics within those domains; findings from those studies begin to show patterns of qualitative age-related changes in social knowledge.

This is not the place for detailed descriptions of the age-related changes found in developmental studies. However, brief mention of some studies will serve to illustrate how several of the topics in Table 2.1 form groupings in accordance with the three domains. In the first place, developmental changes have been identified in the two types of concepts discussed earlier, morality and social convention. Although the distinction between morality and social convention is maintained across ages, changes do occur in the organization of thought within each domain. A narrowly focused analysis of children's moral judgments has been done by Damon (1977), whose research dealt specifically with distributive justice, as one aspect of the moral domain. His formulation of a sequence of six levels (characterizing changes from approximately 4 to 10 years of age) shows that in their development of concepts of distributive justice children form increased understandings of benevolence, equality, and reciprocity (see Damon's chapter in this volume).

In research on social convention (Turiel, 1978a), a sequence of seven levels (characterizing changes from approximately 6 to 25 years of age) was identified. In contrast with distributive justice, the levels of social convention are structured by underlying concepts of social organization. These levels serve to illustrate the types of changes that occur in thinking within the societal domain. The sequence of social–conventional concepts is one in which there are successive affirmations and negations of conventions. In the sequence, affirmation (Level 1), leads to negation (Level 2), which leads to a new form of affirmation (Level 3). The levels of negation constitute conceptual rejections of the way of thinking characteristic of the previous level and are, therefore, part of a process of development in which change from level to level entails a reorganization of thought. That is, each phase of negation entails a reevaluation of existing concepts of social organization necessary to the emergence of reorganized concepts at the next level (see Turiel, 1978a for detailed descriptions of the levels).

For the present purposes, however, it is the levels of affirmation that are of most relevance because they provide descriptions of concepts of social organization reflected in individuals' understanding of convention. The first of these levels represents a form of thinking that is a precursor to later concepts of social systems. At that level there is a rudimentary understanding of social system based on power and status distinctions, as well as on perceived uniformities in social behavior. At the third level, uniformities in social behavior are tied to a conception of social system based on concrete rules, roles, and authority relations. Beginning in early adolescence, development progresses toward conceptualizations of social systems as hierarchically organized units and toward viewing social systems as serving the function of coordinating social interactions.

The concepts of social organization underlying the levels of social convention correspond to sequences derived from studies of children's concepts of groups and social institutions. In one study, Neiderman (1978) investigated understandings of groups in classroom, family, and peer settings. For each type of group he examined how children think about membership, decision making, and leadership. In another study K. Dodsworth and this author have investigated children's constructions of social communities and their concepts of social structure, institutions, and roles. Again, it was found that development progresses from rudimentary notions of groups and social institutions based on perceived uniformities and power relations, to a conception of social systems based on concrete regularities in rules, roles, and institutions, to a conception of the functions of groups, communities, and institutions as hierarchically organized systems serving to coordinate social interactions.

Likewise, in the remaining category identified in the classification of social concepts—the psychological—several studies have yielded findings of age-related developmental patterns. Age-related changes have been described through studies of concepts of self or personal identity (Broughton, 1978; Lemke, 1973; Nucci, 1977; Wolfson, 1972), of other persons (Pratt, 1975), and of the causes of behavior (Josephson, 1976). The general patterns of development evident in the limited research findings thus far available are characterized in the results of a recent study by Josephson (1977). In that study measures were obtained of the degree to which subjects (from 5 to 20 years of age) made predictions of behavior in hypothetical stories on the basis of personal–dispositional (e.g., timidity, competence) or situational information provided. The youngest children (5- to 6-year-olds), it was found, relied on situational factors to a greater extent and dispositional factors to a lesser extent than older children (7- to 15-year-olds). The use of dispositional factors in predicting behavior first increased with age (from 7 to 15 years) and then decreased with further increasing age (19 to 20 years). In turn, the use of situational factors first decreased with age and then increased. The following developmental hypothesis is suggested by these findings. The youngest children do not have stable concepts of internal processes of persons and, therefore, rely on the external situation to predict behaviors. The formation of stable concepts of internal psychological processes occurs between the ages of 7 and 12 years, resulting in an overgeneralization of the influence of internal dispositions in predicting behavior. Subsequently, there is an increasing view of behavior as determined by the interaction of personal–dispositional and situational factors.

This interpretation of the Josephson findings is consistent with studies of children's reasoning about other psychological topics. As an example, Wolfson (1972) investigated concepts of personal identity by asking subjects a series of questions regarding the stability of identity. For the youngest children (4 to 5 years of age) in the study, identity was based on external physical characteristics. The understanding of identity manifested by somewhat older children (9 to 11 years) focused on perceived consistencies in the behaviors of individuals. By early adolescence (12 to 14 years) there emerged a notion of identity based on concepts of stable internal dispositions, such as personality traits, attitudes, and beliefs.

The types of age-related changes found by Wolfson correspond to the Josephson findings on predictions of the causes of behavior, as well as to another study of personal identity (Lemke, 1973) and studies of concepts of the self reported by Broughton (1978), Nucci (1977), and Montemayor and Eisen (1977). Moreover, these studies are consistent with findings by Pratt (1975) in a study of children's concepts of other persons. In that study children's concepts of persons were also found to change from a focus on physical characteristics, to behavioral consistencies, to internal dispositions.

There are several studies, therefore, that begin to show developmental patterns converging within the three domains. However, the separation of domains of thought raises a question of some importance that should be noted at this point. It may be said that the proposed demarcation of domains could serve to obscure analyses of social cognition because some issues include components from more than one of the identified domains. In such a case, it would be argued, the separation of domains is inaccurate and would fail to account for those aspects of social thought.

However, the distinct domain analysis does not preclude the possibility of identifying issues that include components from more than one domain. Judgments about such issues would entail the coordination of concepts from different domains. If the distinct domain hypothesis is valid, it then becomes all the more important to provide adequate analyses of the domains so as to be able to examine their coordination, or lack of coordination, in judgments about a given issue.

Indeed, there are studies listed in Table 2.1 that investigated issues entailing more than one domain. One such example is the study by Coie and Pennington (1976) of children's concepts of deviant behavior and psychological disorders. Subjects were interviewed about: (1) other children they considered "different"; and (2) stories depicting an aggressive child lacking self-control and a child acting in a paranoid fashion. Although the stated topic of the study was children's concepts of deviance and disorder, two more general categories of thought were being investigated. An understanding of self-control and paranoia entails psychological knowledge; concepts of deviancy entail both psychological and societal knowledge. As a matter of fact, subjects responded to questions about deviance with reference to both psychological (e.g., aggressiveness, withdrawal) and sociological (e.g., social norm and rule violations) constructs.

An understanding of children's concepts of an issue like deviance would benefit from the separation of domains and analysis of their coordination. Such a separation of domains proved fruitful in a study by Smetana (1978) on judgments about abortion. Although abortion is generally classified by researchers as a moral issue, Smetana explored the possibility that it includes both moral and nonmoral judgments. She found that not all subjects applied moral judgments to questions about abortion. Briefly, some subjects treated abortion as a nonmoral issue if it occured prior to a certain time in the pregnancy, others always treated it as a nonmoral issue, and still others dealt with the issue by coordinating moral and nonmoral judgments. In other words, a prior classification of domains produced a differentiated analysis of reasoning about the topic. Consequently, an identification of domains also serves to inform research on topics that include components from more than one domain.

REFERENCES

Barenboim, C. Developmental changes in the interpersonal cognitive system from middle childhood to adolescence. *Child Development, 1977, 48,* 1467–1474.

Bar-Tal, D., Raviv, A., & Sharabany, R. *Cognitive basis of the development of altruistic behavior.* Paper presented at the biennial conference of the International Society for the Study of Behavioral Development, Pavia, Italy, 1977.

Benedict, R. *Patterns of culture.* Boston: Houghton–Mifflin Co., 1934.

Benedict, R. *The chrysanthemum and the sword.* Boston: Houghton–Mifflin Co., 1946.

Bernstein, A., & Cowan, P. Children's concepts of how people get babies. *Child Development, 1975, 46,* 77–91.

Bigelow, B. Children's friendship expectations: A cognitive–developmental study. *Child Development, 1977, 48,* 246–253.

Bigner, J. A Wernerian developmental analysis of children's descriptions of siblings. *Child Development, 1974, 45,* 317–323.

Broughton, J. Development of concepts of self, mind, reality and knowledge. In W. Damon (Ed.), *New directions for child development. Vol. 1: Social cognition.* San Francisco: Jossey–Bass, 1978.

Chandler, M. J., & Greenspan, S. Ersatz egocentrism. A reply to H. Borke. *Developmental Psychology*, 1972, *7*, 104–106.

Carter, D. B., & Patterson, C. J. Sex roles as social conventions: The development of children's sex-role stereotypes. *Developmental Psychology*, in press.

Chomsky, N. *Language and responsibility*. New York: Pantheon Books, 1979.

Coie, J., & Pennington, B. Children's perceptions of deviance and disorder. *Child Development*, 1976, *47*, 407–414.

Damon, W. *The social world of the child*. San Francisco: Jossey-Bass, 1977.

De Vries, R. Constancy of generic identity in the years three to six. *Monograph of the Society for Research in Child Development*, 1969, *34*(3).

De Vries, R. The development of role taking as reflected by the behavior of bright, average, and retarded children in a social guessing game. *Child Development*, 1970, *41*, 759–770.

Emmerich, W., Goldman, K., Kirsch, B., & Sharabany, R. Evidence for a transitional phase in the development of gender constancy. *Child Development*, 1977, *48*, 930–936.

Feffer, M. The cognitive implications of role-taking behavior. *Journal of Personality*, 1959, *27*, 152–168.

Feffer, M., & Gourevitch, V. Cognitive aspects of role-taking in children. *Journal of Personality*, 1960, *28*, 383–396.

Fishbein, H. D., Lewis, S., & Keiffer, K. Children's understanding of spatial relations: Coordination of perspectives. *Developmental Psychology*, 1972, *7*, 21–23.

Fischer, K. W. *Sequence and synchrony in cognitive development*. Symposium presented at the annual meeting of the American Psychological Association. San Francisco, August 1977.

Flavell, J. *The development of role taking and communication skills in children*. New York: Wiley, 1968.

Flavell, J. The development of knowledge about visual perception. In C. B. Keasey (Ed.), *Nebraska Symposium on Motivation, 1977* (Vol. 25). Lincoln: University of Nebraska Press, 1979.

Furth, H. Children's societal understanding and the process of equilibration. In W. Damon (Ed.), *New directions for child development, Vol. 1: Social cognition*. San Francisco: Jossey–Bass, 1978.

Geertz, C. *The interpretation of culture*. New York: Basic Books, 1973.

Gilligan, C., Kohlberg, L., Lerner, J., & Belenky, M. *Moral reasoning about sexual dilemmas: The development of an interview and scoring system*. Unpublished paper, Harvard University, 1970.

Josephson, J. *The child's use of situational and personal information in predicting the behavior of another*. Unpublished doctoral dissertation, Stanford University, 1977.

Keasey, C. B. Implicators of cognitive development. In D. J. De Palma & J. M. Foley (Eds.), *Moral development: Current theory and research*. Hillsdale, N.J.: Lawrence Erlbaum Associates, 1975.

Keasey, C. B. Children's developing awareness and usage of intentionality and motive. In C. B. Keasey (Ed.), *Nebraska Symposium on Motivation, 1977* (Vol. 25). Lincoln: University of Nebraska Press, 1979.

Kohlberg, L. *The development of modes of moral thinking and choice in the years 10 to 16*. Unpublished doctoral dissertation, University of Chicago, 1958.

Kohlberg, L. The development of children's orientations toward a moral order: 1. Sequence in the development of moral thought. *Vita Humana*, 1963, *6*, 11–33. (a)

Kohlberg, L. Moral development and identification. In H. Stevenson (Ed.), *Child Psychology. 62nd Yearbook of the National Society for the Study of Education*. Chicago: University of Chicago Press, 1963. (b)

Kohlberg, L. A cognitive–developmental analysis of children's sex role concepts and attitudes. In E. Maccoby (Ed.), *The development of sex differences*. Stanford: Stanford University Press, 1966.

Kohlberg, L. Stage and sequence: The cognitive–developmental approach to socialization. In D. A. Goslin (Ed.), *Handbook of socialization theory and research.* Chicago: Rand McNally, 1969.

Kohlberg, L. From is to ought: How to commit the naturalistic fallacy and get away with it in the study of moral development. In T. Mischel (Ed.), *Psychology and genetic epistemology.* New York: Academic Press, 1971.

Kohlberg, L. Moral stages and moralization: The cognitive–developmental approach. In T. Lickona (Ed.), *Moral development and behavior: Theory, research and social issues.* New York: Holt, Rinehart, & Winston, 1976.

Kramer, R. B. *Changes in moral judgment response pattern during late adolescence and young adulthood: Retrogression in a developmental sequence.* Unpublished doctoral dissertation, University of Chicago, 1968.

Krebs, D. A cognitive-developmental approach to altruism. In L. Wispé (Ed.), *Altruism, sympathy and helping: Psychological and sociological principles,* New York: Academic Press, 1978.

Kuhn, D., Langer, J., Kohlberg, L., & Haan, N. The development of formal operations in logical and moral judgment. *Genetic Psychology Monographs,* 1977.

Lemke, S. *Identity and conservation: The child's developing conceptions of social and physical transformations.* Unpublished doctoral dissertation, University of California, Berkeley, 1973.

Lockwood, A. L. Moral reasoning and public debate. In T. Lickona (Ed.), *Moral development and behavior: Theory research and social issues.* New York: Holt, Rinehart, & Winston, 1976.

Maratsos, M. P. Nonegocentric communication abilities in preschool children. *Child Development,* 1973, *44,* 697–700.

Marcus, D., & Overton, W. The development of cognitive gender constancy and sex-role preferences. *Child Development,* 1978, *49,* 434–444.

Menig-Peterson, C. L. The modification of communicative behavior in preschoolaged children as a function of the listener's perspective. *Child Development,* 1975, *46,* 1015–1018.

Montemayor, N., & Eisen, M. The development of self-conceptions from childhood to adolescence. *Developmental Psychology,* 1977, *13,* 314–319.

Mossler, O. E., Marvin, R. S., & Greenberg, M. T. Conceptual perspective taking in 2- to 6-year-old children. *Developmental Psychology,* 1976, *12,* 85–86.

Much, N., & Shweder, R. A. Speaking of rules: The analysis of culture in breach. In W. Damon (Ed.), *New directions for child development. Vol. 2: Moral development.* San Francisco: Jossey–Bass, 1978.

Neiderman, R. D. *Development of the social group in childhood and adolescence.* Unpublished doctoral dissertation, University of California, Berkeley, 1978.

Nucci, L. *Social development: Personal, conventional, and moral concepts.* Unpublished doctoral dissertation. University of California, Santa Cruz, 1977.

Nucci, L., & Nucci, M. S. Children's social interactions in the context of moral and conventional transgressions. *Child Development,* 1982, *53,* 403–412.

Nucci, L., & Turiel, E. Social interactions and the development of social concepts in preschool children. *Child Development,* 1978, *49,* 400–407.

Piaget, J. *The language and thought of the child.* New York: Harcourt, Brace, & Co., 1923.

Piaget, J. *The child's conception of the world.* New Jersey: Littlefield, Adams, 1960. (Originally published, 1929.)

Piaget, J. *The moral judgment of the child.* Glencoe, Ill.: Free Press, 1948. (Originally published, 1932.)

Piaget, J. *Play, dreams and imitation in childhood.* New York: Norton, 1962. (Originally published, 1951.)

Piaget, J. *Six psychological studies.* New York: Random House, 1967.

Piaget, J. *On the development of memory and identity.* Barre, Mass.: Clark University Press, 1968.

Piaget, J. *The mechanisms of perception.* London: Routledge, 1969.

Piaget, J. *Genetic epistemology.* New York: Columbia University Press, 1970. (a)

Piaget, J. Piaget's theory. In P. Mussen (Ed.), *Carmichael's manual of child psychology* (Vol. 1). New York: Wiley, 1970. (b)

Piaget, J. *Psychology and epistemology.* New York: Viking Press, 1970. (c)

Piaget, J. *Understanding causality.* New York: Norton, 1974.

Piaget, J., & Inhelder, B. *The child's conception of space.* London: Routledge and Kegan Paul, 1956. (Originally published, 1948.)

Piaget, J., & Inhelder, B. *Mental imagery in the child: A study of the development of imaginal representation.* New York: Basic Books, 1971.

Piaget, J., & Inhelder, B. *Memory and intelligence.* New York: Basic Books, 1972.

Piaget, J., & Inhelder, B. *The origin of the idea of chance in children.* New York: W. W. Norton & Co., 1975.

Pratt, M. *A developmental study of person perception and attributions of social causality: Learning the what and why of others.* Unpublished doctoral dissertation, Harvard University, 1975.

Rest, J. Patterns of preference and comprehension in moral judgment. *Journal of Personality,* 1973, *41,* 86–108.

Scarlett, H. H., Press, A. N., & Crockett, W. H. Children's descriptions of peers: A Wernerian developmental analysis. *Child Development,* 1971, *42,* 439–453.

Schwartz, T. Where is the culture? Personality as the distributive locus of culture. In G. D. Spindler (Ed.), *The making of psychological anthropology.* Berkeley: University of California Press, 1978.

Selman, R. L. The relation of role-taking to the development of moral judgment in children. *Child Development,* 1971, *42,* 79–91.

Selman, R. L. Social cognitive understanding: A ghide to educational and clinical practice. In T. Lickona (Ed.), *Moral development and behavior: Theory, research and social issues.* New York: Holt, Rinehart, & Winston, 1976. (a)

Selman, R. L. Toward a structural analysis of developing interpersonal relations concepts: Research with normal and disturbed preadolescent boys. In A. Pick (Ed.), *Minnesota Symposium on Child Psychology* (Vol. 10). Minneapolis: University of Minnesota Press, 1976. (b)

Selman, R. L., & Byrne, D. F. A structural–developmental analysis of levels of role-taking in middle childhood. *Child Development,* 1974, *45,* 803–806.

Selman, R. L., & Cooney, E. W. Children's use of social conceptions: Toward a dynamic model of social cognition. In W. Damon (Ed.), *New directions for child development (Vol. 1): Social cognition.* San Francisco: Jossey-Bass, 1978.

Selman, R., & Damon, W. The necessity (but insufficiency) of social perspective taking for conceptions of justice at three early levels. In D. J. De Palma & J. M. Foley (Eds.), *Moral development: Current theory and research.* Hillsdale, N.J.: Lawrence Erlbaum Associates, 1975.

Shantz, C. V. The development of social cognition. In E. M. Hetherington (Ed.), *Review of Child Development Research* (Vol. 5). Chicago: University of Chicago Press, 1975.

Shantz, C. V., & Watson, J. S. Assessment of spatial egocentrism through expectancy violation. *Psychonomic Science,* 1970, *18,* 93–94.

Shatz, M., & Gelman, R. The development of communication skills: Modifications in the speech of young children as a function of listener. *Monographs of the Society for Research in Child Development.* 1973, *38*(5).

Shweder, R. A. Rethinking culture and personality theory: Part 1: A critical examination of two classical postulates. *Ethos,* 1979, *7,* 255–278. (a)

Shweder, R. A. Rethinking culture and personality theory: Part 2: A critical examination of two more classical postulates. *Ethos,* 1979, *7,* 279–311. (b)

Smetana, J. G. *Personal and moral concepts: A study of women's reasoning and decision-making about abortions.* Unpublished doctoral dissertation, University of California, Santa Cruz, 1978.

Stein, J. L. *Adolescent's reasoning about moral and sexual dilemmas: A longitudinal study.* Unpublished doctoral dissertation, Harvard University, 1973.

Tomlinson-Keasey, C., & Keasey, C. B. The mediating role of cognitive development in moral judgment. *Child Development,* 1974, *45,* 291–298.

Turiel, E. An experimental test of the sequentiality of developmental stages in the child's moral judgment. *Journal of Personality and Social Psychology,* 1966, *3,* 611–618.

Turiel, E. Developmental processes in the child's moral thinking. In P. H. Mussen, J. Langer, & M. Covington (Eds.), *Trends and issues in developmental psychology.* New York: Holt, 1969.

Turiel, E. Conflict and transition in adolescent moral development. *Child Development,* 1974, *45,* 14–29.

Turiel, E. The development of social concepts: Mores, customs and conventions. In D. J. De Palma & J. M. Foley (Eds.), *Moral development: Current theory and research.* Hillsdale, N.J.: Lawrence Erlbaum Associates, 1975.

Turiel, E. The development of concepts of social structure: Social convention. In J. Glick & A. Clarke-Stewart (Eds.), *The development of social understanding.* New York: Gardener Press, 1978. (a)

Turiel, E. Social regulations and domains of social concepts. In W. Damon (Ed.), *New directions for child development (Vol. 1): Social cognition.* San Francisco: Jossey–Bass, 1978. (b)

Turiel, E. Distinct conceptual and developmental domains: Social convention and morality. *Nebraska Symposium on Motivation, 1977* (Vol. 25). Lincoln: University of Nebraska Press, 1979.

Ullian, D. Z. *The development of conceptions of masculinity and femininity.* Unpublished doctoral dissertation, Harvard University, 1976. (a)

Ullian, D. Z. The development of conceptions of masculinity and femininity. In B. Lloyd & J. Ascher (Eds.), *Exploring sex differences.* London: Academic Press, 1976. (b)

Watson, M. W. *The development of social role concepts in preschoolers.* Paper presented at the meetings of the Society for Research in Child Development, San Francisco, March 1979.

Werner, H. *Comparative psychology of mental development.* New York: International Universities Press, Inc., 1957.

Weston, D., & Turiel, E. *Act–rule relations: Children's concepts of social rules.* Unpublished manuscript, University of California, Berkeley, 1979.

White, E., Elson, B., & Prawat, R. Children's conceptions of death. *Child Development,* 1978, *49,* 307–310.

Whiting, J. M. W., & Child, I. L. *Child training and personality: A Cross-Cultural study.* New Haven: Yale University Press, 1953.

Whiting, B., & Whiting, J. M. W. *Children of six cultures.* Cambridge, Mass.: Harvard University Press, 1975.

Wolfson, A. *Aspects of the development of identity concepts.* Unpublished doctoral dissertation, University of California, Berkeley, 1972.

Youniss, J. Another perspective on social cognition. In A. Pick (Ed.), *Minnesota Symposium on Child Psychology* (Vol. 9). Minneapolis: University of Minnesota Press, 1975.

Youniss, J., & Volpe, J. A relational analysis of children's friendship. In W. Damon (Ed.), *New directions for child development* (Vol. 1): *Social cognition.* San Francisco: Jossey–Bass, 1978.

3 Cognition of Physical and Social Events

Frank B. Murray
University of Delaware

In the *Psychology of Intelligence,* Piaget (1963) claimed that it was self-evident that the intellectual experiences of social and physical environments were: "exactly parallel, . . . since the two kinds of experiences are indistinguishable in reality [p. 60]." Thus, the cognition of social events entails the very same cognitive structures and schemes that are implicated in the cognition of nonsocial or impersonal events and vice versa. The comprehension of social principles is merely a special case of comprehension in general, the difference in content being insufficient to require any unusual cognitive operations in their behalf. Lee (1975), for example, has proposed that children's knowledge of social events, like their knowledge of other events, is critically dependent on the conservation operation.

Similarly, from a psychometric perspective, the structure of the intellect model (Guilford, 1956) does not require additional or different intellectual operations to treat social or behavioral content apart from what is required to treat other intellectual contents, even though the model requires that the domain of behavioral content concerned with interpersonal relations is structurally independent of the other content domains. Incidentally, the age levels for the mastery of behavioral content items seem no different from the levels required for other contents.

Recently some researchers (Bearison, 1975; Clarke-Stewart, 1978; Glick & Turiel, 1978) have suggested that the nature of social events is such that their cognition should be considered as qualitatively distinct from the cognition of other events. Glick (1978, p. 1) writes that: "the simple translation of cognitive processes as applied in the object world to the social world is an enterprise that must be undertaken with great caution" because social events are less stable,

91

more variable, and less determined than physical events and therefore elicit more intuitive, guessing thinking strategies than the more focused, logical strategies that are commonly identified in concept formation tasks that have physical and geometric content. So it appears that the Genevan claim that the social and physical worlds "are indistinguishable in reality" is not "self-evident" after all.

Distinctions Between Social and Physical Domains

But is it self-evident that social events are more complex, variable, or unpredictable than physical events, or is it simply that social psychologists are naive natural scientists who do not appreciate the inherent spontaneity, complexity, and unpredictability of the universe? The differences between naive psychology and naive physics are minimal and, if anything, the latter is more baffling and capricious for most than the former. The naive psychology of interpersonal relations (Heider, 1958), for example, operates successfully with a handful of constructs (viz., ability, effort, chance, difficulty, etc.), whereas the complexity of many physical phenomena (e.g., tides, weather, radio, X-rays) remain simply mysteries in the naive physics and engineering of most of us.

Stability, complexity, variability, determinacy, and predictability are in the end not, as a moment's reflection will show, attributes by which social and physical domains can be distinguished because, in each domain, there are events that run the range of the dimensions of determined–indetermined, constant–variable, predictable–unpredictable, and so on. Brownian molecular motion, Heisenberg's indeterminary principle, sampling requirements of photoelectron spectroscopy illustrate one pole for the physical sciences, whereas certain social routines, conventions, rituals, and operants illustrate the other pole in the social sciences. The notion of greater "context sensitivity" (Glick, 1978) for the social domain will not distinguish the domains either, at least not since the establishment of Maxwell's field of potential concept in physics. Although it is quite true that the significance of the smile as a sign of happiness, boredom, exasperation, etc. would always be dependent on the context in which it occurred, it is equally true that proper interpretation of certain physical events, like mounds of earth or decreases in an object's temperature, depends also on the context surrounding the event in space and time. The knock of a car engine, for example, means different things about its physical state in different contexts and circumstances. Furthermore, it is not merely in the social world that we employ "belief systems" that reduce informational complexity to allow action (Glick, 1978). Such systems are also employed in commerce with the physical environment (e.g., in navigation and orientation strategies).

The relationship of the social and physical domains to most of the dimensions alleged to distinguish them is probably orthogonal with events occurring in all quadrants. Harre and Secord (1972) have proposed in this context a general conceptual scheme: "which will have sufficient generality to encompass both electrons and men, and by implication all degrees of entity between [p. 78].'' It requires recognition by social scientists of a notion of the nature of scientific inquiry that is not restricted to a metaphysics of substances and their qualities, an epistemology of cause in correlation, and logical positivism. It is a view that recognizes an open-ended, indeterminant, relative, spontaneous universe in which the basic unit of analysis is change.

However, as Bearison (1975) has noted, there is still a potentially significant difference between knowing people and knowing other things, because, at least in the immediate case of knowing people, the knower and the known are one and the same. Although it is possible to know people as we know other objects, as perhaps the psychopath knows and thinks about people, it is clear that through introspection and projection we can have a unique knowledge of ourselves and other people that we could never have of physical objects. Even so, does this privileged cognitive position require the postulation of another set of cognitive processes to treat their knowledge? Or is it more likely to be the case that the privileged position is in fact not often fully invoked and that the lack of it in the case of physical objects can be overcome by prolonged experience and special training. It has been observed by some (Argyl, 1978; Nisbett & Wilson, 1977) that despite the closeness of the relationship between the knower and known, there is a certain blindness in people to the nature and order of their social behavior.

Apart from the fact that most people have scanty knowledge of the syntactical rules they follow in their own speech, people also have little awareness of even more obvious features of their own facial expressions, body movements, and stimuli that control or influence their own behavior. Researchers in cognitive dissonance, altruism, psychoanalysis, affective behavior, attribution theory, concept formation, and problem solving regularly find that their experimental subjects' reports of their behavior during experiments are surprisingly inaccurate and misleading (Argyl, 1978). Even simple conversational turn-taking gambits or the structure of forms of address in social exchanges are not readily recognized by their users.

To be sure, the power and certainty in naive psychology is no doubt founded on people's special status as the objects of their knowing, but at the same time, an equally impressive power and certainty is found in the naive physics of artisans and laborers in their special domains. The commercial fisherman's knowledge of the sea, for example, as complex, unpredictable, and unstable as the sea no doubt appears to the shoreperson, may equal or even exceed his knowledge of the social events in which he participates. In the end, the question remains whether an adequate account of cognition would require the consideration of special cognitive processes for the cognition of ourselves and others like us. Even so, the special benefits such processes could bestow on social understanding would no doubt be extended to physical events by anthropomorphic analogies anyway. In the end, it does not seem to be necessary to expect special social–cognitive processes on account of the social world being inherently more complex, variable, and unpredictable than the nonsocial world or on account of the knower being a more intimate member of one than the other.

None of the foregoing should be taken as implying that people do not recognize distinctions between the two domains or that the course of intellectual development isn't marked by construction of hierarchies in the social and nonsocial categories. There can be no question that from early infancy onwards social stimuli are discriminated from the rest. As Bower (1977) notes: "the perceptual and motor capacities of newborn babies, surprising as they are, fade into complete insignificance when compared with their social behaviors [p. 27]." Although his may be an overstatement, the evidence of infants': (1) spontaneous imitation of facial expression; (2) synchronous body movements elicited by human speech; (3) construction of 'mother' permanence at about 5 months; (4) early attachment to salient persons; (5) sensitivity to linguistic stimuli; and (6) nonverbal communication competence underscore the distinctiveness of social stimuli for the developing child.

Although much has been made of some allegedly inherent differences between the physical and social domains, that one is more regular, homogeneous, stable, predictable, more accurately represented, and more controllable than the other, it very well may be that, for the most common events, physical interactions, despite their probabilistic, even capricious character are in most contexts less variable, and so forth than the social interactions. However, it is not at all clear that this is the case for the very young child. It is conceivable that for the young child, particularly an only child, his or her interaction with parents and other friendly and well-meaning adults may be more constant, predictable, stable, and controllable than his or her interactions with the nonsocial environment. It would not be hard to believe that the young child learns how to operate his or her caretakers with vocalizations, eye contact, and smiles long before he or she learns to operate the other parts of the environment, or that the child could acquire person permanence before object permanence.

The question is not whether infants and others make a discrimination between people and things because any number of lines of evidence show that they do. The question is, what are the consequences of the discrimination, if any, for the development of cognitive structure and process.

Decalage in Social and Physical Cognition

In the preceding chapter of this volume Turiel develops the argument that social cognitive development should not be explained by the same global cognitive structures that organismic theories have applied to the development of cognition in general, because unlike the individual's social judgments, logical– mathematical–physical judgments do not form a unified and organized system. Moreover there are not only some non-age-related differences between domains of social understanding, but development takes place in such unique ways within each social domain, that there is no justification for searching for common cognitive structures and operations across the domains.

Although it makes sense to think that the various social domains (morality, social convention, etc.) may be independent and unsystematized with nonlogical or nonnecessary links between them and with their own individual stage or nonstage developmental sequences, it is equally clear that, contrary to what is implied throughout the preceding chapter, the same condition holds in the various physical domains. That social judgments do not form, at the moment, a unified structural system is probably true for the reasons Turiel enumerates, but it is equally true of the cognition of the physical or nonsocial domains—at least insofar as the knower is not an expert in the domain.

In a sense, the claim is that social cognition is concrete operational because particular contexts and contents dominate and so overwhelm any general structural aspect of cognition as to vitiate completely any explanatory power the structural construct might have. The salient feature of social cognition is the *decalage,* perhaps not a decalage of mathematical–logical structures, but a *decalage* with respect to some structure nevertheless. But the preeminent problem in the accounts of logical–mathematical development is the decalage, not just at the concrete operational period, which is defined by it, but at the so-called formal operational period as well.

Although there may be no central unified social–cognitive system, there seems, despite the early Piagetian orthodoxy, to be no such cognitive system for the various physical domains either, notwithstanding the fact the formal study of the domains may eventually provide unified systems for expert cognition. For most of us the various physical domains have the same distinctness and independence that Turiel has claimed for the social domains. That the physical domains, *mass, distance,* and *time* are distinct for most of us and for most children does not mean that there are no necessary structural links between them or that there could not be. It did of course take the development of Newtonian mechanics to make clear the logical entailments by which area, density, velocity, acceleration, force, work, power, and so on were generated from the mass, distance, and time domains.

The Genevan logical–mathematical operativity structures may not be appropriately or profitably applied to the social domains, but neither are they well suited to our understanding of the physical domains, although they have been almost exclusively researched in those domains. The operativity structures are structures of necessity and logical deduction—that is, they are structures of events that must be true, that have to be true, that are necessarily true. Although physical events and social events may be true, they don't have to be, because they could be otherwise, and for that reason operational structures or schemes have limited bearing on most of the informational content of physical and social domains.

"Nothing in nature," Piaget (1960, p. 279) writes in *The Child's Conception of Physical Causality,* "can give the child the idea of necessity." It is a major issue in developmental psychology and epistemology to assess the status of our concept that some events are necessary and some aren't. Operativity concerns the former only and thus is appropriately applied to a very small portion of what we know and believe. As an aside, it should be clear that it really doesn't make much sense to speak of a single Piagetian structural theory, as there are many Piagetian theories of development in various subject matter domains, some with operativity structures as in logic and mathematics, and some without, such as in the morality, perception, creativity, and information-acquisition domains. In some Genevan accounts, stages are salient and in some they are not.

The description of the needed research on the development of the cognition of social domains in the preceding chapter perfectly matches the concomitant research needed in the cognition of physical domains. We have, for example, after all the conservation research, no real idea why certain irrelevant attributes of objects are taken by young children as relevant attributes, or why some transformations produce nonconservation whereas others do not, or why conservation performance is sensitive to such factors as whether the material to conserve is of one material rather than another, is discontinuous rather than continuous, is animate rather than inanimate, and so on (see Murray, 1981, for a review of these factors). Our knowledge of the cognition of the physical or nonsocial concepts can not advance much by the interpretation of them as operativity domains. This is one reason why the implications of Piagetian theory of logical development for curriculum content are so meager (Murray, 1979).

Necessity in the Social Domain

Although it is the case that most of the social and nonsocial information we have and believe is not necessarily true, some of it is necessary and could not be otherwise than as it is. All quantitative and comparative relationships in either domain, for example, are transitive and therefore necessary. The truth of the relationship between John and Mary is guaranteed by their relationship to Jim when it is the case that John is friendlier than Jim and Jim is friendlier than Mary. Even though not all relationships, particular social relationships, are transitive, many have necessary components nevertheless. For example, if A is the father of B and B is the father of C, the relationship between A and C is guaranteed in the logic of necessary kinship relationships. In fact the kinship relationships are the prototypical case of the triangular matrix of an operational grouping from the logical model of concrete operational thought.

The source of the idea of necessity cannot be the physical environment in Piaget's view, which leaves for him the possibility that the source is social interaction. In *The Child's Concept of Physical Causality* and *Judgment and*

Reasoning in the Child, he develops the argument that logical structures have their roots in the child's need to verify and prove his or her opinions when confronted with the contrary opinions of others. Logical proof and deduction is the outcome of arguments in the social domain, as it were. Necessity has its roots here and in the social domain of morality. The necessity of law is initially, according to Piaget, entirely moral. The first events that *must* be the way they are and could not conceivably be otherwise are moral events. Regardless of its ontological status, necessity exists in the social cognition of the moral domain and indeed it may be the critical attribute that distinguishes the moral from the conventional. Insofar as appreciation of necessity is the defining feature of operational thought, operational structures and schemes may not be completely irrelevant to social cognition.

The work of Lee (1975) has already been mentioned in this connection but to it can be added the research program of Saltz and Hamilton (1968), which demonstrated that the conservation paradigm could be applied to social relationships. An analysis of the cognitive requirements in understanding Hieder's (1975) balanced and unbalanced systems of interpersonal relationships indicates a structural basis of the relationships that can be easily related to the operational accomplishment of simultaneously considering two or more attributes of an event. The distinction between logical and nonlogical features of social domains is as clouded as it is for the physical domains. It becomes a moot point whether research on the interpretation of the conditional proposition, for example, as a biconditional, or as a promise, or as a causal statement, etc. is research in social cognition or some other kind of cognition. If a person were to wager that 'if Mondale is a vice-presidential nominee in 1980, he will be president in 1984' the determination of the circumstances in which he *must* win or lose is both a social cognition issue and nonsocial cognition issue if the cognition is to be divided along these lines. The complete account of the wager interaction is probably better served without the division.

Apart from those aspects of social relations that could not conceivably be otherwise, and the limits the various stages of cognitive development place on the understanding of them, the operativity model may have heuristic value for research in the social domains.

Some aspects of social domains may be successfully treated as an INRC group. For instance, it makes sense to consider the attributes, effort and ability, as a Klein four-group in which high effort and high ability are correlates, in which high effort is negated obviously by low effort and high ability by low ability, and in which high effort is nullified or reversed by its reciprocal low ability, and so forth. Or in the morality domain, an action's positive intention and positive consequence are correlates, and an action's positive intention is negated by negative intention, and its positive intention is reversed by its reciprocal, negative consequence, and so forth. These applications to social domains make as much sense as conceptualizing the product-moment relationships of the balance beam as an INRC four-group, the most common application or illustration of this formal operations group to a physical domain.

Cauley and Murray (1982) asked 40 second and third graders to explain how it was that they were unable to read some words they had just been shown and failed to read. After they had read some and failed to read others they were asked whether they would be able to read particular words under the following eight conditions: if they were a year older (or a year younger); if they tried (or didn't try); and if they were older (or younger) and tried (or didn't try). The notion behind the study was that the child's privileged position as a knower of himself or herself would allow him or her to evaluate simultaneously two familiar attributes of the self, namely, ability and effort in the ordinary school task of reading words. The possibility of simultaneous evaluation of attributes sets a condition for operational competence. In this study, being older, and presumably having more reading ability, and trying are taken as correlates for example in the formal operational sense of the INRC group. The other INRC relationships among the eight conditions are shown in Fig. 3.1 along with the percentages of children who thought they could successfully read a set of words they had just failed to read if each of the eight conditions held. It is clear from the data that the effects of the attributes are not additive and the child's effort, particularly lack of effort, is a disproportionately significant determiner of the child's estimate of future success. For the young child the remedies for failure appear to be either increased effort or greater ability. He or she realizes that these remedies can be undone by having lower ability or by being indolent. However the factors, effort and ability, can be evaluated by the child separately and conjointly. The child seems to know that whatever benefit being older and having more ability would bestow can be reversed or can be undone by indolence and/or being younger. In

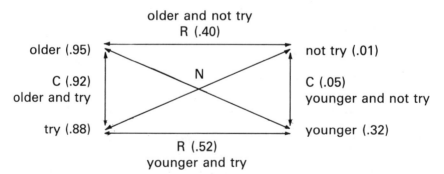

FIG. 3.1. An INRC group for eight conditions, four single attributes at the intersection of lines and four double attributes represented by the vertical and horizontal lines. The percentages of children ($N = 40$) who thought they could read a word they just failed to read under each of the eight conditions are shown in parentheses.

other words he or she seems to be able to combine the negation and reciprocal of each of the attributes of success or failure into a system like that in Fig. 3.1. In that figure, incidentally, all percentage differences greater than 20% were significant by independent chi-square and binomial analyses.

Expert Knowledge and Domains

The research program into the cognition of physical or social domains needs to be, as Piaget, Turiel, and others have insisted, interdisciplinary because the academic discipline in which the domain being researched resides must be consulted, not only as the source of experimental variables, but as a description of the developmental endpoint. How else could the boundaries of domains be established, how can it be known whether a difference makes a difference, or whether an event crosses a domain boundary? Does it make sense, for example, to have a domain of continuous matter or discontinuous matter because some persons treat them differently in conservation experiments? These questions are at the heart of the genetic epistemological research program because the significance of domains and their attribute variables are established teleologically in the collective cognitive structure of the experts in each discipline. Thus, for example, Piaget's work on time and velocity was motivated and made important by the priority of time or velocity in relativity mechanics. To be sure, the research programs are neater in discipline domains, like physics, in which there are large portions of uncontested knowledge.

Such programs, incidentally, may promote development in the academic discipline. The social sciences themselves may develop orthogenetically, thereby integrating hierarchically some of differentiated social domains described in the preceding chapter. Consider, for example, Johnson's work (Johnson, Cox, & Curran, 1970) on the associative structure of physics concepts. In this work, multiple dimensional scaling of physicists' similarity ratings of conceptual equations in analytical mechanics yielded a three-dimensional model solution that had at its nodes various equation concepts, some of which did not yet exist in physics. In other words, the physicists recognized the concepts generated by the associative structure of their judgments as possible concepts in the discipline, but they didn't know what they were.

The interaction of domain, cognitive structure, and interdisciplinary endpoint specification of development can be seen nicely for the concept of weight in physics. Whether weight constitutes a domain or is part of another broader domain is the question raised in the foregoing, but it is clear that the concept undergoes a complicated development. For the expert the weight of an object is a function of three factors—the mass of object, the mass of the nearest largest object, and the inverse square of the distance between their centers. Weight varies only as a function of variation in one or more of the three factors and the equation that relates the three factors constitutes the current endpoint of cognitive development in this domain (Johnson & Murray, 1970; Murray & Johnson, 1975). For the typical adult, weight is a function of only the mass of the object. For the child, weight is also a function not only of the mass of the object, but of its shape, texture, temperature, and continuity. Moreover it is not a function of the mass of the nearest largest object nor the distance between it and the object. Why these other factors should be a part of the child's conception of weight is in part explained by his or her level of cognitive development because cognitive operations are clearly implicated in the child's thinking. But certain peculiarities of the child's appreciation of the domain are also implicated, and these are not well understood (Murray, 1981) and will probably require the kind of nonstructural explanation Turiel has argued for in the social domain. Why should the object's temperature, for example, be a factor? Why should the child consider it a salient factor, whereas the adult ignores it as irrelevant?

In summary, the argument presented in this chapter is that there are few grounds on which to distinguish the so-called physical and social domains that will have any bearing on the psychological explanation of a person's understanding of them. The two domains present equivalent and identical difficulties for developmental cognitive theory and it is a mistake to think that our current explanations of 'physical' cognition are more advanced than similar accounts of social cognition.

REFERENCES

Argyl, M. An appraisal of the new approach to the study of social behavior. In M. Brenner, P. Marsh, & M. Brenner (Eds.), *The social context of method*. London: Croom Helm Ltd., 1978.

Bearison, D. *The comparative development of social and physical knowledge*. Unpublished manuscript. Graduate School of the City University of New York, 1975.

Bower, T. *A primer of infant development*. San Francisco: Freeman, 1977.

Cauley, K., & Murray, F. B. Structure of children's reasoning about attributes of school success and failure. *American Educational Research Journal*, 1982, *19*(3), 473–480.

Clarke-Stewart, K. Recasting the lone stranger. In J. Glick & K. Clarke-Stewart (Eds.), *The development of social understanding*. New York: Gardner Press, 1978.

Glick, J. Cognition and social cognition. In J. Glick & K. Clarke-Stewart (Eds.), *The development of social understanding*. New York: Gardner Press, 1978.

Guilford, J. The structure of intellect. *Psychological Bulletin*, 1956, *53*, 267–293.

Harre, R., & Secord, P. *The explanation of social behavior*. Oxford: Basil Blackwell, 1972.

Heider, F. *The psychology of interpersonal relations*. New York: Wiley, 1975.

Johnson, P., Cox, D., & Curran, T. Psychological reality of physical concepts. *Psychonomic Science*, 1970, *19*, 245–247.

Johnson, P., & Murray, F. B. A note on using curriculum models in analyzing the child's concept of weight. *Journal of Research in Science Teaching*, 1970, *7*, 377–381.

Lee, L. Toward a cognitive theory of interpersonal development: Importance of peers. In M. Lewis & L. Rosenblum (Eds.), *Friendship and peer relations*. New York: Wiley, 1975.

Murray, F. B. The generation of educational practice from developmental theory. In S. Modgil (Ed.), *Toward a theory of psychological development within the Piagetian framework*. London: National Foundation for Educational Research in England and Wales, 1979.

Murray, F. B. The conservation paradigm: Conservation of conservation research. In I. Sigel, R. Golinkoff, & D. Brodzinsky (Eds.), *New directions and applications of Piaget's theory*. Hillsdale, N.J.: Lawrence Erlbaum Associates, 1981.

Murray, F. B., & Johnson, P. Relevant and some irrelevant factors in the child's concept of weight. *Journal of Educational Psychology*, 1975, *67*, 705–711.

Nisbett, R., & Wilson, T. Telling more than we know: Verbal reports on mental processes. *Psychological Review*, 1977, *84*, 231–259.

Piaget, J. The child's conception of physical causality. Paterson, N.J.: Littlefield & Adams, 1960.

Piaget, J. *The psychology of intelligence*. Paterson, N.J.: Littlefield & Adams, 1963.

Saltz, E., & Hamilton, H. Concept conservation under positively and negatively evaluated transformations. *Journal of Experimental Child Psychology*, 1968, *6*, 44–51.

4

The Nature of Social–Cognitive Change in the Developing Child

William Damon
Clark University

Most contemporary theories of cognitive development are built upon a limited view of human behavior. The primary empirical base for Piaget's model, as well as for information-processing approaches, is the child's solitary attempt to master physical, logical, or scientific tasks in a laboratory setting. It is still an open question whether models that draw mainly upon such restricted data will be appropriate for describing the development of human cognition in all its forms. Of all the many manifestations of thinking during the day-to-day lives of children and adults, scientific problem solving is only a part, and for most persons a minor and unusual part.

Recently, and partly in reaction to the predominant way in which psychologists have operationalized cognition in their laboratories, there has been a surge of interest in the *social*–cognitive performances of children and adults. In such studies, social cognition has meant a number of things. Some studies view social cognition as a specific sort of knowledge, pertaining to social interaction, and focus upon the organization of this social knowledge as it develops through the life span. In such an approach, social knowledge is seen as a person's means of interpreting social interaction, and models based on such an approach attempt to define the special categories and principles that structure social knowledge at each level of development. Through the use of interview studies about social phenomena, such approaches have yielded developmental analyses of children's social understanding in a number of conceptual areas: social interactions, like affirmation, kindness, or sharing (Baldwin & Baldwin, 1970; Damon, 1977; Youniss, 1980); social relations like friendship and authority (Damon, 1977); the self (Broughton, 1978; Keller, Ford, & Meachum, 1978); other persons (Lively & Bromley, 1973); social and moral regulation (Damon, 1977; Turiel, 1978);

103

and societal institutions, like money, government, and politics (Connell, 1971; Furth, 1978). On the other hand, other approaches to social–cognitive study have considered social cognition as the process by which persons apprehend one another's meaning in the course of communication. Studies within this approach have observed persons during actual social interaction and have inferred from such observations children's early abilities to engage in reciprocal exchange, perspective taking, and referential communication with others (Asher, 1978; Mueller & Brenner, 1977; Shatz & Gelman, 1973).

In previous writings on the study of children's social cognition, I have lauded both these "social–cognitive" approaches to investigating human knowledge (Damon, 1979, 1981). My view is that, at this phase in the life of developmental psychology, a focus on social cognition is necessary to save us from models of cognitive development distorted by an almost exclusive emphasis on the child-as-scientist. My main concern has been that scientific knowledge, and its acquisition, requires types of understanding that are radically different, in form and substance, from many aspects of cognition that play more prominent roles in our daily social encounters.

In advancing this argument concerning the importance of social–cognitive research, I emphasized the undeniable distinctions between social and nonsocial cognition. The point was that we cannot learn everything there is to know about cognitive development solely from children's responses to physical science tasks administered in isolated testing situations. Social–cognitive study, both in the sense of exploring children's understanding of things social and in the sense of observing and inferring children's thinking during actual social interaction, has an essential role to play.

But despite this essential role, the developmental study of children's social cognition encounters many of the same scientific problems and borrows on many of the same theoretical insights as the study of any aspect of human cognition. In fact, the major controversies and problems currently facing developmental psychologists are equally in evidence on the social–cognitive front as well. In this chapter, I address some of these general controversies and problems through a presentation of my own recent research in social–cognitive development; I focus therefore, on similarities rather than differences between research on social–cognitive development and research on other types of cognitive change. It is my hope that, considered in the light of the relatively new (or at least rejuvenated) research area of social cognition, some troublesome problems at large in the field of developmental psychology may become more amenable to certain intuitively appealing solutions.

The Problem of Stages

A widespread contemporary debate concerns the validity of stage models in describing psychological development (Brainerd, 1977; Flavell, 1977). Generally, the debate is framed around the question of whether or not human cognition has the properties implied by stagelike descriptions of thinking. For example, a stage model implies discontinuity in development, in the sense that any two stages in a sequence are qualitatively different from one another in their fundamental organization. For another example, a stage model implies that developmental change occurs in a fixed sequence across all individuals and social conditions. For a third example, a stage model implies that there is some consistency within a person's thinking and behavior, such that a range of thinking and behavior at any period of life can be accurately portrayed by one or another stage description within the model. The debate over stage, therefore, proceeds along lines of questioning such as, "Is cognitive development really continuous or discontinuous?"; "Are there individuals, or collections of individuals, that undergo psychological change in manners other than the fixed sequences of stage models?"; "Are people consistent in their thinking and behavior from one occasion to the next?" Because there are plenty of data around that support both yes and no answers to all such questions, the stage debate could continue without resolution until psychologists simply tire of the controversy.

Another perspective on this problem is to take a less absolute stance regarding the implications of a stage model. It is possible to recognize that there is both continuity and discontinuity in development, both variance and invariance in the sequence of change, and both consistency and inconsistency in human thinking, while at the same time making fruitful use of developmental stage descriptions. In fact, my own view is that there are characteristics of psychological development that elude any theoretical language currently in our scientific repertoire, other than that that accompanies sequential stage models. This is not to say that all aspects of cognition and change conform to the traditional implications of such models. Nor is it to say that other, better models of psychological development are not possible. It is simply to say that, at the present state of our science, we have two choices: either to ignore in our psychological studies some criterial developmental aspects of behavior, or to recognize and further explore these developmental aspects, however crudely, with stagelike analyses of change.

Continuity and Discontinuity in Development. Children's knowledge changes gradually over time, reflecting only small increments in skill and insight from month to month. In the course of this gradual change, there is also considerable unevenness; normally slow improvements in understanding are often further slowed down by conceptual false starts, wrong turns, or even steps backward. In this sense, any close examination of children's behavior as it develops will unquestionably reveal considerable continuity from day to day. There are few, if any, sudden leaps in understanding that in a short period of time radically alter a child's way of seeing the world. Ideas and concepts, even during the dynamic period of childhood, have a stability that ensures their endurance even as new insights gradually begin replacing them.

Nevertheless, it is paradoxically also true that the most important of these gradual and uneven changes—that is, those that have permanent, long-term consequences for the behavior and further growth of the child—reflect a fundamental discontinuity in children's knowledge as it develops. This is a discontinuity in how knowledge is organized at different developmental levels. In other words, conceptual development is a process of reorganization that proceeds gradually but ultimately results in a radical alteration of the character and quality of a subject's understanding. Although the day-to-day flux of children's behavior may obscure this discontinuous, qualitative shift in understanding, a series of observations over extended periods of time will reveal it as the essence of developmental change.

To illustrate, I describe here the development of one widely recognized aspect of children's social understanding: the notion of reciprocity. Most accounts of social and moral development note the increasing expression of reciprocity in both the judgments and behavior of children as they grow older (Cairns, 1979; Hoffman, 1977; Kohlberg, 1979; Piaget, 1932/1965; Youniss, this volume). The question for the moment is, how is this increasing reciprocity best characterized? Is it most accurate to describe it as a quantitative change, strictly continuous in nature (the child simply becoming more and more reciprocal with age)? Or is there a qualitative shift (or several) in the nature of children's social reciprocations, implying conceptual reorganizations that represent a succession of discontinous changes? In my own descriptions of children's social–cognitive development, I have chosen the latter course; some examples here indicate the reasons behind this decision.

All social concepts require some recognition of social reciprocity. This is because social interaction, the subject matter of social concepts, is at its core a reciprocal phenomenon, generally including some give-and-take of actions, ideas, or objects.[1] The specific nature of the give-and-take varies from social interaction to social interaction, depending on the social relation or regulation that the interaction is intended to serve. For this reason, social concepts, which are the subject's way of organizing the variety of social relations and regulations in the social world, reflect many different uses of reciprocity. In my own social–cognitive research (Damon, 1977), I have investigated four areas of social conception that I believe to be central in children's social lives: authority and friendship, two important social relations from early childhood on; and justice

---

[1]In this use of terms, social interaction refers to interchange during which persons intentionally coordinate their actions, thereby communicating and maintaining a shared relation to one another. (For example, command–obedience is an interaction that maintains an authority relation.) Reciprocity is the means by which interactions are more or less equalized, making possible a sense of mutuality in the shared relation. This (often crude) equalization is achieved through a compensation of one act for another; reciprocation restores a balance temporarily altered. For example, a favor can be compensated for by a thank-you, thereby restoring equality and a sense of mutuality to the relation. It should be noted that this use of reciprocity is broader than that offered by Cairns (1979), because it includes complementary as well as similar actions and reactions. Exchange, or give-and-take, is reciprocity's criterial feature in this current use.

and social rules, two basic means of regulating all social relations. Each of these social concepts relies, in its own way, on the notion of reciprocity.

In the concept of authority, the central issue is the exchange of one party's obedience for the expression of respected leadership qualities by the other. Obedience, or a demand for obedience, without the presentation of respected leadership qualities by the dominant party, would create a conflictual state of imbalance. In the case of the authority relation, this state of imbalance is called "illegitimacy," and the continuance of such a state would ultimately lead to the breakdown of the authority relation. This is true whether the relation is con-stituted formally, as between a captain and a crew, or informally, as between parent and child. Understanding the authority relation, therefore, requries a grasp of the necessary command–respect exchange that is the basis of legitimacy and obedience in any ongoing authority relation.

Children at an early age (by 4 or 5 at the least) are able to express in their reasoning about authority some grasp of this command–respect exchange. With development, however, their ideas about the proper basis of this exchange change quite dramatically. Table 4.1 presents early stages in the development of children's authority reasoning. From the descriptions in this table, it can be seen that children's notions of the reciprocation between leadership qualities and obedience are central to the development of their authority understanding. At the earliest level, obedience is given in exchange for the loved one's expression of desire; in this primitive and subjective conception, it is the subordinate's attach-ment to the leader that itself endows the leader with legitimate qualities and provides the subordinate with a rationale for obedience. At the next level, still reflecting a subjective appraisal of the leader only in relation to the subordinate, obedience is exchanged for the authority figure's ability to reward or punish the subordinate. At 1-A begins a more objective assessment of the leader's actual characteristics, first in terms of physical prowess; then at 1-B, in terms of generally superior knowledge, talent, or skill; and at 2-A in terms of prior experience and specific leadership and organizational know-how. Beginning at 2-A, and culminating at 2-B, appears a new dimension to the command–respect exchange. Respect is no longer invested in *persons,* in their entirety, but rather in the leadership role that persons temporarily fill when appropriate. At 2-A, the subordinate assumes new rights, and the care and respect of the leader for the subordinate becomes a critical aspect of legitimate leadership qualities. At 2-B, the roles of leader and subordinate are only temporarily and voluntarily assumed for specific purposes; command and respect can be exchanged either way be-tween two parties, depending on the circumstances of particular situations. The authority relation itself becomes more flexible, consensual, and equal, due in part to the more mobile means of establishing and maintaining a reciprocal balance between acts of obedience and the respected qualities of leadership.

In the friendship relation, the central issue is the exchange of companionship and affection between the parties. The media of this exchange can range from

TABLE 4.1
Brief Descriptions of Early Authority Levels

Level 0-A:	Authority is legitimized by attributes that link the authority figure with the self, either by establishing affectional bonds between authority figure and self or by establishing identification between authority figure and self. The basis for obedience is a primitive association between authority's commands and the self's desires.
Level 0-B:	Authority is legitimized by physical attributes of persons, particularly those descriptive of persons in command. These legitimizing attributes may be used in a fluctuating manner, because they are not linked logically to the functioning of authority. The subject recognizes the potential conflict between authority's commands and the self's wishes; commands are followed as a means of achieving desires, or to avoid actions contrary to desires.
Level 1-A:	Authority is legitimized by attributes that enable authority figure to enforce commands (social or physical power). Obedience is based on subject's respect for authority figure's social or physical power, which is invested with an aura of omnipotence and omniscience.
Level 1-B:	Authority is legitimized by attributes that reflect special talent or ability, and that make the authority figure a superior person in the eyes of the subject. Obedience is based on reciprocal exchange; one obeys because authority figure helps, has helped, or otherwise "deserves" your obedience.
Level 2-A:	Authority is legitimized by prior training or experience specifically related to the process of commanding. Authority figure is seen as able to lead better than subordinates. Obedience is based on subject's respect for this specific leadership ability, or on the belief that leadership implies a concern for the welfare and the rights of subordinates.
Level 2-B:	Authority is legitimized by the coordination of a variety of attributes with specific situational factors. Subject believes that a person might possess attributes that enable one to command well in one situation but not in another. Authority is seen as a shared, consensual relation between parties, adopted temporarily by one person for the welfare of all. Obedience is seen as a cooperative effort that is situation specific rather than a general response to a superior person.

concrete objects to abstractly expressed sentiments, but without some form of reciprocation that leads to at least an attempt at equalizing the contribution of each party, the relation falters. As with authority, children at an early age (4 or 5) employ the notion of reciprocity in their friendship reasoning and, again, the nature of their reciprocal notions changes with development. As can be seen from Table 4.2, the exchange in friendship is initially conceived as an exchange of favorable actions, such as playing together, taking turns, sharing; or of actual goods, such as food and toys. At the next level, the key exchange in the relation is seen as one of trust between parties: Friends are people who can be trusted to respond to one another's needs, or who can be trusted not to betray each other's interests. At the third level, the key exchange within friendship becomes more psychological in nature and more exclusively limited to the participants of a particular friendship. It is now the secret thoughts and feelings of one another that friends are seen to exchange. But the function of the reciprocation remains the same, as it does in all social interaction; if one party to the relation withholds his or her contribution, the interaction becomes unequal or imbalanced, and the relation becomes endangered.

In justice, reciprocal action establishes a balance between the claims of individuals and their rewards or punishments. In distributive justice—the positive aspect of justice, having to do with the sharing and fair distribution of valued resources—the claims of individuals can include their deeds, their talents, their state of need, their physical attributes, their relations to the controller of the resource, or simply their presence in the distribution situation. A fair distribution calls for a balance between the worth of an individual's claim and his or her share of the resource. Early in childhood, children in their sharing activities demonstrate an awareness of this reciprocal relation between claim and reward, the core of a fair distribution. But as with other social concepts, the quality of children's reciprocation changes with development. Table 4.3 reflects this change; as can be seen in these brief descriptions, both the types of claims that children value

TABLE 4.2
Brief Descriptions of Early Friendship Levels

Level 1

Friendship is established by material acts of goodwill, such as the giving and sharing of food, toys, and other valued resoures. A friendship may be terminated by a negative material or physical act, such as the stealing of a toy, hitting, refusing to share.

Level 2

Friends are seen as persons who assist one another, either spontaneously or when one expresses a need. Accordingly, friendship is seen as a relation that is in the reciprocal interest of the two parties. Friendship is established by demonstrating that one may be relied upon to help: reciprocal trust is a defining element of the relation. Friendship may be terminated by a refusal to help, or by the commission of an act that is considered untrustworthy.

Level 3

Friends are persons who understand one another, sharing with each other their innermost thoughts, feelings, and other secrets. Friendship is now seen as an exclusive and long-term relation, established over a period of time with special people, and maintained through a mutual sharing of personal interests, private thoughts, and psychological comfort. Because friends are capable of mutual understanding and forgiveness, only a continual display of bad faith or disaffection is considered to be grounds for terminating a real friendship.

and the distributional relation between a claim and amount of reward become reformulated as the child's conception of justice develops.

At the earliest justice level, the only claim that is recognized is one of desire, particularly when the desire is associated with that of the self; the wishes of self or someone linked with the self are seen as sufficient for the awarding of a resource. The amount of the reward is proportionate only to the amount of expressed desire, as in "I should get a lot because I like ice cream a lot." At the next level, more objective claims, such as size or other physically linked attributes, are recognized and rewarded, although such claims are still often selected with a view to what pleases the self. Distributions may reflect a balance between the magnitude of the physical attribute and the amount of reward (as in "the bigger they are, the more they should get"). At 1-A begins a more extended system of balance, with the simple participation of a person in the situation justifying that person's share of a reward. Distributions are constructed equally, in compensation for the mere existence of the participant (and, consequently, as a means of preventing trouble, as in "If someone gets left out they will cause a fuss"). At 1-B, the notion of compensation as payback for good deeds or talent emerges; a balance is achieved between the reward and each person's contribution. This is the notion of deserving through merit, and the distributional balance again becomes unequal, now being proportionate to each party's positive investment in the situation. At 2-A the possibility of compromise between different types of claims is realized, with the compensation of need, prior deprivation, or special inability achieving priority in such compromises. Multidimensional and quantitatively complex distributional balances are constructed, as in "This reason is worth this much, this not so much," and so on. Finally, Level 2-B represents a coordination of various claims and rewards that takes into account the demands of specific situations, as in "The situation is cooperative so everybody should get the same but in this situation those who did the best should get the most so that everyone knows to try harder next time." Balances are therefore achieved with an eye toward the function of the reward itself.

The reciprocal balance at the heart of children's social rule knowledge parallels closely the reciprocity established in their authority reasoning, particularly at the early levels where social regulation is often embodied in concrete authority figures (such as parents). As with authority, an understanding of social rules depends on reciprocation between the child's deferral to external requirements and the child's respect for these requirements. The major difference, which becomes increasingly important with development, is that in the case of authority this obedience–respect balance is maintained in the context of a personal relation, whereas in the case of social rules it reflects the child's relations with impersonal regulations inferred from the demands of society at large (as manifested in the conduct of all persons with whom the child comes in contact). Thus, although the reciprocal nature of the obedience–respect balance continues throughout the development of both authority and social rule knowledge, in the

TABLE 4.3
Brief Descriptions of Early Positive Justice Levels

Level 0-A:	Positive justice choices derive from wish that an act occur. Reasons simply assert the choices rather than attempting to justify them ("I should get it because I want to have it").
Level 0-B:	Choices still reflect desires, but are now justified on the basis of external, observable realities such as size, sex, or other physical characteristics of persons (that is, we should get the most because we're girls). Such justifications, however, are invoked in a fluctuating, after-the-fact manner, and are self-serving in the end.
Level 1-A:	Positive-justice choices derive from notions of strict equality in actions, (that is, that everyone should get the same). Equality is seen as preventing complaining, fighting, "fussing," or other types of conflict.
Level 1-B:	Positive-justice choices derive from a notion of reciprocity in actions: that persons should be paid back in kind for doing good or bad things. Notions of merit and deserving emerge.
Level 2-A:	A moral relativity develops out of the understanding that different persons can have different, yet equally valid justifications for their claims to justice. The claims of persons with special needs (that is, the poor) are weighed heavily. Choices attempt quantitative compromises between competing claims.
Level 2-B:	Considerations of equality and reciprocity are coordinated, such that choices take into account the claims of various persons and the demands of the specific situation. Choices are firm and clear-cut, yet justifications reflect the recognition that all persons should be given their due (though, in many situations, this does not mean equal treatment).

former case the reciprocation becomes increasingly informal and "humanized," whereas the opposite is true in the latter case (see Damon, 1977, pp. 228–240 for further discussion).

More to the current point, and similarly with all other social concepts, the nature of the reciprocation in children's social-regulation reasoning itself undergoes radical transformation with development. Table 4.4 demonstrates this change. At the earliest level, deferral to regulation, understood as mere situational regularities, is exchanged for the child's whims and desires of the moment. At the next developmental level, deferral is exchanged for the child's fear of the pragmatic consequences accruing to disobedience, or for the converse (as a means of achieving a desired end). A similar balance is established at Level 2, although here different types of social regulation are distinguished on the basis of the severity of the consequences resulting from their breach. Finally, at Level 3, rules are respected for their intrinsic value in maintaining social order, and deferral to rules is exchanged for this generalized respect.

TABLE 4.4
Brief Descriptions of Early Social Regulation Levels[a]

Level 0

All types of social regulation are seen as situationally specific modes of behavior mandated only by the self's desire to perform such behavior. Observed social conventions and rules are represented idiosyncratically by the child, often being distorted to conform to the child's wishes. Neither conventions or social rules are seen as regulating behavior in any stable, constraining sense. Rather, they are viewed similarly to personal customs or habits, as momentary regularities that may be followed or ignored at will.

Level 1

The potential conflict between social regulation and internal desire is realized. Both social conventions and other social rules are viewed as constraining (unlike personal custom or habit). Social conventions and rules are seen as stable behavioral uniformities that are consistently enforced by the demands of an authority figure or by authoritative social group pressure (such as peer disapproval). Social regulation is deferred to for much the same reason that authority is obeyed: to avoid pragmatic consequences that are disagreeable to the self or to implement the desire of the self. No general distinction is drawn between conventions and other types of social regulation. All social regulation is considered binding, because it is assumed that what uniformly exists will be regularly enforced.

Level 2

Certain social regulations (such as moral ones) are distinguished from most social conventions on the basis that the former are followed more consistently than are the latter. Following this distinction, social conventions are often rejected as arbitrary, or at least are considered relatively unimportant, because they are often not followed or enforced. For example, stealing might be considered worse than sloppy eating because one ends up in jail after stealing, whereas one is only scolded for sloppy eating. Such a basis for distinguishing types of social regulation does not consistently distinguish the conventional from the moral, because conventional infractions sometimes may be more unusual than are certain moral ones or, similarly, may be more strictly enforced than certain moral ones.

Level 3

A respect for all social rules develops, based on an understanding of the social regulating function served by rules. For example, it may be considered wrong to disobey a rule because chaos will result if rules are ignored. Or a rule may be considered mandatory because it serves some necessary social purpose, such as protecting everyone's property. Because rules are considered to be an intrinsic part of the social order, they are seen as inflexible and as equally binding on everyone. Only those conventions that are governed by rules are respected. Conventions that are not rule governed are considered voluntary. Some distinction is also made between "less important" rules (such as dress codes) and "real rules" (such as stealing laws). But it is generally believed that everyone in society shares an equal responsibility to obey all social rules, regardless of the nature of the concern regulated by the rule.

[a]Levels 1, 2, and 3 were adapted from Turiel's social–conventional levels of the same number (Turiel, 1978).

From the preceeding discussion, two points should be clear: that reciprocity of one sort or another is embedded within all social interaction, and that children's conception of the reciprocity within social interaction changes with development. What, then, is the nature of this change? First, it is multifaceted; just as social reciprocity takes many forms, depending on the function of the reciprocal interaction; so does the child's developing understanding of social reciprocity take on many forms, each organized according to the relation or regulation that defines the purpose of the social reciprocation. Hence the different character of friendship exchanges from authority exchanges, and so on. Second, and directly to the point of this section, children at all levels of development use reciprocal reasoning within each area of social knowledge but there are important differences from level to level in the nature of the child's reciprocation. The descriptions already offered were intended to illustrate these radical differences. How are these differences best conceptualized by us as developmental psychologists? Here we have two main types of choices: a continuous model, implying that the reciprocal understanding exists from the start, and that development consists chiefly in quantitative increases in such reciprocal understanding (either in the sense that with age the understanding is applied to an ever wider array of phenomena, or in the sense that children use more and more of it); or a discontinuous model, implying that children's reciprocal understanding is qualitatively different at the beginning of childhood than during subsequent years, and that development consists chiefly in a succession of radical transformations in children's organization and use of their reciprocal reasoning.

The very nature of the foregoing descriptions argues against a solely quantitative and continuous model of social–cognitive change. An attempt to reduce the changes outlined here to statements like "the child becomes more and more reciprocal with age" would be inadequate as well as inaccurate. It is not exactly true, for example, that the succession of obedience–legitimacy exchanges in the authority sequence, or the succession of claim–reward exchanges in the justice sequence, or the succession of companionship exchanges in the friendship sequence, or the succession of deferral–respect exchanges in the social-regulation sequence, become progressively more reciprocal. There is nothing necessarily more reciprocal about exchanges of trust than about exchanges of goods, to take an example from friendship; similar statements could be made about all level changes in each of the aforementioned four sequences. Rather than an increase in reciprocation, each new level represents a new quality of reciprocation, defined by the types of considerations that are being compensated for. In authority, for example, considerations in the compensation equation change from (on the part of the leader) power to ability to experience to caring to respect for subordinate's rights, to name only a few of the changes. In justice, considerations change from (on the part of the claimant) association with the self's wishes, selected physical attributes, participation, merit, need, and situational appropriateness of deed, again to name only a few changes. Such considerational differences can be captured only in terms of what they are: distinct and diverse means of resolving social concerns. They are not quantitatively comparable on any dimension, even though some argument may be made that they *can* be ordered in a sequential developmental model. Such a model, however, will have the characteristics of an ordinal rather than an internal scale; arguments can be made that one type of consideration (and the level of reasoning based on it) is developmentally more advanced than another (see Damon, 1977), but the "amount" of developmental space between the levels is indeterminate. Again, the differences are of quality and order, not of degree.

In emphasizing the necessity of discontinuous descriptions in capturing so-cial–cognitive change in the child, I have focused on the nature of the changes themselves, somewhat distilled for the sake of constructing a systematic develop-mental model. As indicated earlier in this section, the actual character of changes with age in children's daily performances is far more graduate and uneven than discontinuous, models seem to imply. The paradox of development is that dis-continuous changes are brought about in the course of day-to-day activity and flux, which reveals considerable continuity in children's growth patterns. This point is demonstrated and amplified with the presentation of some empirical data in the following section.

Sequence and Reversion in Development[2].   The original empirical evidence that I presented in support of the four social–cognitive sequences outlined in the preceding section was cross-sectional and short-term longitudinal in nature (Damon, 1975, 1977). The cross-sectional data showed that, in children ages 4 through 10, the authority, justice, and social rule were positively age related, with age–stage correlations ranging from .64 (authority), .69 (rules), and .85 (justice). (Not enough friendship data were collected to establish quantitative empirical relations.) The short-term longitudinal evidence pertained only to the authority and justice sequences, and the findings were a bit more equivocal concerning the developmental ordering of the sequences. This longitudinal data came from a 1-year study in which children aged 4 through 9 were interviewed about authority and justice and then reinterviewed 1 year later. The data did show that, by the end of the 1 year, children who changed in their authority or justice reasoning generally did so in a positive direction, normally moving to the next highest level. But, particularly in the justice area, a large number of subjects did not change at all during the 1 year of the study, and a small but noticeable number (as many as 23% on one justice measure) scored lower on the second testing than they did on the first. Thus, although the trend toward progressive movement with age was confirmed among the significant majority of longitudi-nal subjects, there were a large number of no-changes in addition to some actual reversals. Because stage models generally imply invariance of sequence, these

---

[2]The data reported in this section have been more fully elaborated in Damon, 1980.

data lead me to remain cautious in ascribing to the social–cognitive sequences full properties of stagelike development.

At the conclusion of this initial longitudinal study, I suspected that one reason for the tentativeness of its results might be the too-short time interval of the study; a year may simply not be long enough to gain an adequate view of social–cognitive development in individual children. For this reason, I decided to conduct one further follow-up of the children from this original study. This follow-up (Testing time 3) was 1 year from the second testing, or, in other words, 2 years from the initial testing time in the original longitudinal study. By Testing time 3, 34 children from the original sample remained. (Seventeen had been lost through attrition of one sort or another, e.g., moving away from Worcester.) Of these 34, five subjects were 6 years old (the original 4-year-olds at Testing time 1), six were 7 years old, five were 8 years old, five were 9 years old, nine were 10 years old, and four were 11 years old. I shall discuss here the social–cognitive progress of these 34 children during the 2 years between Testing time 1 and Testing time 3.

As at the original two testings, the 34 subjects at Testing time 3 were given clinical interviews on issues of justice and authority. (Interviews of this sort are available in Damon, 1977). The three sets of interviews corresponding to the three testing times were similar in focus but different in specific detail. All the justice interviews probed for children's understanding of fair exchange and distribution of reward, and all the authority interviews probed for children's conceptions of criteria for legitimacy in leadership and the rationale for obedience. Only the story contexts in which these issues were presented differed from testing time to testing time.

Children's individual patterns of change from Testing time 1 through Testing time 3 are shown in Figs. 4.1 and 4.2. In these figures, Testing time 1 is referred to as Year 0, Testing time 2 as Year 1, and Testing time 3 as Year 2. Unbroken lines demonstrate progressive change in any one year, and broken lines demonstrate reversals or lateral movement. Each line represents one subject's progress from Year 0 to Year 2, with each figure therefore being composed of 34 lines. It should be noted here that subjects' justice and authority scores as calculated in this study and represented in Figs. 4.1 and 4.2 were *modal percentage* scores: That is, each score indicates the justice or authority level at which the highest percentage of the subject's reasoning was found. This use of modal (or "predominant") reasoning score was a shift from the "best-level" scoring system used in the previous analysis of the initial year's data in Damon, 1977.[3] Reasons for this shift to a modal-percentage scoring system are given shortly.

---

[3]For this reason, there are some small differences between certain numerical results reported here and the longitudinal results in Damon, 1977. Interestingly, however, these differences are slight: Whether modal or best-level scores are used, the general patterns of change from year to year look essentially the same. Of course, as noted earlier, the 1977 report contained only longitudinal results from Year 0 to Year 1.

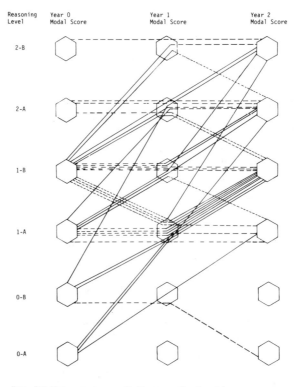

Reasoning   Year 0   Year 1   Year 2
Level   Modal Score   Modal Score   Modal Score

Note: Each line represents one subject's progress from Year 0 to
       Year 2. Solid portions of the lines indicate upward movements
       from one year to the next, and broken portions of the lines
       indicate lateral or downward movements.

FIG. 4.1. Pattern of 2-year change in children's justice reasoning. Each line represents one subject's progress from Year 0 to Year 2. Solid portions of the lines indicate upward movements from one year to the next, and broken portions of the lines indicate lateral or downward movements.

As can be seen from Figs. 4.1 and 4.2, the additional longitudinal testing year did indeed reveal a more complete picture of children's social–cognitive development. Although, as in the previously reported longitudinal data, there were a number of horizontal movements and even reversals in children's social reasoning from year to year, when the 2 years of this completed study are taken together, the vast majority of subjects can be seen to progress forward along the justice and authority sequences. Generally the total change from Year 0 to Year 2 was by no more than one or two levels in a positive direction. Initial downward movements tended to be "corrected" in the following year, as did initial movements of particularly large magnitude (greater than two levels). Thus, although there was considerable unevenness in the direction of children's change from year to year, there was an "evening-out" tendency that, over the space of 2 years, resulted in the vast majority of subjects progressing by one or two levels along the sequences described in Tables 4.1 and 4.3. This magnitude of progressive change was consistant with cross-sectional age trends reported elsewhere for these sequences (Damon, 1975, 1977).

One question that a longitudinal approach is naturally designed to answer is whether there are, at an initial testing time, indications that can predict which children will progress by the time of a subsequent testing. In other words, was there any way to tell from a subject's reasoning performance in 1 year whether or not he or she would advance during the following year?

In order to answer this question I wanted to preserve in my scores of subject's

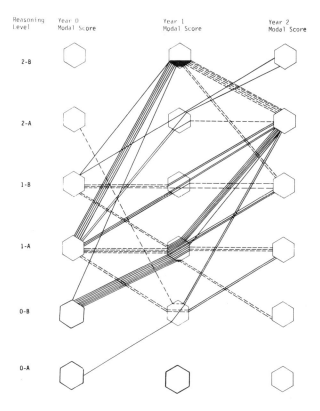

Note: Each line represents one subject's progress from Year 0 to Year 2. Solid portions of the lines indicate upward movements from one year to the next, and broken portions of the lines indicate lateral or downward movements.

FIG. 4.2.   Pattern of 2-year change in children's authority reasoning. Each line represents one subject's progress from Year 0 to Year 2. Solid portions of the lines indicate upward movements from one year to the next, and broken portions of the lines indicate lateral or downward movements.

reasoning performances all available information. For this reason, I switched my scoring system from the "best-level" method previously used (Damon, 1977) to a method representing the entire range of subjects' performances. In the previously used technique, scores for children's justice or authority reasoning were limited to single scores representing the best level at which the children performed on a justice or authority task. Although this means of determining subjects' scores can facillitate the establishing of empirical relations in developmental data[4], it nevertheless does not take into account the total pattern of each subject's reasoning on the task. Most importantly, it ignores the possibility that a child's reasoning may be "spread" across several developmental levels during the course of any task performance.

For the present study, the entire range of each subject's reasoning on every interview was retained, rather than merely the best level displayed per interview. This range was represented as a list of percentages, each indicating the proportion of a subject's responses that was scored at one of the six levels in the justice or authority sequences. For example, Subject 12 on Year 0 justice was scored 0-A (13.5%), 0-B (53%), 1-A (20%), 1-B (13.5%), denoting in this manner the spread of Subject 12's reasoning across four justice levels on the first testing occassion. From this score it was easy to determine the subject's modal levels (in Subject 12's case, 0-B) upon which the sequence findings already reported were based. It was also possible to calculate various measures of reasoning "spread" for each subject: For example, "spread above the mode" was determined by totaling the percentages of a subject's reasoning at all levels above the modal level (20% + 13.5%, or 33.5%, for Subject 12); "spread below the mode" was determined by adding the percentages of below-mode reasoning (13.5% for Subject 12); and "spread away from the mode" was calculated by subtracting the subject's modal reasoning percentage from 100% (47% for Subject 12).

The best predictor of movement on both justice and authority was reasoning spread *above* the mode in the previous year. General spread was no predictor at all, and spread below the mode was inversely correlated only with change on justice, and this to a smaller degree than above mode spread. This last statistic most likely reflects the stronger relation between above-mode spread and positive change, since percentage of spread below the mode is intrinsically related to percentages of spread above the mode.

These findings indicate that stage changes in children's social understanding are anticipated by partial, tentative developments in the child's reasoning long before the predominant pattern of the child's social understanding becomes progressively reorganized. Because of these anticipatory developments, it is possible to predict which children in a sample are in the process of changing their conceptions: The children most likely to advance along a stage sequence are those who *already* show some indication of higher-level reasoning, however

---

[4]See the following section for a further discussion of this point.

slight or ephemeral this indication may be. "Transition" from one social–cognitive stage to the next, in other words, is most clearly signaled by the initial appearance of some reasoning in advance of the old stage.

Although this conclusion does not violate common sense, it does contradict certain other uses of the stage model in developmental psychology. For example, Flavell and Wohlwill (1969) once presented a model in which consolidation of a previous stage's cognitive achievement was seen as a necessary condition for movement to the next stage. From the model, we should expect very little "spread" in a subject's reasoning prior to progressive stage change. This clearly was not the case in the findings reported here, where spread of one type (*above* the previous reasoning mode) was indeed associated with subsequent stage change. Another notion of stage change was advanced by Kohlberg and Kramer (1969) and also in early writings by Turiel (1968): According to this notion, a general "stage mixture" was expected to be a precursor to developmental change. From this notion, we should expect that subjects who demonstrate reasoning spread upwards *and* downwards from their predominant stage should be the ones most likely to change. Again, the present findings do not suggest this notion, particularly with regard to the role of downward spread as a positive predictor of subsequent stage change. The present findings, rather, are more in line with writings by Inhelder, Sinclair, and Bovet (1973), and later writings by Turiel (1974), in which it is suggested that transition from stage to stage is heralded by a child's beginning attempts to reason in a more advanced manner.

In this sense, the findings of this study support the notion presented previously that even stagelike development proceeds with considerable continuity in the child. Despite the qualitative discontinuities that define the organizational changes described by a stage model of development, the child's actual month-to-month movement along the sequence of stages is a long, gradual process. It is not an abrupt series of changes in which children wake up on Tuesday understanding the world differently than they did on Monday. Rather, the acquisition of new concepts begins long before the new concepts come to dominate the child's understanding. The eventual reorganization of a predominate pattern in a child's social–cognition pattern is only one part of a story that has an earlier history.

The message from the research, therefore, is the following: Although stages of social cognition express important qualitative differences between distinct social reasoning patterns that appear in sequence throughout childhood, the actual month-by-month growth of children's social cognition is gradual, continuous, and often uneven. This is quite a different use of a stage model than has appeared throughout the prior psychological literature. Nevertheless, I believe it to be the only way to retain the stage notion, given data such as I have presented here, as well as data presented by many others working in other areas of cognitive development (see, for example, Brainerd, 1978). And I do believe it essential to retain the stage notion, at least until we have a viable alternative, simply because the essence of psychological development can be captured only in models that are sensitive to qualitative differences in cognitive organization. (This was the point that I have already illustrated in my discussion of reciprocity development.) Unless we are to forgo the possibility of describing and analyzing qualitative changes, and by so doing forgo the study of long-term human development, we will need to rely on stagelike models to characterize development. But such models must be adapted to the realities of gradualism, unevenness, and flux in children's cognitive growth.

Consistency and Inconsistency in Development.   Another widely held notion concerning stage models is that, at any stage of development, there is a consistency in the child's behavior that is a result of the child's "being" at that stage. This is the notion that stages must be to some degree "holistic"; that, in other words, each stage in a sequence can be used to describe the major part of a child's behavior (as related to that sequence) at some point in the child's development. Langer (1969), for instance, has written: "each stage in the child's development must be defined by a writing or organization that characterizes all his new conduct at that stage [and not by a simple dominant property] [p. 8]."

Such claims, however, have run into an indisputable feature of mental life: variation. Study after study of psychological processes have shown that there is considerably less than perfect stability in subjects' cognitive performances. In fact, the preponderance of data seems to indicate that situational flux (or context dependency) is more truly characteristic of human judgment than is uniformity or consistency. Further, developmentalists even more than other psychologists have had to confront this problem of cognitive variability, because children seem particularly prone to impulsive shifts in their performances. Many psychologists, recognizing the fact of cognitive inconsistency, have cited this as reason enough to question structuralist notions like stage or level (Brainerd, 1978; Flavell, 1977). And virtually no one is satisfied with the old Piagetian solution of naming this problem decalage, comparing it with the problem of friction in physics, and then moving on to other problems.

In fact, the issue of consistency (or its lack) in an individual's behavior is a timeless and central problem in psychology and deserves our most careful attention. As already noted, variation, or inconsistency, is a fact of life but it is not the only fact. It is also possible to make a convincing case for the existence of uniformities within individuals' behavior. But how can we decide if human behavior has the consistency necessary to conform to stage-model expectations of some fundamental integrity, or "wholeness" of behavior? This is a question whose complexity has been greatly underestimated in recent developmental debates. One problem is that consistency is not a characteristic that can be objectively measured, because the determination of consistency is itself relative to what the investigator chooses to look at. What seems consistent from one point of view may be inconsistent from another. For example, if one is a good structuralist, there are always ways to find uniformities even across behavior that appears fragmented. One might say that young children's behavior is "consistently primitive" even though there are no actual commonalities among various aspects of the behavior other than certain specifically defined confusions or inabilities (i.e., "primitivisms"). This was precisely Piaget's approach when he tried to explain an apparent contradiction or "paradox" in the moral behavior of young children with regard to social rules. Piaget noticed that the same young children who claimed that rules were sacred and immutable were also the ones who in practice frequently broke the rules, or who at best obeyed them only irregularly. Although this appears to be an inconsistency, Piaget (1932/1965) wrote that: "this paradox is general in child behavior and constitues . . . the most significant feature of behavior belonging to the egocentric stage. [p. 61]." According to Piaget, both parts of the paradox—a belief in the sacredness of rules and irregular rule following—are really two aspects of the same moral structure: the primitive and egocentric mode of heteronomous morality. Further, Piaget treats the paradox itself as an index of childhood egocentrism.

In general, there is always a way, at some level of abstraction, to find uniformities in any array of phenomena, including human behavior. The issue in social science is always the heuristic value of the hypothesized uniformities in describing, explaining, and predicting human behavior. A notion like "egocentrism" is quite global and is difficult unambiguously to apply to human behavior. Perhaps for this reason, Piaget himself long ago gave up on this as a definer of early developmental levels. However, the logical–mathematical structures (concrete operations, formal operations) that Piaget later introduced are also global, as well as highly formal in nature. The usefulness of such formalistic, structural descriptions in predicting the range of children's everyday behavior is still an open question, even in the areas of scientific content to which they most directly apply.[5] There is little evidence that children's behavior across a range of logical–mathematical tasks consistently conforms to one or another of Piaget's formal stages. Nor has Piaget himself made such claims for his model (which he has presented rather as a general framework outlining the boundaries of epistemological development throughout the history of society as well as of the individual).

Stage models that aspire to capturing more of the variance of individual human behavior must be more content bound and less formalistic than Piaget's logical–mathematical structures. Such models must be capable of making distinctions between cognitive development in different conceptual areas—recognizing, for example, the distinction between physical and social understanding or, within the social domain itself, the distinction between friendship and authority conceptions, or between justice and social regulation. It is such a model that I

---

[5]As I noted at the beginning of this chapter and have extensively argued elsewhere (Damon, 1979, 1981), such logical–mathematical structures have limited applicability to other areas of understanding, such as the social domain.

have attempted in my own stage descriptions, presented in Tables 4.1 through 4.4, or that Turiel, in his distinguishing of moral from social–conventional understanding, is working on in his own developmental-level descriptions (Turiel, 1978). In such models, uniformities in children's behavior are defined according to children's cognitive performances within specific conceptual areas. That is, each developmental level within a particular sequence (authority, justice, or whatever) describes a set of behavioral uniformities that is expected to lead to some degree of consistency in the related behavior (that is, the authority behavior, the justice behavior, and so on) of children operating at that level.

The empirical question than remains: To what extent do children in their daily lives operate consistently at one or another developmental level in a sequence like the ones I have described here? Here, again, we must keep in mind that the determination of consistency is relative to where we look for it. Within the entire scope of children's daily lives, we should entertain only the most modest expectations concerning consistency of behavior. But it is nevertheless possible, within the flux and variety of children's behavior, to isolate threads of uniformity that emanate from the developmental levels of children's understanding. The manner in which a child organizes knowledge in a given area has a muted though discernable influence on the range of the child's behavior relative to that area. It is this influence that establishes some consistency in the child's behavior, and that justifies our use of developmental stage models for description and prediction.

In other words, there is both inconsistency *and* consistency in children's behavior. Any sensible use of a stage model focuses on the latter but also must recognize and come to terms with the former. These are not contradictory goals, as long as we remain aware of the limitations of structural descriptions. First it must be remembered that any structural description, however content bound, defines only the organization of behavior. For this reason there will always be aspects of behavior that do not fall under its rubric, and for which the issue of consistency is therefore irrelevant. (At justice stage 0-B, for example, it does not matter whether a child one day decides that girls should be treated better and the next day decides that boys should be treated better; according to the organizing principles of 0-B justice, there is no inconsistency in these contradictory beliefs.) Second, we should remember that childhood is a dynamic period developmentally, and that some inconsistency of stage-related performances is to be expected for this very reason. The data from the longitudinal study presented earlier are evidence enough of this point. And third, behavior from occasion to occasion, and even within single occasions, varies because of situational as well as performance reasons. No two life situations are alike; each calls for a different application of knowledge, or for unique interactions among various types of knowledge (justice, authority, and so on), depending on the specific situational parameters. For optimal functioning in a diverse world, children must entertain some such inconsistency in the name of flexibility. As for performance variables, the role of fatigue, inattention, and hosts of other factors in influencing behavior is self-evident and, of course, contributes significantly to inconsistency within a developmental-stage framework. The lesson here is that, even with a focus on manifestations of cognitive organization, our expectations of consistency must remain modest.

In order to tease out the consistency that does exist in children's expression of their social understanding, I have constructed for my studies a particular kind of method that focuses on a certain aspect of children's behavior. This method is an adaptation of Piaget's *methode clinique,* in which an interview about an area of interest is administered to children at various ages. Two principles of administration distinguish clinical-method interviews from standardized tests. First, a clinical interview must be given flexibility enough to allow all children to express their full range of knowledge about the topic of interest. This may entail thorough probing of a child's initial responses with follow-up questions. Second, in probing, the interviewer must establish a balance between suggesting too much to a child on the one hand and allowing the child to discourse aimlessly, without direction, on the other hand. I (Damon, 1977) have described my social– cognitive interviews for children, and the scoring procedures for them, in the following manner:

> As in all clinical interviews, the questions following the story are only the skeletal outline of the interview. For purposes of comparability between subjects, each subject must be given an opportunity to respond to all of these questions; but the order or wording of the questions may vary from subject to subject, depending upon the needs and interests of the individual child. For example, if a child spontaneously brings up an issue before the appropriate question has been asked, it is wise to explore the issue at that time, while the topic is hot. Also, to clarify the child's response, probe questions—"Why" or "What difference does that make?"—must be asked after virtually all of the basic questions listed above. In addition, countersuggestions are an important tool of this sort of interview. Clearly, the countersuggestion will vary according to the nature of the child's statement. If for example, the child decides that Billy should get a free candy bar because he is poor, the countersuggestion might be, "Is that fair to Johnny, who has to pay for his?" If the child's decision is not to give Billy the free candy bar, the countersuggestion might be, "Well, what if Billy says he never gets to eat candy bars because he can't afford them?" [pp. 68–69].

> The unit of scoring in a protocol is called a "chunk" of reasoning, a chunk being any statement or group of statements by the child that convey a coherent idea or meaning. After all of the reasoning chunks in a given protocol are scored, a composite . . . score for the protocol is obtained [p. 89].

As noted earlier, there are at least two means of obtaining a composite score from the scored "chunks" (the number of which vary of course from protocol to protocol). One means is by representing the range of subjects' reasoning by percentage scores, as was done in the longitudinal study described previously. In my initial studies, however, I used a ''best-level'' means of arriving at composite scores, selecting for the composite score only the highest level of reasoning unambiguously displayed by the subject during an interview:

> The final consideration of only the subject's highest reasoning is consistent with the ''testing-the-limits'' philosophy of the clinical interview method employed in this study. In a sense, the interview and scoring techniques when combined may be seen as a means of obtaining the best performance, or the reasoning competence, of children [p. 89].

Now it should be clear that the clinical interview, when combined with the best-level technique of scoring, yields only a restricted view of children's social behavior. That is, the view is restricted to the well-reflected, well-probed reasoning of children in verbal and often hypothetical context and, even at that, only the child's highest-level communications are selected for the final score. Given this restricted view, the issue of consistency is put to its truest test. If we are ever to expect consistency in the expression of children's knowledge, we should most confidently expect it under such ideal circumstances.

In fact, under such circumstances we do find moderately high consistency within and across occasions. In my earlier studies, for example, I reported that the association between subjects' best scores on two separate positive-justice dilemmas given on or around the same testing occasion was r (38)= .73, p < .001; and the association between two authority dilemmas given on the same occasion was r (34) = .83, p < .001. Further, there is evidence of consistency across time, the rank-order association between children's justice reasoning from one year to the next on different justice interviews, r (38) = .48, p < .01 for the authority interviews were similar, only a bit lower in magnitude.

Even aside from the best-level means of selecting composite scores, there is evidence for some consistency in children's expression of social knowledge during a clinical interview. For example, in the longitudinal study reported earlier, when all interviews from all three testing occasions were considered, children's *modal* reasoning on justice constituted a mean 64.7% of their total reasoning, with a standard deviation of 15.5%. (In other words, on the average, 64.7% of children's justice reasoning on all three testing occasions was at one level in the sequence). Further, a mean 92.2% of children's justice reasoning on all three occasions was within one level of the mode (that is, at the mode or plus or minus one level). Authority statistics were almost identical, with 64.5% of children's reasoning at the mode, standard deviation of 20.0%, and 91.69% of their reasoning within one level of the mode.

It must be remembered, and in fact emphasized here, that the clinical technique itself selects for a certain kind of performance. The method, when properly administered, encourages children to give thoughtful, reasoned statements. Further, only well-probed chunks of reasoning are scored. Thus, even in the range-or-percentage technique of composing final scores, the scoring system is highly attuned to the subjects' well-thought-out performances. This feature of the scoring system is highlighted by the close correspondence between children's best-level performances and their modal performances. For example, on the three occasions of the longitudinal study reported here, 78% of subjects had the same justice scores regardless of whether their best-level scores or their modal scores were taken for a composite final score. This was also true in 75% of cases on the authority interview. Clearly, therefore, my use of the clinical technique generally draws for subjects' best reasoning performance; and it is in this best performance that we are able to see some consistency in children's social understanding from situation to situation.

Such consistency should not be confused with stability, inasmuch, as noted earlier, childhood is a dynamic period developmentally. In the long run, children are constantly changing their beliefs and conceptions, as the foregoing study demonstrates. But they do so in an orderly manner. This is the meaning of the rank-order associations presented in the preceding paragraphs; the associations mean that children who are relatively high in one year will be relatively high the next, and similarly for the low scorers; they do not mean that children have not moved forward during the year. It is just that most of the children have moved at a fairly regular pace, retaining their relative developmental positions amongst themselves. Consistency in children's developmental levels of understanding, therefore, means two things. First, within the short term, it means that children, when given the opportunity to reason thoughtfully and carefully about an issue, will organize their thoughts on that issue at or near the same developmental level. This should hold true across situations, as long as the task requirements of the situations do not vary significantly. Second, within the long term, consistency means that changes will take place in an orderly fashion, with new modes of cognitive organization replacing old ones in (roughly) sequential, steplike fashion. I add the modifier "roughly," because as demonstrated previously, there is a good deal of unevenness to the developmental process. But in the long run there is regularity as well, and from this regularity derives the second kind of consistency already noted.

Now consistency of well-reflected reasoning is one thing; but we must also ask the extent to which the entire range of children's social reasoning, or even of children's social behavior itself, is consistent with this restricted aspect of children's cognitive performance. This is an important question in behavior science, for it ultimately asks what role is played by cognitive organization in the daily life of child or adult. Unfortunately at this point in our behavioral science this problem is a long way from being clearly illuminated; appropriate studies are difficult to do properly, and consequently data are scarce. What data there are seem to demonstrate the point that I made previously, which is that there are as many reasons to expect inconsistency as consistency in the total scope of children's performances. To cite an example related to the social–cognitive focus of the present chapter, Larson and Kurdek (1979) administered my justice interview to children aged 6 through 10 in an attempt to assess intratask consistency in children's moral reasoning. It is important to note that both the interview and the scoring procedures in the Larson–Kurdek study differed considerably from my own practices. First, their testing procedure was described as: "brief and standardized and may have been more representative of immediate rather than optimal levels of moral judgment [p. 463]." Second, Larson and Kurdek scored components of their protocols (such as "spontaneous resolutions") that were not in themselves samples of thorough reasoning. (In my own procedures, choices without reasons are not scored.) The end result was that Larson and Kurdek obtained a series of more broadly based justice scores from their adaptation of my procedures than I myself do. Interestingly, with these broadly based scores, Larson and Kurdek reported intratask correlations ranging from .18 to .31, depending on which aspects of the protocols were being correlated (spontaneous resolution, spontaneous justification, and so on). They concluded that: "Children's level of moral reasoning increased with grade level, but performance was inconsistent both at the intratask and intertask[6] levels [p. 462]." We might only add Larson and Kurdek's low but positive correlations for the justice task do indicate some core of consistency, although it is certainly small in magnitude.

It seems clear from the Larson–Kurdek findings that children's reasoning can vary quite a bit in the course of their responding to questions from adults. Unless efforts are made in testing procedures to encourage and select children's well-reflected statements, performance scores are likely to reflect a good degree of fluctuation and mix. There are important lessons that we can learn from this fluctuation and mix; one of these is that a child's capacity to organize his or her thinking about a certain issue has only a partial influence on the child's actual expression of reasoning about the issue during normal circumstances. I do not consider a well-probed clinical interview to be normal circumstances. The Larson–Kurdek procedures come closer than my own to eliciting and scoring children's spontaneous thinking and, as we might expect, there is less than overall consistency in such ideas.

In my own studies of relations between children's hypothetical moral reasoning and their real-life moral behavior (Damon, 1977; Gerson & Damon, 1978), I have found a similar picture: some fundamental coherence, most clearly expressed under ideal circumstances, amidst a web of variation and flux. When considering social behavior during real-life social interaction (as opposed to during a verbal interview), variables intervening on consistency become even more numerous as well as more strongly felt. Self-interest, force of habit, and

---

[6]The Larson–Kurdek study also included tests of relations between children's performances on the justice task and children's performances on social reasoning tasks adapted from Selman and Piaget.

specific situational considerations all interact with children's social conceptions in influencing children's real-life judgment and conduct. Gerson and Damon (1978) have discussed the problem in the following manner:

> It should surprise no one that we expect (and have found) only modest consistency in children's moral behavior. After all, the situations that a child may encounter are widely varied. The child's developmental capacities are often in flux; his or her objectives are many. The specifics of most situations are open to many interpretations. The child's interactions may be deliberate or habitual. Or the situation may demand an immediate intuitive response, and it may arouse disturbing and compelling moral emotions. With all these possibilities, why should we expect any consistency at all? Yet in spite of life's diversity, there are some continuities. Children are not totally different people in each new situation; they bring with them a limited range of developmental capabilities, a unique history, and a personality. To the degree that the child can assimilate a situation to past experience, the child's moral behavior will be informed by previous efforts at moral understanding (sometimes to the point of being habitual). What we are proposing is a modified "doctrine of specificity," which asserts that moral behavior is not specific to context alone (as Hartshorne and May wrote), but that it is specific in interaction with all the variables discussed above. That is, the child constructs a specific understanding that derives from the child's developmental capabilities, the child's objectives, the child's particular interpretation of the situation, the context, and the type of interaction (deliberate, habitual, intuitive). The consistencies that are seen are due to certain continuities in the child and to recognized similarities across situations [p. 56].

As for the problem of stages in developmental psychology, it must be re-emphasized that a stage description expresses only the manner in which a child may organize his or her thinking around a particular issue. At any point in a child's development, we might well expect more than one manner of organizing beliefs to exist simultaneously. This alone is reason enough to expect some variation in children's performances. Beyond this, the further one departs from observing children's thinking under ideally restricted circumstances, the more variation one introduces into the system. The data that we now have supports the notion that there is some integrity and some uniformity in children's social knowledge, despite the normal mix of levels due to the frequent developmental transitions of childhood. Such consistency is observable in settings such as well-probed clinical interviews, but has only a partial and muted influence on children's behavior in other laboratory and real-life contexts. Further, one aspect of the consistency is a mobile and dynamic one, in the sense that consistency during development must be assessed not simply by stability of conception, but rather by a regularity and order in the process of individual change. Among certain kinds of interview data we have been able to witness such regularity and order over the long term, and a good deal of short-term stability as well.

Structure and Process[7]

In the foregoing section, I have argued for the validity of structural models (as in stage sequences) for describing children's social-cognitive development. In fact, I have made the claim that structural descriptions are necessary if the qualitative organizational changes that are the heart of long-term development are to be adequately and accurately conveyed. My only qualification has been that our uses of stage models must be adapted to the realities of gradualism, continuity, and unevenness in development, and to the reality of relative inconsistency in children's everyday behavior. Such realities need not be incompatible with the implications of a sequential structural model, so long as our use of the model is properly restricted to analyzing the developmental levels of children's cognitive organizations. Beyond such use, questions like the role of cognitive organization in the total behavior of an individual must remain open to empirical investigation. In short, developmental psychology must maintain a middle ground between forgoing structural descriptions and expecting them to explain all of human life.

There has been, however, a more serious challenge to structural descriptions than the challenges that have already been discussed. This has been the claim that structural descriptions are insensitive to the dynamic aspects of cognition. These dynamic aspects have been called "processing" features by one school of psychologists and "dialectical" features by another, but, whatever the language, the point has been to emphasize the cognitive mechanisms that provoke developmental change by gathering new information, storing it, encoding it, processing it, substituting it for old ideas, and so on. This is quite a different emphasis than the structural focus on the organizational characteristics of cognitive systems in themselves.

In fact, it is true that developmental psychologists generally have found it very difficult to talk about the structural and processing aspects of cognition in the same breath. Structural explanations have emphasized the pattern in children's thinking, describing progressive changes in thinking as reorganizations in the pattern: Advanced structures incorporate primitive ones, forming new and more complex patterns, and so on throughout development. Although this progressive reorganization is considered to be a transformational process, there is nevertheless a static quality to the structural descriptions of developmental stage models. These descriptions convey the competence and the understanding of the subject in a given area, but do not convey the means by which the subject seeks to improve that competence and understanding. In order to capture this dynamic aspect of cognition, developmentalists have often turned to a different type of language, borrowing words like "encoding," "recall," and "evaluation" from computer models of intelligence. In this way, the "learning potential" of chil-

---

[7]Some parts of this section have been adapted from Damon, 1981.

4. SOCIAL-COGNITIVE CHANGE

dren may be discussed, and it even becomes possible to investigate individual differences in such potential. But exclusive reliance on processing language misses both the child's overall conceptual abilities and the child's developmental status in relation to its past, present, and future understanding of the world. Nor is "tacking-on" processing to structural language a very satisfactory way of telling the whole story of development. The two languages are different enough in origin and assumption to abrogate the possibility of establishing intrinsic relations between them. The interesting problem is not to describe how the child understands the world in addition to describing how the child seeks and receives new information. Rather it is to explain how the child's mode of understanding the world carries with itself the seeds of its own future transformation. How, in other words, can an organization of thought function simultaneously as a means of: (1) understanding the world; (2) seeking new information; (3) receiving environmental feedback; (4) critically questioning itself; and, ultimately, (5) prodding its own transformation? In order to address this problem, a developmental model needs not two languages but one, capable of discussing both structure and process in thinking.

Piaget's model, perhaps more than any other, has been attacked for emphasizing the structural at the expense of the processing aspect of cognition. But this is a misguided attack. Piaget's approach to this problem is through his equilibration model, which is at the heart of his lifelong view of the relation between the knowing subject and the object of cognition. It is a view that does full justice to the dynamism of cognitive processes. Equilibration is the central process that Piaget invokes to explain the process of development, and in recent writings (Inhelder, Garcia, & Voneche, 1976; Piaget, 1932/1965), he has outlined three phases of the equilibration process. These phases consist of three developmentally ordered reactions by a subject to a new experience that may potentially have a "perturbing" effect on the subject's prior way of understanding things. According to Piaget, quoted in Inhelder et al. (1976):

> The initial reaction, named "pattern alpha," consists only in an attempt to neutralize or suppress the perturbation by a voluntary ignorance comparable to a kind of repression. The second reaction, or "pattern beta" consists in taking the perturbation into consideration but doing so by seeking a compromise resulting in some displacement both of the perturbing experience and the subject's original system. Finally, the gamma reaction results in a genuine incorporation of the perturbation into the system itself, where it becomes an intrinsic and deducible new variation. In these processes, therefore, there is a simultaneous re-equilibration and construction of structural novelty; and one recognizes in them what Foerster expressed by his celebrated phrase "from noise to order" [p. 28, my translation].

The three phases of equilibration describe the progressively adequate manner by which the subject comes to terms with new information in the world, particularly information that contradicts the subject's previously held beliefs. But the phases can also be read as process parallels to the three basic stages by which Piaget has described children's developing conceptions of number, time, space, geometry, logic, and so on. (Here I refer to Piaget's many content-specific stage sequences that focus specifically on one or another type of concept acquisition, not to his broader four-stage model of operational development from infancy to adolescence). It is easy to see the parallel between an alpha-type reaction, in which there is a rejection (sometimes playful, sometimes serious) of perturbing new information, and a Stage 1 approach to a Piagetian task. Whatever the nature of the task—and this has been reported in any number of conceptual areas—the Stage 1 response avoids coming to grips with the task requirements, either through playful ''romancing'' or through an inappropriate perseverance of the subject's usual orientations into the new sphere of questioning. Similarly at Stage 2, where intermediate solutions of one sort or another parallel the ''compromise'' beta reaction, and at Stage 3, where the subject is capable of anticipation, flexibility, mobility, and systematic compensations—just as in Piaget's descriptions of equilibration's gamma phase (Piaget, 1975, pp. 71–75). Piaget's equilibration writings, therefore, can be read as his attempt to explore the dynamic potential of cognitive stages. By adding a new dimension to his model of developmental progression, Piaget attempts to express both the comprehending and the knowledge-generating (or ''ever-increasing,'' as in the French *dépasser*) nature of cognition. Further, he is able to do this systematically, using one language and one set of consistent assumptions, which is certainly a step in the direction that I outlined previously.

Nevertheless, my reservations (alluded to at the beginning of this chapter) about the nonsocial nature of Piaget's approach still remain. It could hardly be any other way, of course, for, as just noted, the equilibration model is simply another side to his stage model, compatible in all respects. The fundamental problem has to do with Piaget's view of knowledge acquisition as a gradual construction by the subject of the properties of an objective world. Starting from this initial subject–object dichotomy, Piaget is led to a feedback model of development in which the subject, through active manipulation of the world, reorganizes its own thinking as it discovers new, unsuspected features of reality. Despite the enormous inroads that Piaget has made in applying this model, in my opinion he has yet to speak convincingly to the fundamental mystery of cognitive development: how the subject is able to grasp features of the world that are initially beyond the reach of its own consciousness. In Piaget's equilibration model, this question may be focused at, and prior to the alpha phase. Given the initial tendency of cognitive structures to reject information that they cannot assimilate, how are contradictions ever recognized to begin with? That is, how do new experiences become perturbing, given the model's position that all experience is known only through the subject's existing structures? Piaget in all of his theoretical writings has struggled to portray cognition as an open rather than a closed system—hence the ''expanding equilibration'' model. But the implications of the original subject–object dichotomy are that things originally lie outside the consciousness, waiting to be grasped. Combined with a constructionist viewpoint that emphasizes above all the primacy of the subject's own activity and understanding, this position leads inexorably to the closed system that Piaget has tried to avoid. The key problem is that there is no means within such a system for feedback "external" to the subject (whatever that could be) to register itself on the subject's consciousness.

Within Piaget's theory, the way out of this closed system is to postulate "other" factors, beyond the equilibration process, that contribute to intellectual development. Piaget has done exactly this (Piaget, 1964), citing maturation and social experience as two such factors. But this is hardly a satisfactory solution, because again it results in a developmental model consisting of several unconnected languages and several orders of explanation. It leaves unclear the relation between these factors and equilibration, and relegates equilibration to an uncertain position in the overall developmental scheme of things. What is needed is a model that expresses one cause of developmental change in terms of the other causes, rather than a model that not only distinguishes between causes but offers no means from within the system of ordering or relating these distinctions. However great a contribution the equilibration model will prove to make, this essential achievement stems beyond its powers.

One alternative approach is a study of cognition that is more truly social in character, an approach that denies the distinction between social experience and equilibration to begin with. From such an approach, one is led to examine critically the original split between subject and object, at least insofar as consciousness is concerned (see Macmurray, 1957, 1961, for a fuller discussion of this alternative view). If one begins with the assumption that all human knowledge is fundamentally social in nature, and that all subsequent restructuring of children's knowledge proceeds under the past or present influence of social interaction in some form, then one is left with a model that envisions social experience as an integral part of the developmental process. Rather than the view that the subject discovers properties of an external object, sometimes with the aid of social feedback, this alternative approach presents the view that knowledge is from the start motivated, organized, and communicated in the course of social interaction. It is co-constructed, rather than unilaterally constructed.

The experimental work of Willem Doise and his collaborators (Doise & Mugny, 1979; Doise, Mugny, & Perret-Clermont, 1975; Mugny & Doise, 1978; Perret-Clermont, Mugny, & Doise, 1976) has lent support to such an alternative approach. Although Doise has not expressed his own theoretical model in quite the manner presented here, his operating assumptions are closely compatible. According to Doise and Mugny (1979): "our hypothesis states that conflicts of cognitive centrations embedded in a social situation are a more powerful factor in cognitive development than a conflict of individual centrations alone [p. 361]." In his studies, Doise has compared the cognitive performances of children working singly with the performances of children working in social interaction with other children or with adults. Presenting subjects with a spatial perspective-taking task, Doise found (Doise et al., 1975) that: "two children, working together, can successfully perform a task involving spatial coordinations; children of the same age, working alone, are not capable of performing the task [p. 367]." Even more interesting were the results from a similarly-presented conver-vation-of-quantity task: "subjects who did not possess certain cognitive operations . . . acquire these operations after having actualized them in a social coordination task [op. cit., p. 367]." It seems that children in social interaction must restructure their cognitive performances in order to coordinate them with others and, further, that this act of restructuring may have some direct influence on the organization of each participating child's thinking. This suggests a model of development with social interaction as an intrinsic feature, rather than as an additional, external factor.

In his series of studies, Doise has demonstrated that developmental progress is achieved through the coordinating of a child's perspective and actions with those of another, rather than through the simple transmission of information and ideas from one child to another. Basic mechanisms of change are shown to be coordination and social conflict, rather than learning or imitation. As an illustration of this, Doise (Mugny & Doise, 1978) found that during a spatial perspective-taking task: "collective performances were structurally superior to those of the group members taken individually [p. 190]" in cases where children are paired with peers *either* less advanced *or* more advanced than themselves. Progress, therefore, was not so much a result of imitating another with superior knowledge as it was a result of coordinating one's approach with that of another. Interestingly, in this and other studies, Doise has found that "more progress takes place when children with different cognitive strategies work together than when children with the same strategies do so [op. cit., p. 181]." He has even shown this to be true in cases where both children's initial strategies were incorrect (Doise & Mugny, 1979). Thus, to have a significant effect, the act of social coordination must require a child to alter his or her standard way of approaching the problem. This is to say that coordinations that are successful in leading to a progressive restructuring of children's cognition must consist of an initial social conflict imbedded within a context[8] of cooperation.

Doise's studies are an important first step toward an experimental paradigm that does justice to the social foundation of cognitive growth. In observing children working through cognitive problems in the course of social interaction, such a paradigm is capable of examining cognition as a process rather than merely as a product. Further, Doise's approach has also shown that the structural

---

[8]It should be noted that such developmental social interactions need not be limited to the sphere of child–child relations: Doise has established essentially the same pattern of results in studies of children in social interaction with adults (Doise, Mugny, & Perret-Clermont, 1976).

aspects of cognition need not be overlooked in the study of developmental process. For example, not only has Doise used children's developmental levels of understanding as a dependent variable; he has also investigated the role of the child's developmental level in enabling a child to benefit from his or her social interactional experience. In one such study (Perret-Clermont et al., 1976), it was found that children's cognitive "readiness" (indicated by their developmental levels of understanding) did indeed influence their likeliness to progress during the experiment. In this manner, the mutual influence of a child's cognitive structure and the social-interactional process upon one another is recognized and investigated in Doise's approach.

But the work of Doise and his colleagues requires more of a social–cognitive process analysis than has yet been achieved. We need to know more about how children establish the social interactions that enable them to restructure their own collective and individual cognitive performances. This, of course, is a social–cognitive question because it entails explaining how children comprehend the thoughts, intentions, and actions of another, as well as how they contribute to the developmental social interactions by communicating their own thoughts and perspectives. Related to this question, one is led to the children who did not change during their exposure to Doise's experimental conditions. Part of the answer no doubt lies in the initial state of cognitive "readiness" that varies from child to child, as noted previously. But even among children at similar initial readiness levels some change positively and some do not. It seems that some children seem particularly able to benefit from their social interactions, whereas others at the same cognitive level (cognitive, that is, in a task-specific sense) are unable to benefit in similar conditions. This may well reflect differences among children in social-interaction skills. Such skills, of course, may be expected to derive directly from children's comprehension of other persons, of themselves, and of social relations. To tap such comprehension, one needs to introduce into the experimental paradigm indexes of social–cognitive development, such as measures of perspective-taking ability, communication skill, and interpersonal awareness, as well as measures of social and self understanding.

Introducing such measures into a social–cognitive study may be done in either of two ways: Children's social interactions may be directly observed, and their social-interactional styles and abilities may be inferred from such observations; or children's social competence can be measured by standard social–cognitive testing procedures, and such assessments can be related to children's performances during and after social interactions. In my own current work I am trying out both types of approaches. Although it is too early yet to guage the merits of such efforts, I describe them here as an illustration of my own attempt to investigate both the structural and processing aspects of children's social cognition during the course of development.

In some previous research (Damon, 1977), I placed children, three at a time, into a "real-life" distributive-justice situation. The children's task was to divide among themselves (and a younger child removed early) a reward for making bracelets. The reward was 10 candy bars, and the children were asked to determine among themselves a fair way to split it up. Built into the situation were conditions that allowed the children to include in their decision-making processes considerations of merit, equality, sex, age, physical prowess, and special need. In the original version of this experiment, each subject was individually interviewed about his or her decision prior to the group debate; then the three subjects together were observed as they attempted to arrive at a consensus concerning the problem of fair distribution.

My interest in this experiment was initially centered around what its results could tell us concerning relations between hypothetical and actual social action. Children's performances in the course of this "real-life" social interaction were compared with their responses to similar hypothetical–verbal interviews dealing with the issue of positive justice. As noted earlier in this chapter, both consistency and inconsistency between the two types of behavior were found to some degree; these results are spelled out in Damon, 1977, and in Gerson and Damon, 1978. But beyond this problem of consistency, some results from this study shed light upon other interesting aspects of children's peer-group interactions. These aspects have to do with how children communicate with and influence one another in the course of arriving at a group decision. Although the original version of this experiment was not set up to explore directly this issue, some results nevertheless suggested certain possibilities regarding it.

First, one very simple finding may be noted: There seemed to be an increasing ability, with age, of children to reach agreement with their peers.[9] In the oldest groups (the 8- and 10-year-olds), all children reached some sort of consensus by the end of the group session. This consensus in some cases resulted from all three children coincidentally agreeing from the start, and in other cases resulted from one or more of the group changing decisions for the sake of agreement. But for none of the older groups was the experimenter forced to arrange a compromise for the children. On the other hand, 8% of the 6-year-old groups and 22% of the 4-year-old groups failed to reach a consensus among themselves, no matter how long they argued or disagreed. It should be noted that all groups were given as much time as they needed to come to an agreement, and the experimenter encouraged agreements by refusing to distribute candy bars until the group was in accord about how the bars were to be given out. Only after it was clear that there would be no progress toward a consensus did the experimenter step in. In spite of all this encouragement, a sizable number of younger children failed to arrive at a group agreement.

A closer look at the nature of the children's actual decisions before and during the group debate reveals a finer-grained picture of the differences between the older and younger groups. Table 4.5 shows the raw number of children who

[9]A fuller report of their data is presented in Damon, in press.

constructed equal versus unequal distributions, broken down by age group (4, 6, 8, 10), and by choice point (before the group session, at the beginning of the group session, and at the end of the group session). An equal distribution was one in which 25% of the candy bars were given to each of the four original participants; an unequal distribution was one in which at least one child was given more than 25% of the candy. (Percentages rather than raw number of candy bars was used as a measure because some children refused to distribute all 10 candy bars).

As can be seen in Table 4.5, there were two similar and dramatic movements in the use of equal solutions among the children in this study. The first movement coincides with the progressive increase in age represented by the four age groups; the older children construct equal solutions more often than do the younger ones, at each of the three choice points. Similarly, there is a continual increase in equal distributions that coincides with the amount of time the children spend in the group session. This increase occurs at each of the four age levels. In other words, the longer the child spends in the group, the more likely he or she is to distribute the candy equally, regardless of age, but the older children tend to do so more quickly than the younger children. The two movements toward equal distributions reinforce each other, so that all 72 of the oldest two ages of children construct equal distributions by the end of the group session.

Equality is one of the fundamental elements of justice, though it certainly does not, in itself, represent the most advanced form of justice principle. Many of the older children in this study showed themselves capable, prior to the group session, of constructing more sophisticated kinds of justice solution than simple equality: for example, solutions that employ the notion of merit (reciprocal payback for investment of talent or work), the notion of benevolence (inequality in the service of special need, or to remedy prior deprivation), and so on. (Many of the younger children constructed solutions that were even *less* sophisticated than simple equality, e.g., purely selfish solutions.) Although the use of equality

TABLE 4.5
Number of Subjects Constructing Equal and Unequal Distributions at
Each of Four Age Levels, and at Each of Three Choice Points

	Choice Point					
	Before Group Session		*At Start of Group Session*		*At End of Group Session*	
Age	=	Not =	=	Not =	=	Not =
4	7	29	6	30	15	21
6	19	17	22	14	24	12
8	22	14	32	4	36	0
10	28	8	34	2	36	0

as a means toward fairness is a notion that must develop, children by the age of 5 or 6 normally have consolidated this notion and are ready to construct more sophisticated justice principles. But even though strict equality is fairly primitive as a justice principle, it nevertheless is an excellent way to reach agreement in a group. Equality is a perfect leveler of differences, a means of compromise *par excellence*. In an equal solution, a person's full "deserving" may not be recognized, and yet no one's claims are to any great degree ignored. In most peer-group distribution situations—as in the one used in this study—it is to everybody's advantage to reach some consensus, because only then may the disputed reward be distributed. The accomplishment of the older children in our study was to anticipate quickly that, whatever their personal beliefs about fairness, it was equality that would work best in this group situation. Many of the younger children also came to recognize this, although it often took some exposure to peer conflict and debate to get them there.

Here, in this initial finding, we can glimpse a suggestion of the reciprocal influence between development and social interaction. The older children (who, it was also shown in this study, generally operate at higher levels of social knowledge even in the real-life situation) clearly approached the group situation with a different orientation than did the younger children and consequently came more easily to a consensus (the "task requirement" in this situation). In this sense, the child's developmental status can be seen to influence the nature of the child's participation in the social interaction. But in the finding that younger children, after some exposure to the group situation, tended toward the same solutions as the older children, we have some indication of the influence of the social interaction upon the child. We have no evidence from this experiment that the change brought about by this influence was a *developmental* change—that is, that the younger children's adoption of equality represented a permanent reorganization of their thinking in a progressive manner. But even the indication of short-term changes in these children's choices is itself suggestive, especially as these changes were in the direction of solutions constructed by the more advanced children.

As noted in the foregoing, the initial version of this experiment was not designed to explore the two-way relations between social–cognitive development and peer interaction. The findings reported here were a by-product of the original study, one at best tentative in nature. In a subsequent adaptation of this experiment, (Damon & Killen, 1982), we explored more directly the process of social influence during such an encounter. This time we looked for the long-term effect of this peer influence on individual children's conceptions of fairness. Pretests and posttests on positive-justice measures establish children's levels of reasoning about fairness before and after the group encounter. (Children in this study ranged in age from 5 through 8, and represented three basic levels of justice reasoning—0-B, 1-A, and 1-B). The children placed in this peer-group situation were compared with children who engaged in a discussion with an adult about identical issues for a similar period of time, as well as with a control group who were simply pretested and posttested on the justice measures. With the sample of children exposed to the peer encounter, there were several experimental variations. For example, some groups consisted of children who reasoned at the same developmental level on the justice pretest, whereas other groups consist of subjects at different levels. Some groups consisted entirely of relatively advanced reasoners, others entirely of relatively primitive reasoners. We also had children from different backgrounds, such as a middle-class sample versus a lower-class Hispanic-speaking sample.

Results from this study have shown that children in the peer-group conditions were indeed more likely to change positively in their reasoning about justice than were children in the adult discussion group. Overall, 56% of the children who experienced the peer situation showed a small degree of progressive change[10] in their reasoning, as opposed to 34% of the children in the adult-oriented setting, a statistically significant difference. Results from the control group showed that the children exposed to no treatment at all were even less likely to change positively than those in the adult condition.

Now these findings are not so much interesting in themselves—the training potential of peer interaction has already been amply demonstrated in developmental research—but in the questions that they open up for investigation. The major question of interest is, how do the 56% of children who changed differ from the 44% of children who did not? Through an analysis of the children's videotaped peer debates, sessions, we attempted to answer this question in social-interactional terms. A full report of this analysis is available in Damon and Killen (1982). Briefly, we found that children who engaged in rejecting, conflictual modes of interaction with one another tended not to advance. The younger children who advanced tended to accept or transform, through collaboration or compromise, the arguments of their peers. Older children who advanced did so through social-interactional processes that were more varied and diverse than those of the younger children.

This initial study was exploratory in intent, and the findings must be supplemented with findings from further studies in order to gain a complete picture of how social interaction influences social-cognitive development. As a means of conveying the quality of the social-interaction processes examined in this study, I quote here from a transcript of three children during their peer debate. All three children who experienced this particular interaction were among the 56% of the children who subsequently showed some advance in their positive-justice reasoning. At this point in our study, before we have any definitive quantitative results,

---

[10]This change was not by an entire developmental level, but rather an increased percentage of reasoning above the child's previous modal response level. The longitudinal results reported in the first section of this chapter indicate the significance of this type of change to children's future social–cognitive development.

it is interesting to speculate how and why this experience had a progressive influence upon these children.

Matthew: You can't do it when they're all mixed up.

Jennifer: Oh, I know how I'm going to do it (looks closely at bars).

(Girls start dividing candy bars up.)

Matthew: I forgot how much I was supposed to get. I'm all mixed up.

(Jennifer picks up candy bars and gives 2 to Nathan and keeps 2 for herself)

Matthew (takes 3 candy bars):   I got stuck with 3 candy bars. (To Jennifer): Hey, you got 4.

Jennifer (picks up Nathan's 2 and giggles):   Yeah, I got 4.

Sarah: I got 3.

Matthew: Take one away. That's all I would say. Take one away.

(Jennifer takes away 1 of her candy bars and then puts it on Nathan's pile).

Jennifer: Nope I want it. (Picks up the 4 candy bars for herself).

(Jennifer puts her 4 candy bars in the center, takes 3 from Matthew and puts those in the middle.)

Matthew: Hey, (grabs 3 candy bars and one more) Now I got all of them.

(Sarah grabs one more bar for herself, now has a total of 4).

Sarah: I know—take one away—that would be the best—3 each. . . .

Jennifer: Do we have to use all of these candy bars?

Sarah: Now, I know. We all have 4 the same.

Matthew: I know (Takes candy bars and gives them out to Sarah and Jennifer. The girls each have 3 and he has 4). I got 4!

(Now they all start shuffling the candy bars around until finally Sarah has 4 and Matthew and Jennifer each have 3)

Matthew: See! Three! Hey, I know how you got 3! (Notices that Sarah has 4). Oh, You!

Sarah: Give one to him (Pointing to Nathan's pile).

Matthew: (to interviewer) Can you take bars away? Oh, boy, There's an extra one.

(Sarah collects them all and divides them 3, 3, 3, 1.)

Jennifer: No, that's not even. I know—2 and 2 then 2 and then you break it in half and then you put 2 . . .

Matthew: That's what I said. That's what she wrote on my thing. You can't do it when they are all mixed up.

(Girls grab. Jennifer has 4. Sarah has 4. Matthew has 2.)

Matthew: It's not fair, you got 4.

Jennifer: You only got 2.

Sarah: I got 4.

Matthew: I made my decision (He gets up and walks around tables).

Jennifer: I already know.

Sarah: Hey, take one away (Holding one bar behind her back) and we'll all have 3. (Redistributes candy bars to be 3, 3, 3, and 1).

Matthew: Only if we take one away.

Sarah: And give it to him (Nathan).

Jennifer: No.

Matthew: No, then it won't be even. All of us will have 3 and he'll have one.

Sarah: Because he's the youngest.

Jennifer: No, all of us will have 2 like this.

Matthew: Then we'll break two in half. That's what she wrote on my thing, that's why.

Jennifer: That's what he wrote on my thing.

Matthew: Oh, No! Remember when I said I'm gonna faint (falls back). We're going to break 2 in half. That's what he wrote on my thing.

Jennifer: Me too. You take 2, 2, and 2 and break 2 in half and then it'll be even.

Matthew: That's what I am saying. That's what he wrote on my thing.

Jennifer: That's what I'm saying.

(Sarah picks up Matthew's candy bars and then puts them back.)

Jennifer: It won't be even and if it won't be even it won't be fair.

Sarah: But he ain't here.

Matthew: But he's gonna' come back. This will be fair if we give it back.

Jennifer: Break it in half and then you'll have half, he'll have half, I'll have half and he'll have half.

Matthew: O.K. We all agreed, right?

Jennifer: Um, mmmm, we made up our minds!

Matthew: Yes, we all agreed.

Jennifer: We'll have 2, he'll have 2, and he'll have 2 and then we break the candy bars in half and we'll all have halves.

This session was fairly typical of the sessions in which one or more of the participants subsequently showed some progressive change in their justice reasoning. Some such sessions were longer, some shorter; in some the children were more verbal, in some less verbal, and so on. Interestingly, in this and other sessions, children's progress in justice reasoning does not seem to be directly related to reasoning that they offered or were exposed to during the session. In the sample session quoted here, the debate concerns issues of evenness and whether or not to treat the absent younger child equally. Subsequent to the session, one of the children (Sarah) showed some partial movement towards 2-A in her justice reasoning, a movement that could be explained by her exposure to the problem of a younger child in special circumstances. But for the other two children, progress on the posttest meant an increase of reasoning at the 1-B level. This is surprising because nowhere during this session was the issue of merit or payback, the major organizing principle of 1-B reasoning, raised. Many (though not all) sessions that provoked change were similar in this regard. It seems that, in many cases, experiencing collaboration with peers was enough to instigate progressive reasoning change, despite the absence of specific experiences that directly connect with the new level of reasoning.

140 DAMON

REFERENCES

Asher, S. The development of referential communication skills. In G. Whitehurst (Ed.), *Child language*. New York: Academic Press, 1978.

Baldwin, C. P., & Baldwin, A. L. Children's judgments of kindness. *Child Development*, 1970, *41*, 29–47.

Brainerd, C. J. Feedback, rule knowledge, and conservation learning. *Child Development*, 1977, *48*, 404–411.

Brainerd, C. J. The stage question in cognitive-developmental theory. *The behavioral and brain sciences*, 1978, *2*, 173–213.

Broughton, J. Development of concepts of self, mind, reality, and knowledge. *New Directions for Child Development*, 1978, *1*, 75–101.

Cairns, R. *Social development: The origins and plasticity of interchanges*. New York: Harper & Row, 1979.

Chandler, M. J. Social cognition: A selective review of current research. In W. F. Overton (Ed.), *Knowledge and development*. New York: Plenum Press, 1977.

Connell, R. W. *The child's construction of politics*. Melbourne, Australia: Melbourne University Press, 1971.

Damon, W. Early conceptions of positive justice as related to the development of logical operations. *Child Development*, 1975, *46*, 301–312.

Damon, W. *The social world of the child*. San Francisco: Jossey–Bass, 1977.

Damon, W. Why study social–cognitive development? *Human Development*, 1979, *22*, 206–210.

Damon, W. Patterns of change in children's social reasoning: A two-year longitudinal study. *Child Development*, 1980, *51*, 1010–1017.

Damon, W. The developmental study of children's social cognition. In J. Flavell & L. Ross (Eds.), *New directions in social cognitive development*, New York: Cambridge University Press, 1981.

Damon, W. Justice and self-interest in childhood. In M. J. Lerner & S. C. Lerner (Eds.), *The justice motive in social behavior*, New York: Plenum, in press.

Damon, W., & Killen, M. Peer interaction and the process of change in children's moral reasoning. *Merrill-Palmer Quarterly*, 1982, *28*, 347–367.

Doise, W., Mugney, G., & Perret-Clermont, A. N. Social interaction and the development of cognitive operations. *European Journal of Social Psychology*, 1975, *5*, 367–383.

Doise, W., Mugny, G., & Perret-Clermont, A. N. Social interaction and cognitive development: Further evidence. *European Journal of Social Psychology*, 1976, *6*, 245–247.

Doise, W., & Mugny, G. Individual and collective conflicts of centrations in cognitive development. *European Journal of Social Psychology*, 1979.

Flavell, J. H. *Cognitive development*. Englewood Cliffs, N.J.: Prentice–Hall, 1977.

Flavell, J. H., & Wohlwill, J. Formal and functional aspects of cognitive development. In D. Elkind and J. H. Flavell (Eds.), *Studies in cognitive development*. New York: Oxford University Press, 1969.

Furth, H. Children's societal understanding and the process of equilibration. *New Directions for Child Development*, 1978, *1*, 101–123.

Gerson, R., & Damon, W. Moral understanding and children's conduct. *New Directions in Child Development*, 1978, *2*, 41–60.

Inhelder, B., Garcia, R., & Voneche, J. *Epistomologie genetique et equilibration*. Neuchâtel, 1976.

Inhelder, B., Sinclair, H., & Bovet, M. *Learning and the development of cognitive structures*. Cambridge, Mass.: Harvard University Press, 1974.

Keller, A., Ford, L., & Meachum, J. Dimensions of self-concept in preschool children. *Developmental Psychology*, 1978, *14*, 483–489.

Kohlberg, L. Justice and reversibility. In P. Laslett & J. Fishbein (Eds.), *Philosophy, politics, and society*. (Fifth Series), Oxford, Eng.: Blackwell, 1979.

Kohlberg, L., & Kramer, R. Continuities and discontinuities in childhood and adult moral development. *Human development,* 1969, *12,* 93–120.

Langer, J. *Theories of development.* New York: Holt, Rinehart, and Winston, 1969.

Larson, S., & Kurdek, L. Intratask and intertask consistency of moral judgment indices in first-, third-, and fifth-grade children. *Developmental Psychology,* 1979, *15,* 4, 462–463.

Lively, W. J., & Bromley, D. B. *Person perception in childhood and adolescence.* London: Wiley, 1973.

Macmurray, J. *The self as agent.* London: Faber & Faber, 1957.

Macmurray, J. *Persons in relation.* London: Faber & Faber, 1961.

Mueller, E., & Brenner, J. The origins of social skill and interaction among play-group toddlers. *Child Development,* 1977, *48,* 854–861.

Perret-Clermont, A. N., Mugny, G., & Doise, W. Une approche psychosociologique du developpement cognitif. *Archives de Psychologie,* 1976, *44,* 135–144.

Piaget, J. *The moral judgment of the child.* New York: Free Press, 1965. (Originally published, 1932.)

Piaget, J. *Logic and psychology.* New York: Basic Books, 1957.

Piaget, J. Comments on Vygotsky's critical remarks. In L. Vygotsky, *Thought and language.* Cambridge, Mass., MIT Press, 1962.

Piaget, J. Development and learning. In Ripple & Rockastle (Eds.), *Piaget rediscovered.* Ithaca, N.Y.: Cornell University Press, 1964.

Piaget, J. *Etudes sociologiques.* Geneva: Droz, 1966.

Piaget, J. *Biology and knowledge.* Chicago: University of Chicago Press, 1972.

Shatz, M., & Gelman, R. The development of communication skills: Modifications in the speech of young children as a function of listener. *Monographs of the Society for Research in Child Development.* Chicago: University of Chicago Press, 1973.

Turiel, E. Developmental processes in the child's moral thinking. In P. H. Mussen, J. Langer, & M. Covington (Eds.), *Trends and issues in developmental psychology,* New York: Holt, Rinehart, and Winston, 1969.

Turiel, E. *Conflict and transition in adolescent moral development.* Child development, 1974, *45,* 14–29.

Turiel, E. Social regulations and domains of social concepts. In W. Damon (Ed.), *New Directions for Child Development* (Vol. 1). San Francisco: Jossey–Bass, 1978.

Youniss, J. *Parents and peers in child development.* Chicago: University of Chicago Press, 1980.

5 Who Killed the Epistemic Subject?

David J. Bearison
City University of New York

There are two themes that run through William Damon's chapter. One is about the *social* development of cognition and the other is about the development of *social* cognition. All cognition has a social origin in that cognitive development is motivated by social interaction. However, what Damon refers to as the "direct clash of children's ideas" has its own structure. Thus, there is a structure to the social context and a structure to children's knowledge that is derived within that context. These structures progressively interact with each other in the course of cognitive development. However, it is important to recognize that Damon is not proposing the existence of social–contextual structures that are independent of our knowledge of them. The social–contextual structures are a product of a knowing system that is itself structured. Thus, the developmental relationship between social–contextual and cognitive–organismic structures is understood without recourse to any type of external motivating factors or feedback systems between the knower and the known. According to Damon, "the subject is able to grasp features of the social world that are initially beyond the reach of its own consciousness" by interacting with others who share similar conceptions of the social world. He says that "knowledge is from the start motivated, organized, and communicated in the course of social interaction. It is co-constructed, rather than unilaterally constructed."

In this way, Damon has achieved an integration of the two themes he has introduced. The development of social cognition is also the social development of cognition. In other words, children's acquisition of social concepts reflects universal cognitive processes as well as content-specific knowledge. Therefore, studies of social cognition not only inform us of the development of social knowledge, but also of the processes by which all knowledge is acquired.

143

The idea that structures embody their own change processes is, of course, the hallmark of Piaget's theory. However, Damon modifies the theory in two significant ways. These modifications have to do with his criticism of Piaget's principle of equilibration, which is the self-regulating mechanism of structures, and the nature of developmental stages, which are the expression of structures in performance.

Like many other investigators today, Damon finds that the principle of equilibration fails to capture the social dialectics of cognitive development. Of the motivating factors in development—social interaction, maturation, experience, and equilibration—equilibration serves for Piaget as the central organizing force. However, according to Damon, social interaction has its own levels of organization. The ways in which social interaction organizes cognition have been masked in the traditional Piagetian research paradigms. They have emphasized children's reasoning about object relations, such as the conservation of physical matter, instead of children's reasoning about social relations, such as positive justice and authority. Thus, the social foundation of cognitive development is more apparent in children's reasoning about social than about object relations.

Damon's second modification of Piaget's theory is in the way in which he conceptualizes the nature of developmental stages. The stages of social concept development that Damon proposes are different in significant ways from the stages of impersonal concept development proposed by Piaget. Whereas Damon's earlier research focused on the relationship between children's reasoning in hypothetical and actual social contexts, his current research focuses on the problems of stage transition. The data from his 2-year longitudinal study of children's conceptions of positive justice and parental authority are impressive evidence for the progressive development of children's social reasoning. Findings from the modal change scores showed that over a 2-year period more than 90% of the children who showed change on positive-justice concepts changed in a progressive direction, and 100% of the children who changed on concepts of authority changed in a progressive direction. Findings from scores of the percentage of spread across levels of children's responses over 2 years indicated that reasoning above the modal level in the previous year was the best predictor of stage development.

As informative as these findings are of the nature of stage transition, they do not imply that the transition is the result of any type of cognitive–structural reorganization of children's thinking. Piaget's stages are structurally organized and they are formulated a priori to the data. Damon's measures yield stages that are context specific and are deduced from the data once they have been obtained. I suspect that for this reason, Damon refers to his findings as "stagelike descriptions of the children's acquisition of specific concepts" and recognizes that different "sorts of developmental predictions may follow" from a stagelike descriptive model than from a truely structural model.

An essential difference between Piaget's use of the stage construct and Damon's is that for Piaget stages are defined according to the structure of logicomathematical transformations. Although their expression in performance is contextually and culturally influenced the stages are logically related such that the transition from one stage to the next successive stage involves a structural reorganization of knowledge. Damon, on the other hand, makes no assumptions regarding the logical operations that underlie his stages. Consider the transition between Stages 1-B and 2-A in Damon's stage model of concepts of positive justice. At Stage 1-B, conceptions of justice are based on the principles of merit and reciprocity and, at Stage 2-A, they are based on the principle of need. Yet I don't think that Damon could maintain that judgments predicated on the principle of need are logically more complex or represent structurally more advanced forms of reasoning than judgments predicated on the principles of merit and reciprocity. Isn't it likely that among some cultures, this sequence might be reversed, need being antecedent to reciprocity? Thus, the stage transitions that Damon proposes are contextually specific, culturally specific, and without logical structure. Also, I don't see in Damon's stages the strong assumptions regarding role taking that have been the focus of so many previous studies of social cognition, including our own.

Although I believe that Damon's approach to developmental changes in children's social understanding is a bellwether, it is a significant departure from a Piagetian approach. This is probably why Doise, working in Geneva, feels more comfortable studying the process of social interaction in the domain of children's reasoning about physical quantities. In that domain, measures of change are more neatly tied to structural transformations. In the social domain we are much less aware of how logical transformations are embedded in children's reasoning. Attempts to delineate these transformations were seen in some rather basic hypotheses regarding the nature of role taking (i.e., the logical coordination of perspectives) in social cognition. However, findings have not generally supported these hypotheses and today we recognize that many forms of social knowledge are not predicated on the logical coordination of perspectives. There is social–conventional knowledge that is arbitrarily ascribed. There is social knowledge derived from imitation, which determines some forms of social interaction, although its meaning is not assimilated by the subject. As a clinician, I am continually impressed by the extent of social knowledge that is blatantly irrational and derived from psychological defense mechanisms such as projection and paranoia.

It appears, therefore, that the direction for future research that Damon has brilliantly laid down by example of his own studies in this area is toward contextual analyses, with less regard to the formalization of underlying structures. This is not to imply that context is the sole determinant of social knowledge. If that were so we could never explain the developmental changes we find in children's social reasoning. But reasoning from one contextual domain to the next is not bound necessarily by Piaget's principle of *structures d'ensemble*.

This move away from logical formalism toward social contextualism, as a method of analyzing social-cognition development, poses the problem of losing the developmental aspects of change. Differences between contexts are not developmentally ordered, nor can age-related changes within a certain context be explained by contextual constraints. If, as Turiel has said, age-related changes are not ''stages'' in the Piagetian sense, and social judgments don't form unified structural systems, then what role does the organism play in the construction of his or her knowledge and why does such knowledge change qualitatively across age? Another way of posing this question is to ask, what are the logical necessities in social cognition?, assuming, of course, that moral necessities are not predicated on logical necessities.

I think that future studies of social cognition will increasingly examine social–cognitive development in the context of social interaction rather than trying to understand social interaction by constructing theories of social cognition. Social interaction will no longer be seen as subordinate to social–cognitive development or as a by-product of cognition. It will be recognized as the process by which social cognition develops. This, I think, is the central message of Damon's chapter and the contribution that his research has made toward understanding the nature of social–cognitive change in the developing child. Nevertheless, I am personally disturbed by the contextual specificity of his stages and the findings they yield. I can't help but wonder whatever happened to Piaget's ''epistemic subject'' that we all loved so dearly.

6

Children's Understanding of Multiple Emotions: A Cognitive–Developmental Approach

Susan Harter
University of Denver

The study of the child has witnessed very definite trends in the past decade. Hyphenation provides a powerful clue to our new vision. It has become increasingly fashionable to adopt a cognitive–developmental approach to whatever particular content domain we deem worthy of study. Social cognition and socioemotional development are trendy topics. The Zeitgeist is well documented in developmental analyses of moral judgment (Kohlberg, 1969), interpersonal relations (Selman, 1971, 1976), empathy (Hoffman, 1975), egocentrism (Chandler & Greenspan, 1972), perspective taking (Flavell, 1968), and role understanding (Fischer, 1980). The general conceptual strategy has involved an examination of the cognitive skills necessary for the performance of a particular type of behavior in the socioaffective realm.

The present chapter focuses on a cognitive–developmental analyses of children's understanding of *emotions*. At the outset it is necessary to specify the origins of my interest in this topic. One possible approach, consistent with trends already described, would involve the direct application of Piagetian theory to the domain of emotional understanding (Borke, 1971). Within such a hypothetico-deductive framework, predictions concerning the relationship between cognitive–developmental level and a child's comprehension of emotional content could be tested.

This was not the approach I adopted. The story told here can best be characterized as an inductive effort that began in the play-therapy room and only much later found its way into the research laboratory. To set the stage, for a number of years I have been seeing children, referrals to an outpatient clinic, in once-a-week play therapy. My initial orientation, although eclectic, could best be described as psychodynamic.

An important feature of many psychodynamic approaches to therapy with children has been the emphasis on the expression of feelings, emotions, and affect. One finds this focus among a number of different schools of therapy. It is evident among psychoanalytically oriented approaches espoused by such proponents as Anna Freud (1965) and Erikson (1950, 1968); among more nondirective child therapists, such as Axline (1947); and among those who emphasize certain existential considerations with regard to therapeutic change, such as Moustakas (1959). A major concern within each of these treatment modes is the child's *affective* development. The more developmentally oriented ego psychoanalytic approaches such as those of Anna Freud and Erikson place particular emphasis on certain milestones, stages, hurdles, or potential conflicts with regard to the emotional development of the child. As a result, therapy is typically directed toward facilitating the child's expression, as well as his or her understanding, of these emotions. Indirect or displaced expression through play or activity is encouraged as one powerful therapeutic tool. However, the thrust of most psychodynamically oriented therapies involves the eventual goal of conscious access to these feelings as manifest in verbal expression. Play is viewed largely as a means to an end, which is the acknowledgement, acceptance, and understanding of the nature and the implications of one's emotional life.

Although an understanding of the nature of a child's affective development is obviously central to the therapeutic tasks one faces with children, it became increasingly clear that a sensitive appreciation for the child's level of cognitive development was also essential. Through what type of cognitive filter does a child process information about his or her options? And how does one's emotional understanding change with age? What implications do possible ontogenetic shifts have for our attempts at therapeutic intervention?

In my own therapeutic efforts these questions were not raised in the abstract but emerged in relation to a phenomenon that began to emerge as I observed client after client. All these young children seemed to have considerable difficulty acknowledging seemingly contradictory feelings. While one feeling might be expressed, the child couLd not simultaneously acknowledge its seeming opposite, in situations where one would expect both to be manifest. A child I will call K was a classic example.

THE CASE OF K: AN ILLUSTRATIVE EXAMPLE

The major referral problem involved K's poor school performance. At the end of her kindergarten year, she was described as considerably below her peers in reading readiness skills. She was very insecure, and her feelings of competence and self-esteem were extremely low. Even though she was promoted to the first grade, her learning problems continued in each of the basic skill areas of reading, writing, and arithmetic. Psychological testing revealed that she had particular difficulty on a variety of auditory tasks, particularly subtests that required listening to instructions and/or giving an oral response. Although these observations suggest some basic auditory deficit, they were also consistent with her mother's report that K did not seem to pay attention to what was said to her, that she did not listen, and that things simply "went in one ear and out the other." K was also a rather fearful or anxious child. She was living with her natural mother and a stepfather (her mother's second husband). The stepfather vacillated between being psychologically distant from K and her older brother and being extremely harsh, demanding, and punitive. The erratic and unpredictable nature of his behavior made the household a particularly tense environment for the children.

Finally, in terms of the remaining presenting problems of this case, K was described as having a particular fear about people leaving her or going away. This anxiety was understandable in terms of certain events in her life. Her grandmother, of whom K had been very fond, moved away to remarry when K was about 5½, and K seemed to experience this as a tremendous loss. An additional source of potential confusion and ambivalence was the fact that the grandmother had been married several times before. Leaving one husband for another had become a habitual pattern for her. In addition, one of K's favorite uncles died unexpectedly, creating another emotional vacuum. Also there had been a constant train of aunts moving in and out of the house because of interpersonal problems in their own lives, typically because they had left someone, for example, a husband, or someone had left them. Several such people have lived with the family during the past year, although eventually they moved out, leaving K and the family.

One obvious inference from the extended family situation is that among these people, relationships are not very predictable or permanent. This pattern of instability had undoubtedly been a source of both confusion and concern for K, although it has been difficult for her to acknowledge these feelings. The most recent crisis in this regard has been the relationship between her parents, who are living an on-again, off-again existence. Each has talked of leaving the other, the stepfather has been away from the home for temporary periods, and the issue of separation and divorce has finally been raised as a possibility.

K's mother is a well-meaning woman who very much wants to do the right things for her children. However, she herself has difficulty getting in touch with her own feelings and is a very nonanalytical person when it comes to understanding or describing her own motivations and behavior. As a result she has little capacity to facilitate her children's understanding and expression of their own feelings. Very little is verbalized in this household with regard to explanations for events such as the unexpected presence of visiting aunts or the absence of father. Reasons for people's actions, cause-and-effect links, verbalization of thoughts and feelings—all these are extremely rare in this particular family milieu. As a result, the children seem to manifest a generalized anxiety about the unpredictable events that frequently can and do occur. Their environment has taught them not to ask questions and not to verbalize their thoughts and feelings, as neither answers nor approval for such expression will be forthcoming. There is a great source of conflict and confusion, much of which they do not understand.

As a result of this history and family background, there have been a number of areas in which K has had great difficulty dealing with what would appear to be contradictory feelings. Her conceptualizations of several emotional opposites have fit the pattern described previously. That is, until very recently, she has only been able to focus on one aspect of an apparent dichotomy of feelings at any given point in time. The most prevalent of these has been the smart–dumb distinction. One could readily infer from her comments and her play during our sessions that she was viewing herself as virtually "all dumb," that there was little if anything she could do competently in the realm of scholastic achievement. Later in treatment the happy–sad dichotomy emerged. Here the focus was on the issue of people leaving her, and in this arena K could only envisage sadness, which became her predominant reaction. During one particular period she had great difficulty conceptualizing any happy parts of her personality or any pleasant occurrences in her life. However, at other times she vacillated to the opposite extreme, acting as if she felt completely happy, as if the sad parts of her personality and her emotions simply did not exist.

Another theme had to do with the rather chaotic life-style of certain of the extended family members. At the peak of this instability, K's anxiety seemed to increase considerably, and every part of her life seemed confused and uncertain; there was no part of herself that she could conceptualize as stable, consistent, and understandable. Nor, during the earlier phases of treatment, could she deal adequately with the ambivalence that she felt toward her stepfather. Once again, she could acknowledge only one part of herself, the positive part that loved her father and she adamantly insisted this was the only emotional reaction she felt toward him.

Finally, a common theme throughout the therapy has been the issue of talking, of exploring and verbalizing feelings. K, until recently, has outspokenly resisted my attempts to discuss her thoughts and feelings. Such talking was viewed as dangerous, anxiety provoking, and as an activity to be avoided at all costs. Here again, her rigid black-and-white conceptualization of the talking versus no-talking distinction was such that for a long period, talking was not a part of her personality that she could acknowledge or accept.

K's problems are not unique in this regard. I have seen this problem almost universally among the clients I have encountered in play therapy, the problem of not being able to conceptualize realistically the different facets of one's own emotional responses. These particular clients have been in the 5- to 9-year-old age range, of average to above average intelligence, with referral problems that included school learning difficulties and/or various other childhood adjustment problems. None would be considered seriously emotionally disturbed. A common theme among many of these children has been the smart–dumb dichotomy For example a bright sensitive 7-year-old boy, who had been diagnosed as dyslexic, was convinced that there wasn't a smart bone in his body. Like K, he felt "all dumb." In another case, where there was a great deal of latent hostility that an 8-year-old felt toward his father, the boy insisted that he felt nothing but love and admiration for the parent. How could he possibly harbor any ill feelings toward his own father?

Another client, a bright 6-year-old boy, was referred because of a tremendous problem of acting out aggressively both at home and school, where he demonstrated extremely poor impulse control. He was convinced that he was "all bad" and that there was nothing commendable about his behavior. Another 7-year-old girl, from an orthodox Jewish family, the third girl born to these parents, developed an extreme case of sibling rivalry when the family was finally "blessed with"a boy, the longed-for son. She could only acknowledge her extreme hate for her new brother, there was no part of her that could express any positive feelings toward him. Then there was the case of an 8-year-old adopted boy from a very religious Catholic family that insisted that babies came from God and forbid any further discussion of this issue. The boy developed a pervasive learning block, largely reflecting a general stifling of his curiosity about any topic. With tremendous cognitive rigidity, he insisted that he was devoid of any curiosity about anything, that he simply didn't want to learn new things, that in effect he felt totally noncurious.

Repeatedly I have seen young children adopting this kind of all-or-none conceptualization of their own affective life, accepting a very one-sided view of their feelings. That is, they deny alternative emotions and experience great difficulty in accepting the possibility that seemingly contradictory feelings might simultaneously exist. Another related manifestation is the tendency for some young children to *vacillate* from one extreme to the other. Whereas today they may feel "all happy," tomorrow some event may cause a dramatic shift toward the opposite pole where they can only express their strong feelings of anger. At one level, it could be argued that such difficulties stem from the fact that due to certain environmental or familial considerations these particular children have specific adjustment problems, emotional difficulties, and conflicts in the areas cited. Thus it is understandable, from a psychodynamic point of view, why such children should deny certain feelings, should have difficulty acknowledging or expressing what appear to be contradictory feelings or polar opposites. Although this is undoubtedly a valid assumption, it would also appear to be the case that the child's difficulties are a function of certain cognitive–developmental factors, namely age- or stage-specific conceptual limitations that are present in the young child. Thus, initially it seemed fruitful to explore what implications Piagetian theory would hold for comprehending this phenomenon (Harter, 1977).

IMPLICATIONS OF COGNITIVE–DEVELOPMENTAL
THEORY

The developmental shift in Piaget's theory that seemed particularly relevant was the transition from prelogical to logical thought. Specifically, in Piaget's system, this represents the shift from the stage of preoperational thought to the stage of concrete operational thought. For it is this particular transition, and the gradual developmental and solidification of logical operations during the concrete operational period, that seem intimately related to the child's comprehension and construction of a logical system of *emotional* concepts that define the affective spheres of his or her life.

The present analysis concentrated only on those features of Piaget's system that are most relevant to an understanding of this aspect of the child's emotional development. (For a more detailed account of Piagetian theory, see Fischer, in press; Flavell, 1963; Piaget, 1967; Piaget & Inhelder, 1958.)

There are a number of important general hallmarks with regard to preoperational thinking. Principally, the child is unable to reason logically or deductively. Rather, his or her judgments are dominated by his or her *perceptions* of events, objects, and experiences. A further limitation is the fact that he or she can only attend to one perceptual dimension or attribute at a time, to the exclusion of all others.

The preoperational child is also extremely "egocentric." Here Piaget does not mean that the child is selfish per se. Rather, Piaget uses this term to refer to certain cognitive limitations of this period, namely that the young child is conceptually unable to view events and experiences from any point of view but his or her own. He or she is clearly the center of his or her own representational world. Relatedly, the young child is unable to differentiate clearly between himself or herself and the world, between the subjective realm of thoughts and feelings and the realm of objective or physical reality.

In addition, at the preoperational level, the child's reasoning is neither inductive nor deductive but what Piaget terms *transductive*. That is the young child tends to relate particulars in an alogical manner. Events may be viewed as related not because of any inherent cause-and-effect relationship but simply on the basis of spatial and/or temporal contiguity or juxtaposition. Furthermore, the child at this stage is unaware and therefore unconcerned about possible contradictions in his or her logic.

Fischer (in press) has summarized certain of these limitations in the following terms:

> The child does not yet have the ability to organize his thinking into coordinated systems that he can direct and control. His intelligence is dominated by whatever thought strikes him at the moment, whatever characteristic is prominent in a situation. His thinking is egocentric because he cannot coordinate various viewpoints

into a single system that takes all of them into account. . . . His thoughts run on of themselves and he flits from one idea to another, because he cannot coordinate his ideas around a single concept. . . . He cannot coordinate his knowledge of people and objects into systems that allow him to deny his immediate impressions and maintain a consistency to his interpretations. Similarly, he cannot carry out a task that requires him to coordinate his thinking unless he has the help of salient concrete clues [chap. 3, p. 13].

The question, then, becomes: What are the implications of these cognitive-developmental limitations for the child's understanding and expression of his or her emotional feelings and, in particular, the difficulty in simultaneously acknowledging seemingly contradictory emotions? A more detailed look at the *conservation* task, which is central to a Piagetian analysis of the transition from prelogical to logical thought, provides some initial clues. For example, in the classic water beaker experiment, the child is asked to make a judgment about the amount of water poured from one standard-sized glass into a second taller but narrower glass. The typical preoperational child will insist that there is more water in the taller glass. That is, his or her judgment is dominated by his or her perceptions of the most salient physical dimension or attribute, in this case height. Of critical importance is the fact that the child is able to focus on only *one such dimension at a time.* He or she is incapable of reasoning that the amount of liquid remained invarient, that is, was *conserved,* despite the transformation.

The concrete operational child, on the other hand, will assert that the amount of liquid has remained the same because, to take one typical explanation, the "new glass is taller, but it's also thinner." That is, the concrete operational child is able to consider simultaneously more than one attribute and is thus capable of understanding the reciprocal relationship between the two dimensions of height and weight. This realization allows the child to deduce logically the fact that the amount has not been changed—the basis for the concept of conservation. Thus the major advance in the period of concrete operational thought is that the child can apply basic logical principles to the realm of concrete experiences and events, without letting his or her perceptions interfere. Gradually his or her logical thought processes become coherently organized into an increasingly complex and integrated network through which he or she confronts and systematically responds to the world around him or her.

It should be noted that Piaget largely restricts his theorizing to those processes that involve judgments about physical quantities and/or the mathematical sphere. He has not extended this particular type of analysis to judgments in the affective realm. However, it would seem that one can readily extrapolate certain of these principles to the child's developing system of *emotional* concepts. The most obvious link involves the processes underlying the conservation task. Just as the preoperational child has difficulty focusing on more than one *perceptual* dimension at a time, the child also has difficulty focusing on more than one *emotional* dimension at a time. Thus, when the young child is faced with judgments based on such affective opposites as smart versus dumb or good versus bad, his or her cognitive limitations make it difficult to view both as simultaneously operative. Rather, the young child's thinking tends to focus on only one of these emotional dimensions, thereby leading to such all-or-none conclusions as "I feel like I am all dumb" or "I'm completely bad." He or she simply lacks the conceptual capacity to entertain the other possibility simultaneously.

The child's difficulty in responding to more than one dimension at a time, in addition to his or her general inability to coordinate various viewpoints into a single system that takes all of them into account simultaneously, also suggests why the child may sometimes vacillate in his or her affective judgments. That is, the knowledge of these cognitive limitations illuminates those occurrences in which the child may feel "all loving" at one moment and "all nonloving" the next. To take another example, yesterday's assertion implying that "there is only one part of me, and it is happy" may then dramatically shift to the conviction that "I feel all sad" today. The suggestion here is that just as transformations may alter prelogical children's judgments about physical quantities, certain transformations can also change one's judgments in the affective realm.

To pursue this analysis, some particular event, such as a certain parental behavior, may temporarily but dramatically alter the child's emotional frame of reference. For example, at a given point in time, the young boy may staunchly insist that he only has feelings of *love* for his father. However, in the face of some upsetting punitive act on the part of the father, the child in a burst of emotion may blurt out "I hate you, I wish you were dead." He may find that at this point in time, he can only experience and express the emotion of anger for his father. That is, he cannot simultaneously acknowledge both love and hate, he cannot conceptualize the temporary anger within the context of a larger emotional network, of an affective conceptual system, which at the same time includes both positive *and* negative emotions. He has yet to achieve what metaphorically might be termed *affective conservation,* which implies that particular events do not transform the entire emotional system, even though they may distort the balance of feelings temporarily. Rather, the young child is cognitively at the mercy of immediate emotional events to which he or she can only respond in a unidimensional manner at any given point in time. Relatedly, he or she does not have the phenomenological experience of cognitive conflict over the presence of what would appear to be contradictory feelings.

Another Piagetian task involving *multiplication of classes* also provides a direct example of how the cognitive limitations of the young child may be related to his or her difficulty in conceptualizing the emotional realm. For didactic purposes, first envisage a 3 by 3 matrix in which the column labels are different colors (e.g., red, green, blue) and the row labels are different shapes (e.g., square, circle, triangle). The matrix thus depicts two separate dimensions, color and shape, with three specific instances of each. The intersection of the particular colors and shapes in the matrix produce nine different categories or combinations, that is, red squares, green squares, blue squares; red circles, green circles, blue circles; and red triangles, green triangles, and blue triangles.

Now consider a particular task that could be administered to a child in which these categories could be concretized. One can provide a child with numerous blocks that represent each of these nine combinations or cells and ask him or her to *sort* them into different piles. What is discovered on such a task is that the preoperational child sorts them into three categories based on their shape or color. What the preoperational child *cannot* do, however, is to sort them into all *nine* categories utilizing the shape and color dimensions simultaneously. He or she can only focus on one perceptual dimension at a time. In contrast, the concrete operational child can appreciate the intersection or the ''multiplication'' of these dimensions and can effectively construct the entire matrix of nine categories. That is, he or she will sort the blocks into nine separate piles.

To pursue the application of this developmental shift in the realm of emotional concepts, now imagine that we are going to relabel the matrix, designating the columns as negative emotions and the rows as polar positive emotions. For example, the negative emotions might consist of feeling dumb, sad, and mad, whereas the positive counterparts would be feeling smart, happy, and loving. We are no longer in the realm of physical attributes in which one may translate the concept of the matrix into a concrete task such as sorting blocks. However, we can more abstractly imagine the conceptual problem that the young child must have in comprehending such emotional categories. Just as in the Piagetian sorting task, the child can only focus on one dimension at a time—in this case one emotional feeling. He or she cannot envisage the intersection of positive and negative emotions. Thus he or she cannot acknowledge the fact that part of him or her can feel dumb and part can feel smart or that part can be happy and part can also be sad. Again, it is not until the child has developed greater cognitive sophistication that he or she can appreciate these conceptual intersections and apply them to his or her own feelings and self-perceptions.

Werner's cognitive–developmental formulation (Werner, 1948) clearly compliments this Piagetian analysis. Werner's general thesis is that the essence of development is: ''the steadily increasing differentiation and centralization, or hierarchic integration, within the genetic totality [p. 53].'' Two basic pairs of concepts seem particularly relevant to the present topic, the developmental shift from behavioral or cognitive systems that are first: (1) rigid and then flexible; as well as (2) initially labile and then stable. For example, Werner (1948) refers to the all-or-none thinking of the young child and describes such rigidity as if: ''one sphere succeeds the other like scenes on a revolving stage [p. 381].'' He goes on to note that: ''Only when the spheres are not rigidly divided off from one another but intercommunicate—where, in consequence things can be grasped on the basis of different distinct aspects either simultaneously or as rapidly succeeding each other—is it possible to have an identity and constancy of things [p. 381].''

This kind of rigidity and separation of spheres that Werner ascribes to young children is analogous to the formulation couched in Piagetian terms, namely that the young child is unable to consider more than one dimension or sphere simultaneously, whether in his or her judgments of the physical or the emotional realm.

Although considerable emphasis has been placed on the shift from preoperational though to concrete operational thought, this transition is not nearly as abrupt or discrete as this discussion may have implied, or as many reading Piaget have inferred. (See Fischer, 1980, who has articulated the more gradual nature of the child's development through the Piagetian stages.) For example, considerable progress occurs *within* the period of concrete operations itself as the child gradually integrates and coordinates what were previously somewhat isolated operational systems. In Piaget's own writings, he has recognized this feature of development through his concept of "decalage," which refers to an "uneveness" in the ontogenetic emergence of certain logical operations. The clearest example is the development of the concept of conservation that does not appear "full-blown" as an operation that can be applied to any and all realms of logical deduction. Rather, the child typically achieves conservation of number and of amount first, followed by conservation of weight somewhat later in the period of concrete operations, with conservation of volume appearing toward the end of this period.

It seems reasonable to assume, both intuitively as well as on the basis of observation and experience with young children, that there is also a discrepancy with regard to the application of logical thought processes to the physical realm in comparison to the emotional realm. That is, it would appear that the ability to consider different or alternative dimensions simultaneously would appear developmentally earlier for concepts involving physical quantities and concepts than for emotional or affective concepts. One explanation for this assertion is that whereas the concrete operational child has achieved the capacity to apply logical reasoning to certain realms of his or her life, these areas, as the title of the stage implies, are by definition "concrete." They tend to be concrete in the sense that they can be tangibly observed, visualized, and manipulated. The child's approach to more abstract hypothetical considerations at this stage is piecemeal at best. A related feature of the concrete operational child's functioning is that he or she cannot yet think about his or her own thinking.

Given this, what can we expect with regard to his or her conceptualization of his or her *emotions?* The most plausible conclusion is that the emotional arena is much more difficult to conceptualize because it is less concrete, less directly observable, and involves constructs that are both less tangible and more psychological in nature. This suggests what one might consider to be an "affective decalage" to the extent that the conceptualization of an emotional network of concepts may lag considerably behind the application of logical principles to the more physical, observable, or tangible realms of experience. Thus, it is not surprising that children in the 7- to 9-year-old range are still struggling with emotional concepts and are still subject to the kind of unidimensional all-or-none thinking that has been the focus of this chapter. It is understandable why even concrete operational children have some difficulty in simultaneously acknowledging or understanding seemingly conflicting feelings.

It should be emphasized that the actual examples of this type of difficulty cited earlier in the chapter pertain to clinic cases referred for child therapy. The preceding cognitive–developmental analysis was clearly meant to be relevant to the issue of *normal* development. However, to the extent that children referred for therapy are typically experiencing particular problems with regard to the understanding and expression of emotional feelings, one would expect such children to have even greater difficulty in dealing with those contradictory feelings that are central to the domain in which they are experiencing difficulty.

At the time this analysis was first advanced, my interest in the topic was primarily within the clinical realm. I went on to advance the notion that these clients do not seem to consciously experience the cognitive conflict underlying their adjustment problems. Thus, it seemed that at least in the initial phases of treatment one would attempt to promote the expression of conflict (i.e., the acknowledgment of the contradictory feelings). During my work with K, a drawing technique was devised that appears to hold promise as a therapeutic tool to assist children in labeling such emotions, and to appreciate the fact that they can coexist. However, given the argument that stage-specific characteristics of *normal* cognitive development are in part responsible for the difficulty children have in conceptualizing their emotions, it was essential that I embark on a normative cognitive–developmental program of research.

INITIAL RESEARCH CONSIDERATIONS

The research described in the subsequent sections of this chapter represents a collaborative effort with two colleagues, Christian Miner, currently at New York University, and Jim Connell, at the University of Denver (see Harter, Miner, & Connell, 1979). They are an integral part of this program of research and have contributed richly toward every phase of this project, including its conceptualization, design, data collection, modification of our procedures, data analysis, and interpretation.

The Domain of Inquiry

It was important, at the outset, to specify the domain of inquiry, inasmuch as one may well question whether one can actually *feel* two emotions such as loving and mad at the same time. Can one phenomenologically experience two different emotions that seem to constitute polar opposites? These questions raise the thorny definitional issue of precisely what is an "emotion." We have not addressed this question directly. Rather, the choice was made to focus on the child's *conceptualization* of emotions, the child's understanding of the manner in which conventional emotional labels are applied to the self and to others. Thus, the research goal was to indicate how a cognitive–developmental approach could illuminate changes in the child's understanding of emotional concepts. Ultimately it will be important to relate a child's understanding of emotions to his or her ability to experience or express them. This issue has obvious clinical implications. In fact, a major tenet of many forms of psychotherapy, dating back to Freud and Breuer's early studies of hysteria, is that the client not only must verbally acknowledge or label a feeling, but must experience it affectively, in order for curative change to occur. This issue is extremely far-reaching, requiring a comprehensive attack beyond the scope of our current program of research.

General Research Strategy and Its Relationship to Theory

The preceding analysis focused primarily on a two-stage model, highlighting the implications of the shift from preoperational to concrete operational thought. Given the paucity of evidence relating to children's emotional understanding, we did not want to confine our empirical efforts to a test of the applicability of Piagetian theory. Additionally, although the application of Wernerian principles was basically consistent with a Piagetian analysis, the metaphorical nature of Werner's constructs makes them less than adequate as conceptual springboards to empirical research.

Although both approaches lend much to an interpretation of the phenomenon under question, recent advances within the field of cognitive–developmental theory emphasize the need to articulate the stages of cognitive development in a more precise and differentiated fashion. One such position, Fischer's (1980) cognitive–developmental theory, goes beyond Piaget's four-stage model in articulating seven levels of intelligence, each of which is spelled out in considerably more detail than are Piaget's stage descriptions. Because we wanted to allow for the possible demonstration of a sequence of several levels of emotional understanding, Fischer's theory appeared to hold considerable appeal.

At this juncture, two research strategies were considered. One was to take Fischer's levels of intelligence, generate predictions concerning how emotional understanding would be manifest at each of these levels, and design tasks appropriate for each level. This is the strategy that Fischer has utilized in some of his own collaborative work with Watson, on role understanding, and Bertenthal, on the understanding of the self. Although I have utmost respect for Fischer's model, we decided, at least in our initial efforts, to choose an alternative strategy. I did not want to predict the sequence from theory, but rather to allow the data to dictate the sequence. My rationale for such an inductive approach was that at this nascent stage of the research, we know relatively little about the development of children's understanding of their emotions. To superimpose a theoretical structure upon this phenomenon seemed premature. Thus, we began by studying the phenomenon itself, very directly, in the absence of any potential theoretical blinders. At some subsequent stage of this research we will attempt to relate our findings to Fischer's model.

Emotional Concepts Versus Personality Characteristics

The preceding analysis referred primarily to the child's understanding of his or her emotions, and the problem in acknowledging seemingly contradictory feelings. However, it would appear that at least two different types of personal attributions were subsumed under the general label of emotions. Although certain conflicts, such as the happy–sad dichotomy, appear to refer to actual *emotional* concepts, other dichotomies (e.g., smart–dumb) appear to reflect the domain of a child's perceptions of his or her abilities, characteristics, etc. Thus, it seemed fruitful to distinguish between the child's acknowledgment of a *feeling,* such as happy, sad, scared, surprised, mad, excited; and characteristics falling under the rubric "self-concept," (smart, dumb, popular, attractive, unathletic, etc.). Our research to date has been restricted to an examination of the domain of emotional or affective constructs.

Range and Content of Emotional Concepts

Although the ultimate purpose of the research was to illuminate children's understanding of seemingly contradictory feelings and multiple emotions, a prior question concerns the number and range of *single* emotions that a child can comprehend. What ontogenetic shifts can one document with regard to the specific emotional labels utilized by children? Basically, such questions address the issue of how a network of emotional concepts emerges with development. Although a cognitive–developmental analysis typically involves a specification of the *structure* of a given domain (e.g., how this network becomes more complex, more differentiated, with age), we also wanted to direct our attention to changes in the specific *content* of emotional concepts.

Situational Determinants of the Ability to Acknowledge Opposing Feelings

The general thesis advanced has been that young children have difficulty in acknowledging opposing feelings (e.g., that they can simultaneously feel both happy and sad). This ability may in part depend on whether the *same* situation is presumed to evoke different emotions, or whether two different situations each evoke a different emotion. On intuitive grounds, the former ability would appear to be more difficult, such that developmentally it would be observed at a later stage. It may be more difficult for a child to acknowledge that he is both happy and sad over the same event, for example, receiving a new bike for Christmas. That is, it may be difficult to admit that one is happy because one very much wanted a bike, but also sad because one wanted the more expensive flashier model. In contrast, it may be easier to feel happy over one event (e.g., getting the new bike) and unhappy over another (e.g., having to do one's homework or clean one's room instead of riding the new bike). To take an example from another realm, it may be easier to realize that one feels very loving because of what mom did but angry about what dad did, than to realize that one can be both loving and angry toward dad. We wanted to explore this issue developmentally.

The Understanding of Self Versus Others

The discussion has focused entirely on the child's understanding of his or her own emotions. However, an interesting question involves the degree to which the same underlying processes are applied by the child in understanding the emotions of *others*. For example, to what extent can the child appreciate the fact that a parent may be both loving and angry? An extension of the basic cognitive–developmental analysis to the child's perceptions of other's emotions raises the interesting question with regard to possible differences in the emergence of an understanding of self versus others. For example, does a child first learn to acknowledge contradictory emotions in himself or herself, and then apply this understanding to others? Or is the converse the case, in that one must first witness the demonstration of emotional expression in others, see this phenomenon modeled, as it were, before one can appreciate complex emotional concepts in one's self? The former analysis would be consistent with the cognitive–developmental emphasis on egocentrism and decentering, whereas the latter viewpoint would be more consonant with a social learning theory interpretation.

These were several of the initial issues that provided a backdrop for our developmental inquiry. We planned to focus on children in the 3- to 12-year-old age range. The next step required the designation of a research methodology appropriate to the study of these issues.

THE DEVELOPMENT OF A RESEARCH METHODOLOGY

There was some precedent in the existing literature on emotional development for the use of pictorial materials. However, the previous research did not address the question of the understanding of multiple emotions, nor was it intuitively obvious how pictorial stimuli would be selected or designed to meet this need. Thus, we decided to begin our empirical journey with an open-ended interview.

In this interview, children were first asked to generate single feelings, and we then asked a series of questions about each separate emotion. A second set of questions was designed to ascertain the extent to which the child could understand how two feelings could go together.

This initial pilot phase, in which we talked with children between the ages of 3 and 12, was extremely encouraging, both from a methodological as well as a conceptual standpoint. We first learned that the interview procedure netted a very rich yield, for children at all age levels. They had a great deal to tell us about their feelings and were extremely eager to do so. Although there are those investigators who feel that verbal interview procedures have severe limitations with young children, there is no dearth of verbiage among our preoperational subjects. As our data will indicate, they can talk about their feelings, are responsive to the questions, and their responses are interpretable. Thus, we learned that we could comfortably employ the same type of interview procedure at different developmental levels and meaningfully code the verbal responses.

We later conducted extensive pilot work with both a pictorial task depicting the most commonly described situations in which emotions are experienced, and with a photographic task in which we had child models facially express those emotions most typically mentioned in the interview. After considerable experience with these different pilot procedures, we decided to place major emphasis on a semistructured interview that evolved during this exploratory phase. Although the pictorial task had the advantage of presenting every subject with the same set of situations, thereby allowing for a more systematic coding of the data, there were difficulties in utilizing the same situations across the age range sampled. Additionally, this task did not provide subjects with an opportunity to demonstrate the full complexity of their emotional understanding, in that we frequently obtained the most sophisticated responses when subjects were allowed to discuss the situations of their choice in the interview procedure.

Our photographic task also posed problems in that subjects across our age range could only reliably label four basic emotions, happy, sad, mad, and scared. Although this series of four photographs allows us to address certain research questions of interest, it does not permit an inquiry into the understanding of more complex emotions.

Thus, the data presented in this chapter are based primarily on our interview technique. Children's responses to earlier versions shaped our emerging formulations about the categories of emotional understanding, which in turn dictated the specific questions asked in revisions of the interview. One major insight was gleaned from the very first responses to a general question probing into how two different feelings could go together. Two very clear categories of responses emerged. One category made explicit reference to the fact that two emotions could be expressed in temporal sequence, that is, one could first feel one emotion, and then at some later point in time, one could experience a second emotion. These responses were in contrast to examples of how one could have two feelings *simultaneously,* at the very same time. This distinction was highlighted in our subsequent interview format in that we specifically probed for emotions in temporal sequence, as well as for emotions that could be expressed simultaneously.

Specific Interview Format Upon Which the Reported Data Were Based

The data presented here were based on the following interview format. A child was first asked to name all the different feelings he or she could think of, and then to give an example of a situation in which he or she would have that feeling. To date, we have focused on nine different emotions, happy, sad, mad, scared, loving, jealous, ashamed, proud, and nervous. If a child did not spontaneously mention one of these nine, we asked him or her about each feeling, and in what situation such an emotion would be experienced. These questions have provided us with information about the nature and number of single emotions that children at different developmental levels comprehend.

In the second part of our interview, we have systematically probed about the experience of two emotions, asking about what other feelings could coexist with the basic four, happy, sad, mad, and scared. We have referred to these as the basic four, as all of our subjects, including the youngest, demonstrate their understanding of these feelings. Almost all children spontaneously generate the first three emotions, happy, sad, and mad. Although the youngest subjects typically do not spontaneously mention feeling scared or afraid, when this feeling is *presented* to them, they readily supply an appropriate situation in which they have felt scared. (Why it is consistently necessary to probe for this particular feeling is an interesting empirical question in and of itself.)

Our first interview question concerning the experience of two emotions is designed to elicit a response relevant to the *temporal sequence* of each feeling. Thus we say to subjects: "You told me that one thing that made you happy (mad, sad, or scared) was when" (and then we repeat what the child initially described as the situation making him or her happy). We then continue with "That was one feeling, but sometimes you can first have one feeling, like happy, and then you can have another feeling, a different feeling, *after* you feel happy. What feeling could you have after you feel happy?" After the child described another feeling, we ask what would make him feel that emotion.

In order to address the *simultaneous* expression of two emotions, we next say to the child: "O.K., now that was how you could first have one feeling and then have a different feeling after it. But sometimes you can have two different feelings at the *very same time.* Tell me how you could have another feeling at the very same time you were feeling happy?" The child's response is then followed by a question asking him to elaborate on the situation in which he would feel those two feelings.

The child is asked this same series of questions about each of the four basic emotions.

Subject Population

Our subjects, between the age of 3 and 13, have been drawn from predominantly middle- and upper middle-class families. The majority of children have been interviewed in our laboratory facilities where their responses have been recorded on either an audio- or videotape. One sample of children was interviewed at a summer day camp. Over 100 subjects comprised the earlier samples on which our procedures were revised. The data presented in this chapter were collected from 45 children, all of whom were given the interview described previously.

INITIAL EMPIRICAL FINDINGS

Range and Content of Emotions

The number of emotions generated, in our sample of 3- to 13-year-olds, was between three and eighteen, for a given subject. We were able to code a total of 40 discrete emotions spontaneously mentioned by our entire sample. The correlation between number of emotions generated and chronological age across our sample was .38.

The youngest children, 3-year-olds, could consistently generate three emotional labels, happy, sad, and mad, and in certain cases a fourth, scared. They clearly understand all four of these feelings and can give rich and appropriate examples of events or experiences in which they have had these emotions. For the most part, our youngest subjects, in the 3- to 5-year-old range, do not have a clear understanding of ashamed, proud, nervous, or jealous. This is *not* to say that they have not experienced these feelings at some level. Recall that our focus is on the child's ability to conceptualize these emotions, as reflected in their capacity to describe verbally appropriate situations in which they have experienced these feelings.

With increasing age we find that children not only understand all the nine target emotions we selected but demonstrate their comprehension of a wide range of additional feelings that they generate (e.g., annoyed, disappointed, relieved, discourageo, anxious). These particular examples are typical of the older children in our sample, between the ages of 10 and 13. Our younger subjects typically mentioned a minimum of six feelings. Often, however, these constituted synonyms for the basic four emotions or closely related affects (fine, good, great, unhappy, dizzy, hate, yukky, etc.). The correlation reported for the relationship between age and number of emotions mentioned does not reflect the increasing sophistication and differentiation of the emotional network generated by children as they become older. Thus it will become necessary, in our future data-analytic efforts, to determine how to document this type of ontogenetic shift.

Initial Trends in the Data

Inspection of the data from our earliest interviews clearly revealed qualitatively different levels of understanding, which we then tested more systematically in subsequent samples. Thus, our initial efforts indicated that we could broadly categorize children's responses as falling into one of the following three levels:

1. *Only one feeling can be experienced, two feelings cannot go together.*   Although the youngest children can give appropriate examples of situations in which they have felt, or might feel, happy, sad, mad, scared, and loving, they cannot envisage any way in which two feelings could go together. This conceptual inability was manifest in a number of ways. Some children vehemently deny that one could ever have more than one feeling in the same situation. These statements take the form of such verbalizations as: "You *can't* have more than one feeling!" or, for those more engrossed in the vernacular, "No way!" Other exclamations have included: "It's hard to think of this feeling and that feeling cause you only have one mind!" "I'd be sad if my friends don't want to play with me but that's the only feeling I could have then." "I've never done that before, you know I've only lived 6 years!" Other young children gave more indirect responses such as "I don't want to think so hard" or "My brain doesn't know the answer to that one."

2. *Two feelings in temporal sequence.*   The first indication that a child can conceptualize two different feelings take the form of expressing them in a temporal sequence. Samples in this category are: "I would be sad if my friends wouldn't play with me but then if my mommy gave me a toy I'd be happy." "I'd feel excited about getting on the roller coaster but scared once it got going." "I'd feel happy that the present I was getting might be something I liked and then mad if it was something I didn't like." "I'd feel fine because my aunt and uncle were coming to my house and later I'd feel happy because another friend came over to play with me." "I'd be proud cause I thought my report card was going to be good but then later I'd be disappointed that it wasn't as good as I thought."

We are documenting a clear developmental progression in that many of the children who are able to describe two feelings in sequence cannot give an acceptable response to our question asking how they could have two feelings at the very *same time*. Some children simply deny this possibility (e.g., "I've never had two feelings at the same time."). One child exclaimed: "Another feeling with happy at the same time? That's a toughie. Well, it sure couldn't be sad or scared!'' Another child came up with the general conclusion that ''You just can't have opposite feelings at the same time.''

There are other conceptual strategies that children employ in coping with this question. Many children will give responses that indicate that the emotions are expressed in temporal sequence, not simultaneously, despite the fact that the question specifies ''at the same time.'' For example, one child remarked: ''Yes, I could have two feelings at the same time, like if my grandparents came to visit, that would make me feel happy that they came but then I would get sad because I had to go to bed earlier than I wanted to and I couldn't be with them.'' Another child responded: ''Yea, you could feel two things at the same time if you were seeing a monster movie, you'd feel scared when you were watching it and glad when it was over.'' Typically there are linguistic clues, as well as indications from the situational context supplied by the child, that allow us to determine whether the emotions should be viewed as occurring sequentially or simultaneously, and we have found that this distinction can reliably be judged by different raters.

3. *Two feelings simultaneously.*   When asked to indicate how two feelings can go together at the same time, we initially observed that children deal with this question in a variety of ways. The following sample responses give some flavor for this diversity. ''I'd feel mad 'cause my brother knocked down my blocks and sad 'cause I called my mommy and she didn't come.'' ''I'd feel loving about going to see my grandma but grouchy about packing up to go and see her.'' ''If I was watching a Godzilla movie I'd be scared if he attacked someone but excited to see what was going to happen.'' ''If my friends wouldn't play with me, I'd feel sad and angry and disappointed. I'd feel sad that I couldn't play, and angry at them, and I'd also feel disappointed that I didn't try to do anything about it.'' ''Well, if my dog was hurt I'd feel happy if her front legs were O.K., but I'd feel sad because her back legs were hurting.''

All these responses appear to reflect the ability to conceptualize two feelings simultaneously. With regard to their face validity, they are quite convincing.

Consider some additional examples to the same question regarding the simultaneous co-occurrence of two feelings. ''I would be very happy that my Grandma and Grandpa came and visited me but sad because the kitty scratched me.'' ''I'd be sad if something happened to my bunny but happy because my mommy likes me.'' ''I'd be happy about getting straight A's and glad that I'm smart.'' ''I'd be mad that someone wrecked my blocks and angry because I didn't know who it was.'' In the first two examples the children do describe two different feelings, however the first is attached to one situation whereas the second is related to a very different event. The second two examples reflect another strategy for handling this question. Here, the children seem to focus on one situation or event; however, the two feelings are extremely similar (e.g., happy and glad, and mad and angry).

Although the three levels, one feeling only, two feelings in temporal sequence, and two feelings simultaneously, provided us with the general outline of an age progression, the variations within the second two levels gave us pause. There seemed to be qualitative differences in the manner with which different children dealt with the questions at each of these latter levels. Our next task, then, was to determine whether it was possible to categorize these different types of response into a system that was psychologically meaningful, reliably codable, and which might reveal a more differentiated sequence with regard to emotional understanding.

DIMENSIONS UNDERLYING THE UNDERSTANDING OF MULTIPLE EMOTIONS

In keeping with the original strategy, to allow the data to dictate those categories that might define a possible sequence, we began to look for dimensions along which we might organize children's responses. Our previous efforts at systematizing the interview data revealed that the temporal relationship between the emotions, either sequential or simultaneous, was one such dimension. Our examination of the responses within each of these two broad categories suggested two additional dimensions that account for the diversity and the qualitative differences among responses that were cited in the previous section.

Affective Valence

In addition to the temporal relationship, children's responses seem to vary with regard to the affective tone or the valence of the emotions described. That is, certain children produced two emotions that were *similar* in valence, either both *positive* (happy and excited, loving and glad) or both *negative* (sad and mad, worried and disappointed). Other responses described emotions of difference valences, that is one positive and one negative feeling (happy and sad, excited and scared). This particular dimension was of interest to us for a number of reasons. At an empirical level one can ascertain whether there might be developmental differences in the ability to generate examples of the co-occurrence of feelings of a similar valence compared to those of different valences. Intuitively, one might hypothesize that it would be easier for children to describe two feelings of a similar valence. The identification of this dimension also permitted us to examine the interaction between valence and temporal relationship. Is it possible that the ease with which similar valence and different valence pairs can be described is related to whether children are questioned about emotions in temporal sequence versus emotions conceptualized as simultaneous?

This dimension also seemed intriguing given the clinical origins of this research. In the introductory sections of this chapter, many examples of children's difficulty in acknowledging seemingly contradictory feelings were cited. Our data suggest one way of operationalizing the term "seemingly contradictory," namely emotions of different valence. This definition characterizes the emotional opposites that the clinic children had difficulty integrating (happy and sad, or loving and mad). Similarly, the pilot data from our normative developmental samples suggested the possible hypothesis that emotions of different valence may be more difficult for children to conceptualize than those that are more similar.

This conceptual distinction, between emotions of either different or the same valence, raises an empirical question: To what degree do subjects across the age range sampled reliably rate feelings as similar or different? We have utilized two methodological approaches to address this question. With our initial samples of children, we showed them line drawings that depicted children expressing each of our target emotions. Although I indicated earlier that we had difficulty obtaining a series of photographs when we asked child models to produce these facial expressions, we were more successful with our drawings that depicted the entire child. Thus, we were able to include bodily and postural cues that could be utilized by subjects in making their judgments.

With these drawings we employed a very simple sorting task, asking children to sort the drawings into two piles, good feelings and bad feelings. Later, with our interview procedure, we also asked whether each of the target emotions was a good feeling or a bad feeling. Children have no difficulty responding to either request. Our observations indicate that even the youngest children can readily and reliably categorize feelings into good and bad.

Our reasons for phrasing the question in this manner stemmed from earlier observations, particularly with the youngest children. Some of these subjects were not yet 3-year-olds. Common responses to our open-ended question "Tell me all of the feelings you could have that were "good" and "bad." The verbal responses given by these children were understandably meager; however they were psychologically meaningful. Good feelings occur when you get candy, when mommy loves you, and bad feelings happen when you fall down, and when you cry. By the time children are well into their third year, they can make further differentiations among these two categories, and they begin to apply the term "bad" to the emotions sad, mad, scared, and "good" to happy, great, fine. Although we have not pursued this issue systematically, our observations suggest that the most rudimentary emotional understanding involves the dichotomy between good and bad feelings. Within each of these two categories more specific emotion labels become differentiated.

Interestingly, we have also found that although the youngest children are not able to give us adequate definitions for emotions such as proud and jealous, they can appropriately identify the valence as good or bad. Furthermore, their erroneous definitions are fascinating in that they also reflect the valence of the feeling. For example, one 5-year-old defined proud as "it's when I'm doing much of something good like building." When asked the meaning of ashamed he replied "I'm not sure but I think it's when someone doesn't have a friend." Other definitions of proud within this same age range were: "You're happy you can ride your new bike a lot" and "You get to have fun at the amusement park." Sample definitions of nervous also suggest that the young children perceive it as a negative emotion, even though they cannot give us an adequate definition: "It's sort of like when you're mad if someone hits you." "You can't go out and play." "You're driving down the street and you forgot your sister." (Clinicians may question the latent valence underlying this last response!)

I indicated that two methodological approaches have been utilized. In addition to asking the child to designate the goodness or badness of a particular feeling, we have also asked one sample of children to rate the similarity of emotion pairs on a 4-point scale, ranging from very similar to very dissimilar. We have taken pairs of emotion labels, comparing each of the basic four with each other, as well as with each of the other five target emotions. Although we have not yet analyzed these data systematically, we anticipate that they will provide us with information of a slightly different nature. In this task the range of judgments is broadened from a two-choice format to a 4-point scale. The procedure also allows us to examine the similarity of judgments *within* the realms of both positive and negative emotions. Whereas in the previous task, emotions such as happy, proud, glad, and loving would all be categorized as positive, we can now determine how the possible pairs of these emotions vary with regard to perceived similarity.

It is our conjecture that the only manner in which certain subjects can handle the question of the simultaneity of two emotions is by supplying two emotion labels that appear to us to be virtually synonymous (e.g., happy and glad, or mad and angry), as in the examples given earlier. To the extent that subjects rate the emotions in these pairs as basically the same, we can make more direct inferences about the conceptual strategies that these children employ. More generally, we can calculate a similarity–dissimilarity score for each emotion pair that we can relate to the ease with which children can conceptualize the co-occurrence of two emotions.

Object of the Two Emotions

The third dimension that has emerged from our inspection of the interview data has been the object or the target of the emotions. As some of the examples indicated, certain of the emotion pairs appear to be directed toward the *same* object or situation (e.g., "I'd be mad because they knocked my blocks down, and miserable because I'd have to build it up again"). In other examples, each of the two feelings mentioned are attached to *different* events ("I was frightened that my mom was going to punish me for not cleaning my room and happy 'cause I was watching TV'').

The emergence of this third dimension raised another series of questions concerning its relevance to a developmental progression of emotional understanding. In addition, it provoked questions with regard to the interaction of this dimension with the previous two, valence, and temporal and relationship. This third aspect would also seem to have clinical implications that can be related to the initial clinical observations. The examples from clients typically reveal their difficulty in appreciating how one can have different feelings about the same target, primarily people. For example, K initially had difficulty realizing that she might have more than one feeling about her grandmother, toward whom she could only express feelings of sadness at the beginning of treatment. Similarly, she could express only one emotion toward her stepfather, claiming that the feeling of love was the single emotion she experienced. Although the *clinical* material gave ample evidence for her ambivalence toward both of these very significant adults in her life, consciously she could only acknowledge a single feeling toward each, negative feelings concerning her grandmother and positive feelings about her stepfather. These clinical observations, in conjunction with our initial interview data, suggested the fruitfulness of examining the relationship between the target of each emotion, the valence of the emotion pair, and the temporal relationship between the two feelings.

POTENTIAL RELATIONSHIPS AMONG THESE THREE DIMENSIONS

Once having identified these three basic dimensions, we turned our attention to their interaction in determining children's responses. From a conceptual standpoint, we could readily map out the eight possible combinations of these three dimensions, which are given below.

Temporal Relationship	Valence of the Two Emotions	Object of the two Emotions
Sequential	Different	Different
Sequential	Different	Same
Sequential	Same	Different
Sequential	Same	Same
Simultaneous	Same	Same
Simultaneous	Same	Different
Simultaneous	Different	Different
Simultaneous	Different	Same

Although each of these eight combinations could hypothetically exist, it was next necessary to ascertain whether children in the age range sampled actually generated responses that could meaningfully be placed in these categories. An examination of the responses of our 45 subjects between the ages of 3 and 13 revealed clear examples of each of these eight combinations. Sample responses for each category are given in the following Table 6.1.

One methodological consideration should be highlighted at this point. Our interview questions *explicitly* probed for the child's understanding of the temporal relationship between two emotions in that we first asked what emotion could follow a particular feeling, and then asked how that feeling could occur simultaneously with a second. We did *not* specifically probe, however, for either the *valence* of the emotions or their *target*. These latter two dimensions emerged in our scrutiny of the actual responses generated. I return later to the implications of our methodology for data analysis, interpretation, and possible refinements in our interviewing procedures.

In considering the listing of the eight possible combinations among our three dimensions, one may ask what governed the order in which they are presented. At this point in our story, the order should not be interpreted as the specification of a developmental progression. However, it was also not arbitrary. Based on some intuitive hunches, and a global inspection of some crude age trends in the data, we very tentatively placed them in that order. Our next step was to examine the data more systematically to determine whether there were age differences in the usage of these eight combinations of responses.

DEVELOPMENTAL DIFFERENCES IN THE UTILIZATION OF EACH DIMENSION

Temporal Relationship

To review our procedure, we asked each of the 45 subjects about both the sequentiality and simultaneity of different emotions that could accompany each of the basic four feelings understood by all of the children, happy, sad, mad, scared. Figure 6.1 presents both the frequency of subjects and the mean ages for children in three categories: those who (1) could neither adequately respond to the simultaneous nor the sequential question; (2) could give acceptable responses to the sequential question; and (3) could give appropriate examples concerning both the sequential and simultaneous occurrence of two emotions. The emotion labeled in each of the four graphs represents the first emotion in the pair. Each child had previously described a particular situation evoking that single feeling. Our questions reintroduced the situation and required that the subject first describe a second feeling that could occur sequentially, and then describe a feeling that could accompany the first feeling simultaneously.

As can be seen in Fig. 6.1, for all four basic emotions there is a general linear

TABLE 6.1
Sample Responses

Sequential / Different Valence / Different Objects

In the wintertime I get *sad* because I can't go swimming but then I feel *happy* because I can go ice skating.

I would be *scared* going in a haunted house and then *happy* going on a trampoline without my shoes cause you can fall and bounce.

Sequential / Different Valence / Same Object

I was *mad* when my brother Peter got into my stuff and wrecked it—very mad—and then I was very *happy* when Peter put the stuff back to shape.

I'd be real *happy* to see Star Wars three times and then *sad* because my Father promised we'd see the starting and we got there late.

Sequential / Same Valence / Different Objects

I would be *scared* if the robots spit fire at me and then I would be *mad* because the kitty scratched me.

I'm *happy* when my cousin visits me and *excited* cause my Aunt is going to have a baby, it's in her tummy.

Sequential / Same Valence / Same Object

I get *angry* when I'm trying to read and my brother pokes me and then *discouraged* because I couldn't read the book I just started.

I feel *happy* when I hit a home run and *proud* cause your teammates would keep on respecting you.

Simultaneous / Same Valence / Same Object

On the roller coaster I was *scared* cause I thought I was going to fall off the on hills and turns and also *anxious* to see what it would really be like.

When my brother wrecks my stuff I get *mad* and I could be *angry* cause I was *upset* that he messed up my stuff.

Simultaneous / Same Valence / Different Object

I get *mad* if the bug bited me and *sad* cause I lost my ring.

It was raining and there was nothing to do and I was *bored* cause there was nothing to do and *mad* cause Mother punished me.

Simultaneous / Different Valence / Different Objects

If somebody took my dollar or my two pennies of my necklace that would make me *sad* but I would be *happy* and smiling if we went to Elitches (amusement park).

I was *frightened* that my mother was gonna punish me for not cleaning my room and *happy* cause I was watching TV

Simultaneous / Different Valence / Same Object

On my birthday I was really *happy* about going sledding but I was *scared* cause we were going down a really steep hill.

When I went horse-back riding by myself I was *glad* cause it was good to be away from my brothers and sister but I was *lonesome* all by myself cause there was no one to talk to.

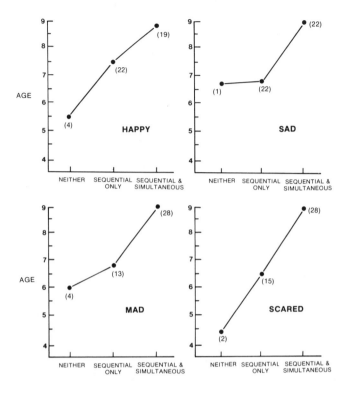

Note: Numbers in parentheses are the frequencies for each group.

FIG. 6.1.   Ages at which children: (1) cannot put two emotions together; (2) can put them in sequence only; or (3) can view them both sequentially and simultaneous, for each of the four basic emotions.

trend with age, indicating that those children unable to conceptualize two emotions as co-occurring under any circumstances were the youngest. The mean age at which children can give acceptable responses to the sequential occurrence of two emotions is between 6½ and 7½, and the average age by which children can conceptualize the simultaneity of two emotions is 9.

The data in Fig. 6.1 are presented with chronological age as the dependent variable, in that we first categorized children into one of three categories, neither sequential nor simultaneous, sequential only, and both sequential and simultaneous. As the frequencies in the parentheses indicate, the number of children in the first category was extremely small. Whereas in our previous samples, the youngest children have included subjects in the range from 2 years, 10 months to 4 years, the youngest child in the present samples was almost 4, and the majority of our preschool children, tested late in the school year, were between the ages of

4 years, 6 months and 5 years, 10 months. Thus, we found relatively few children falling in the first category where one can neither acknowledge sequential nor simultaneous feelings. Across previous pilot samples, however, the findings clearly indicate that children in the 3½- to 4½-year-old range have considerable difficulty conceptualizing the integration of two emotions, despite the fact that they can readily give compelling examples of situations that provoke single feelings.

Given the small frequencies of children in the first category, therefore, we confined our tests of significance to the mean age differences between those subjects who could adequately respond to the question regarding sequentiality, and those who could give appropriate answers to both the sequential and simultaneous question. For each of the four basic emotions on which this inquiry was conducted, the age difference between those answering the sequential compared to the simultaneous question was significant. In addition, all subjects who could successfully answer the simultaneous question also gave a satisfactory answer to the question involving the sequentiality of two feelings.

The Interaction of Valence and Temporal Relationship

Our isolation of the valence dimension allowed us to examine its possible interaction with the temporal relationship between the two emotions. Thus, for the sequential and the simultaneous question separately, we examined the frequency of children generating same valence and different valence responses. These frequency data are presented for the four target emotions in Figs. 6.2 through 6.5. The ages of the children falling into those groups is given in parentheses below each data point.

In examining responses to the *sequential* question plotted in the upper left of each figure, the same pattern was obtained for three of the four emotions, happy, sad, and scared, in that *more* children reported an emotion pair of a *different* than of the same valence, and the mean age of the children describing an emotion of a different valence was 1 to 2½ years lower than those supplying an emotion of the same valence. When *mad* is the first emotion in the pair, the differences in the frequencies of children reporting same and different valences for the second emotion are negligible, and the age trend is the converse of the effect found for the other three emotions.

When one examines the children's responses to the *simultaneous* question, the general pattern for the frequency data is the opposite of that obtained in response to the sequential question. When forced to deal with the issue of simultaneity, *more* children gave *same* valence replies than give different valence responses. Age differences were not found for the two groups categorized according to valence, which is most plausibly attributed to a ceiling effect due to the greater difficulty of the simultaneity question in general.

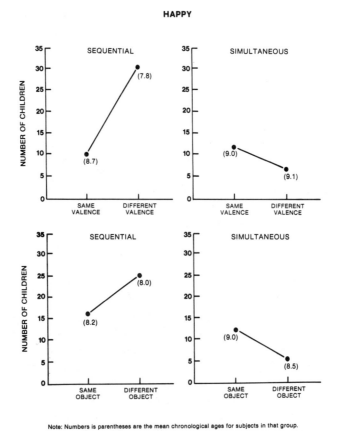

HAPPY

Note: Numbers is parentheses are the mean chronological ages for subjects in that group.

FIG. 6.2.   Frequency of children generating responses about their understanding of the co-occurrence of two emotions in the designated categories below.

The Interaction of Object and Temporal Relationship

The lower half of Figs. 6.2 through 6.5 presents the frequency of children generating same-object and different-object responses to the sequential question, plotted on the left, and the simultaneous question on the right. In first considering the *sequential* question, for all four emotions the pattern is very similar. More children spontaneously make reference to the *different* objects of the two emotions than to the same object. In addition, the children generating different-object responses were younger than those who focused on the same object as the target of both feelings.

The pattern for the *simultaneous* question, plotted in the lower left, is the reverse, for three of the four emotions. When asked about the simultaneity of two emotions, children are more likely to attach these two feelings to the *same* object than to a different object.

IMPLICATIONS OF THE FINDINGS

How might we interpret these patterns? Cautiously! However, the data do suggest some intriguing hypotheses for further study. When one considers responses to the question requiring children to place two emotions in temporal *sequence,* more children are likely to describe emotions of a different valence, and to attach the two feelings to different objects. Additionally, children who focus on differences for both of these dimensions tend to be younger than those who generate

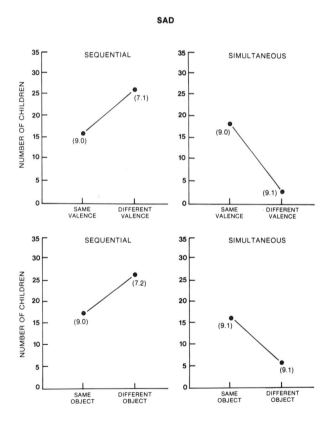

Note: Numbers in parentheses are the mean age for subjects in that group.

FIG. 6.3.   Frequency of children generating responses about their understanding of the co-occurrence of two emotions in the designated categories below.

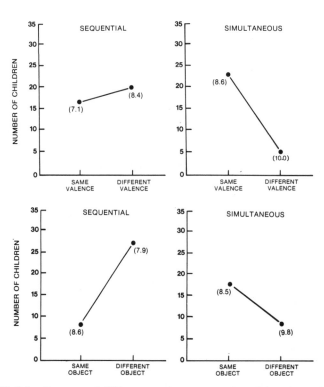

FIG. 6.4.   Frequency of children generating responses about their understanding
of the co-occurrence of two emotions in the designated categories below.

emotions of the same valence, and emotions directed toward the same object. The opposite pattern was obtained in response to our question requiring that two emotions be conceptualized as co-occurring simultaneously. Of those children who could give an adequate response to this question, more made reference to emotions of the same valence, and more attached the emotion pair to the same object. The frequency of different-valence and different-object responses to this question was extremely small.

From a developmental standpoint, one is tempted to interpret those categories with higher frequencies and lower ages as representing potentially "easier" responses. Thus, when asked to supply an emotion that follows the first in time or sequence, it appears easier for children to generate an emotion of a different valence and attach it to a different event, person, or situation. In part, the phrasing of this question may pull for such responses in that we ask the child: "Now tell me how you have a *different* feeling *after* you felt (happy); first you could feel (happy) and then you could feel *what*?"

When given this option why do children tend to shift both the valence and the object? In examining the responses where *happy* is the first emotion in the pair, by far the most common second emotion mentioned was *sad*. When sad was the first emotion in the pair, *happy* was typically the second feeling described. Is it possible that these tend to be "natural opposites," that children learn to conceptualize happy and sad as a dichotomous pair at a relatively early age?

Although this possible interpretation may speak to the sequential responses obtained for happy and sad, how do we view the similar trend for the emotion label "scared" where children also tend to shift both the valence and the target of the second emotion? One "psychodynamic" interpretation might be that when given the opportunity (by our question) to think of a *different* feeling *after* you were scared, children attempt to "escape" conceptually from scary situations by generating a positive emotion attached to quite a different event.

Why doesn't the affect of anger follow this same pattern for the sequential question? The younger the child, the greater the tendency to supply an emotion

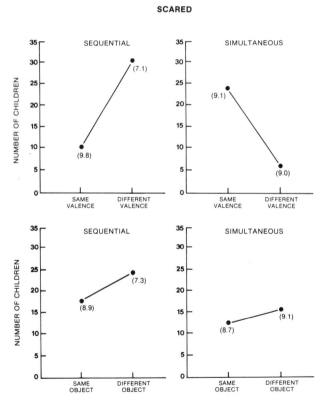

FIG. 6.5. Frequency of children generating responses about their understanding of the co-occurrence of two emotions in the designated categories below.

of the *same* valence, another negative feeling, which is attached to a different object. Is there something unique about the emotion of anger that makes it more difficult to switch one's set to a positive feeling? Are the data consistent with the expression "consumed with anger" and its implication that this particular emotion mobilizes one to remain within the bailiwick of negative affects? Does the fact that the second negative feeling is typically directed toward a different object have any implications for the "displacement of anger?" All these interpretations are highly speculative at this point.

What are the conceptual demands put on the child by the question requiring that one supply two emotion labels that can *simultaneously* co-occur? Why does it appear "easier" for children to generate emotions of the *same* valence, and to attach the second emotion to the *same* situation, event, or object? When forced to consider another feeling that one could experience at the very same time, is it more difficult to conceptually shift moods and situational targets? Intuitively this seems plausible. We need to be much more precise, however, in defining what we mean by such terms as "conceptually shift," "natural opposites," "psychodynamic interpretations," and so on.

The Limitations of Categories Based on Spontaneously Generated Responses

The implication, in delineating the eight possible combinations of our three dimensions, was that we would examine our data with the hope of specifying a developmental sequence. The interview procedure we utilized did not permit this type of analysis. Recall that the only dimension we inquired about directly was the temporal relationship between the two emotions. We required that the child demonstrate his or her ability to produce a sequential as well as a simultaneous emotion pair. We did not specifically ask children to give us both same valence and different valence responses, nor did we require that they deal with both same and different targets or objects of the emotion pairs. That is, we did not systematically probe for a child's understanding of those eight possible combinations. We did not test for the *ability* to conceptualize each of the possible relationships among our three dimensions. Two of the dimensions, valence and object, had not been identified prior to our examination of the data. As indicated earlier, these dimensions emerged upon our scrutiny of the responses themselves.

Thus, at present, we must be cautious in our inferences about which combinations are "easier," because this term implies an ability component for which we have not yet tested directly. Based upon both the frequency of children generating a particular response, as well as the ages of children in a given category, we can *hypothesize* that the ability to specify how emotions of different valence can occur in temporal sequence precedes the ability to specify how emotions of similar emotions occur sequentially. Conversely, we can hypothesize that the ability to conceptualize the simultaneous occurrence of emotions with a similar valence developmentally precedes the ability to apply such a conceptualization of two feelings of different valences. Analogous predictions can be made with regard to the object dimension.

Although our present data, therefore, cannot speak to the question of a scalable sequence, we can address this issue in future research. An adequate test of such a progression requires that we formulate interview questions that specifically ask about *each* of the eight combinations of the three dimensions. These data can then be analyzed utilizing scalogram techniques. We can determine whether the combinations we have identified can be cast into an acquisition sequence such that particular combinations of these dimensions systematically precede and follow other combinations. We can also examine the ages at which each of these combinations is manifested, as a second approach to the demonstration of a developmental progression in the understanding of multiple emotions. We are currently in the process of revising our interview in order to address these very questions.

Content Versus Structure and the Issue of Décalage

The attempts to demonstrate a systematic developmental progression that defines the structure of the child's thought has historically been plagued by a pesky problem: The nature of this progression, and the age at which particular cognitive structures appear to emerge, may in large part depend on the particular content domain sampled. Perhaps the most classic example is the demonstration that conservation skills do not emerge full-blown in the repertoire of the concrete operational child but develop in the order of conservation of matter, weight, and volume. Furthermore, one may find differences depending on the task domain, nature of the stimulus materials, and so forth (see Fischer, 1980). Although Piaget has chosen not to highlight this type of horizontal décalage, but rather to focus on the general pattern of cognitive–structural change, more recently others, specifically Fischer, have made the consideration of skill domain a dominant focus.

In our own efforts to understand how children conceptualize emotions, we need to give serious attention to both structure and content. Within our conceptual framework one may conceive of the eight possible combinations of temporal relationship, valence, and object as the structural component. What developmental differences can we demonstrate with regard to children's ability to conceptualize the combinations of these dimensions? *Content,* within our realm of inquiry, can be viewed as the particular emotion labels to which children apply these structures. Although we did not predict differences associated with the specific emotion labels we have investigated to date, our findings have alerted us to the possibility that certain emotions (for example mad) may not follow the same pattern as other feelings (e.g., happy, sad, and scared). Although we could sweep such findings under the empirical rug, and choose to highlight global patterns of ontogenetic change, we have not opted for this choice. We feel that such a strategy not only obscures an important general consideration for developmentalists, but places blinders on our efforts to understand how and why particular emotion labels differ from one another. Such an understanding not only has theoretical ramifications, but has practical implications for our educational and clinical efforts with children.

FURTHER CONSIDERATIONS

Chronological Age Versus Mental Age and the Concept of Ability

Midway into the interview, we administered the Peabody Picture Vocabulary Test, in part to give our young subjects a conceptual "breather," as our questions did require considerable cognitive effort. (Comments such as "I can't think that hard" and "My brain just doesn't know the answer" were not infrequent among our 4- and 5-year-olds!) This task also provided us with a mental age, albeit based only on the child's recognition vocabulary. Because these scores were available for only 31 of the 45 subjects in our most recent sample, the findings presented earlier in this chapter related emotional understanding to chronological age. However, analyses performed on the subsample of 31 children indicated that mental age correlated more highly with the number of single emotions generated and with children's ability to conceptualize the simultaneous occurrence of two emotions than did chronological age.

These findings are related to a critical issue we plan to address, namely: What are the underlying abilities, the cognitive processes, that are predictive of a child's level of emotional comprehension? Several possibilities come to mind. Are we dealing primarily with a child's ability to *verbalize* his or her understanding of emotions, such that a production vocabulary task would capture a significant part of the developmental variance in the responses? Or, to take our Piagetian analysis seriously, are the skills involved in tasks such as conservation and multiplication of classes necessary, if not sufficient, precursors of children's ability to integrate emotional concepts? Are there other problem-solving tasks, either verbal or nonverbal, in our armamentarium of standardized tests and experimental procedures that might be more thoughtfully related to our task of emotional understanding?

Chronological age is a crude developmental index of conceptual level at best, as I have pointed out in another context (Harter, 1967). What is required is an analysis of the possible skills that are necessary to perform the various levels of our interview task. Here we feel that it would be fruitful to examine the implications of Fischer's theory of cognitive development, which not only delineates seven levels of intelligence, but attempts to specify the transition rules governing the shift from one level to the next. Such an analysis will then hopefully dictate our strategy with regard to the identification and measurement of those underlying cognitive processes that are predictive of a child's level of emotional understanding.

Ultimately it will also be necessary for us to broaden our perspective and to consider what *experiential* factors contribute to the child's comprehension of emotional concepts, independent of cognitive–developmental level. We have observed striking individual differences within a particular age range that do not appear to be mere reflections of some intellectual ability factor. There are those children who are extremely facile in their descriptions of emotional content, who manifest considerable sensitivity to the affective domain. Conversely, there are those children who appear to be as intellectually competent as their age peers yet struggle with the emotional concepts we ask them to discuss. Our goal, therefore, must include the specification of those cognitive processes undergoing normative developmental change that may predict our sequence of emotional understanding. However, we must eventually address the question of what types of experiences in the socialization history of the child are responsible for individual differences within developmental level. This issue is not only of theoretical interest but has practical implications for our intervention efforts with children.

Personality Characteristics and Self-attributions

The clinical context from which this research emerged dealt with the co-occurrence of different emotions as well as of different attributes such as smart and dumb. Later in this chapter it was suggested that a distinction be made between those concepts that are conventionally defined as emotions, and those that we typically label as personality characteristics. To date, we have confined our normative–developmental research to emotional constructs. In our future work we would like to extend our inquiry to the domain of the child's self-attributions about such characteristics. Does the child's perception of himself or herself as smart or dumb, bad or good, athletic or uncoordinated, popular or unpopular, attractive or unattractive follow a developmental progression similar to the one emerging for emotions? More specifically, are the dimensions of temporal relationship, valence, and object relevant to this class of judgments, and to a similar degree?

In such an analysis, the counterpart of the object designation in our emotion paradigm would be the situation in which a particular characteristic was manifest, and we would examine the extent to which attributions were situation specific. For example, do children consider themselves to be smart in one context, but less intellectually adequate or even stupid, in another? Consider the street-savvy child who is failing in school. Does this child view himself or herself as smart in the first situation or context and cognitively inadequate in the second?

Another interesting question involves the degree to which children view these attributes as "traitlike" in nature. Are characteristics such as smart or athletic viewed as relatively enduring, in contrast to emotions that may be considered relatively transitory? Although it has been cogently argued (Mischel, 1973) that adults treat many trait labels as situation specific, we have little information about how children utilize these concepts.

This general line of inquiry converges with my research on children's perception of their competence (Harter, 1978, 1982). In that work, we have demonstrated one form of situation specificity in that children clearly do not view themselves as equally competent across the three skill domains we have tapped, cognitive, social, and physical competence. However, we have *not* addressed the question of whether *within* a particular domain (e.g., cognitive) children can feel smart in one context and "dumb" or inadequate intellectually in another. The particular question structure devised for the Perceived Competence Scale does not permit that type of response in that we ask children to make a single judgment about their relative competence in a given domain. Thus, we would now like to address the issue of the differentiations a child makes *within* each domain in order to determine whether there is a developmental progression in children's appreciation of attributional dichotomies such as smart–dumb, and whether the three dimensions identified in our emotion research apply to these judgments. On an intuitive basis, one would expect that the *temporal* juxtaposition of two such attributes would be more readily acknowledged than their *simultaneous* occurrence, and as such might occur at a developmentally earlier stage. Within the realm of simultaneous judgments only, one would also predict that attributions of smart and dumb would be much more difficult to conceptualize within the same situation than across different situations. At this point in time, it would seem that we could make certain a priori predictions about the order of these combinations that we could then test directly.

The Relationship Between the Level of Understanding of Emotional Concepts and of Self-Attributions

We can also determine whether these two lines of development parallel one another. Is a child able to make certain types of differentiated judgments in one sphere at a developmentally earlier age than in the other? The answer to this question may ultimately be linked to the hypothesis that attributes are viewed as more stable, whereas emotions are conceptualized as transitory. This prediction would lead to the expectation that children would be able to appreciate the co-occurrence of two *emotions* of differing valence at an earlier age than they would be able to integrate two traitlike *attributes* such as smart and stupid.

Another related line of research involves the *direct* study of children's emotional reactions to the characteristics that they attribute to themselves. What affect labels do children associate with their perceptions of themselves as smart or dumb, popular or unpopular, athletic or unathletic? And at that point in time where they are able to indicate that a part of them can be smart and part of them can be dumb, do they also apply different emotional labels to each attributional component of their personality? One would certainly expect that positive valence emotions would be associated with positive attributes, and likewise that negative affects would be expressed over undesirable characteristics. Beyond that, it would seem critical to determine whether certain classes of emotions become attached to attributes in particular domains. Consider intellectual achievement-related behaviors. What positive affects are related to success? Is happiness largely defined by pride? Is the negative counterpart disappointment in one's self? Is there frustration and anxiety? Are different emotion labels attached to one's successes and failures in the *social* domain? Are successful relationships likely to evoke positive feelings of love and security? Might the negative affects be slightly different from those in the intellectual competence arena, such that the more prepotent emotions are jealousy, anger, loneliness, hurt, and depression? These questions are raised to highlight our need to address such questions from a developmental perspective in that the relationship between particular domains and their related affects may undergo ontogenetic shifts, particularly as the child's network of emotional concepts becomes more differentiated with age. Additionally, we will need to consider the role of individual differences within developmental level.

Although our developmental focus has been primarily cognitive up to this point, these questions can also be considered within the broader context of Erikson's theory of psychosexual stages and their related nuclear conflicts. Consider those four conflicts most relevant to the age periods we have studied: autonomy versus doubt and shame; initiative versus guilt; industry versus inferiority; identity versus role confusion. Erikson's theory would appear to speak to both the issue of affect and of attributions about competence. However, he seems to confound the two in his stage designations of the potential conflicts represented. For example, a sense of autonomy and of initiative refer more to attributions about one's personality, whereas their "opposites" in these conflicts, doubt and shame, guilt, reflect emotional reactions. In the case of his conflict between industry and inferiority, each of two components seem to refer to characteristics of the self rather than emotions. That one would have emotional reactions to such characteristics is to be expected. But this is precisely the issue that requires clarification in such an analysis. That is, it would seem that we should first distinguish between attributes and emotions, and once having identified members of each class or category, we can then attempt to relate one to the other meaningfully. Whether they follow the pattern Erikson suggests is an empirical question.

Children's Understanding of Parental Emotions

We have recently begun to adapt our procedures in order to assess a child's understanding of his or her *parents'* feelings. Although we are interested in this question in and of its own right, we also want to assess the relationship between the level of understanding of one's *own* emotions and the level at which one can discuss parental emotions. Does the child come to comprehend his or her own affective life first and then apply this understanding to others? Or do the parents, as models, display affects that the child comes eventually to appreciate in adults, after which he or she applies these labels to his or her own behavior? The latter modeling formulation would also imply that children are more likely to imitate the behaviors of the same-sex parent, something we can also address directly.

Our current procedure utilizes a photographic task[1] in conjunction with interview questions. We obtained two sets of four photographs from two adult models, one set that depicts a mother and the other a father. Each series portrays the basic four emotions, happy, sad, mad, and scared. The facial expressions are realistic, without being exaggerated, and when asked to label each, children's judgments are extremely reliable.

To date, we have asked children about single emotions only. Our procedure is as follows: After insuring that each child can accurately identify the four emotions in each parent, we ask the child to tell us what would make each parent experience each of those feelings, and why. This procedure mirrors that employed in the first part of the child interview, which focuses on the single emotions the subject experiences. Thus we can compare the child's responses about his or her own emotions to responses concerning parental emotions.

This research is only in its exploratory phase, however the procedure is quite successful in eliciting rich responses about parental emotions. We have now talked with children between the ages of 4 and 11. Although we have interviewed relatively few children, a very clear developmental trend is emerging. Four- and 5-year-olds give us resonses that are appropriate to their *own* lives, not their parents'. For example, when asked about happy, they will tell us that mommy or daddy would be happy if they "went to the circus," "got a new toy," etc. Events that they report as evoking sadness in a parent are "losing his toy giraffe in the backyard," experiencing the death of a pet, and having to "go to bed when he wanted to watch television." Angry feelings attributed to a parent occur when "her friends won't play with her," and scared feelings are typically attached to monsters that might be under the bed at night, or other mythical creatures that are scary. In many cases, the specific situation that the child describes as evoking the *parental* emotion is identical to the situation he or she described earlier, when asked about his or her own feelings. Thus we see the young child egocentrically projecting his or her own emotional experiences onto that of the parent.

The first evidence of decentering in this realm occurs among our 6-, 7-, and 8-year-olds, who can describe emotions that are appropriate parental responses.

---

[1] I would like to thank Rayma Skeen for her dedicated and successful efforts with adult models to obtain these particular photographic stimuli.

However, the *child* is typically the *target* of the parental affect. Some examples are the following: "My mom gets mad when she has to tell me six times to pick up my room"; "Dad would be happy if I took out the garbage"; "Mommy would be scared if I got lost." Rarely do we see children in this age range describing a situation that involves issues concerning parental life, independent of the child subject.

Our 9-, 10-, and 11-year-olds, in contrast, are capable of describing appropriate parental affective situations in which they themselves are not directly involved. For example, they describe how "mother would be happy if she won a contest cause then she could pay the bills"; "Daddy would be mad if someone wrecked his new chiropractor's table"; "Mommy would be scared if she was home alone and she thought she heard a burglar"; "Daddy would be sad if one of his patients died."

These trends are certainly consistent with the cognitive–developmental literature on egocentricism and decentering. However, any complete understanding of these emerging developmental processes must turn to social learning theory as well. Our findings suggest, as is so often the case, that any explanation of the child's emotional understanding will not rest on the conceptual shoulders of one formulation alone. With regard to emotional understanding and expression, observational learning or modeling processes clearly come into play. Our own procedures reveal this dramatically. At the end of our interview, we ask our child subjects to pretend that they are first happy, then mad, sad, and scared, and they enact each of these feelings in front of our one-way mirror. Their expressions and gestures, indeed, their entire body postures, represent miniature replicas of adult stereotypes. What is of interest, however, is that whereas children at an early age learn to imitate the emotional cues that expressively convey these different affective states, they do not simultaneously develop an understanding of the situations in the parental life that evoke these emotions. Thus, we need to turn our attention to the cognitive–developmental limitations of the young child in order to understand fully the complexities of the child's conceptualization of emotionality.

Undoubtedly, the picture will become even more complex when we address the child's understanding of *multiple* emotions in the parents, something we plan to pursue. Although we will be open to novel dimensions that might possibly emerge, we will be interested in how the dimensions of temporal contiguity, valence, and object are manifest. Additionally, we will be able to determine whether children utilize these dimensions differently for the four emotions (i.e., are there differences in children's description of parental feelings that are consistent with the description of their own affective life).

Our preliminary findings suggest some intriguing practical implications as well. Consider our youngest subjects, who can only entertain the possibility that they can have one feeling at any given point in time. To the extent that this is the only manner in which the child can perceive his or her *own* emotional experience, one would predict that such a child can only view parental emotions from the same unidimensional prospective. Thus, when a parent is mad, they must be "all mad," and the child is undoubtedly unable to interpret parental anger against a backdrop of emotional concepts that simultaneously includes feelings of love and concern. This all-or-none conceptualization on the part of the young child must also have implications for his or her own affective reaction to the perceived parental emotion. The fact that mommy must be "all mad" may evoke considerably more fear, anxiety, shame, or guilt in a child than if one perceived mommy as both angry and loving or caring.

Next consider the child in the 6- to 8-year-old age range who views himself or herself as the primary target of parental feelings. What psychological burden does this place on the child to the extent that he or she is the *cause* of parental anger, sadness, or fear? The suggestion in our data—that the child views himself or herself as the central cause—is not a new thought. For example, psychoanalytic theory has alerted us to the problem of the oedipal child whose momentary angry death wish toward the father may be interpreted by the young boy as a *cause,* should some misfortune subsequently befall the parent. Piagetian theory has described the prelogical mechanisms governing such natural (i.e., stage-appropriate) inferences at this age. The examples typically cited in the literature refer to the child's misperception of actual events in their lives. Why was daddy in an accident? Why are mommy and daddy getting divorced?

Our own domain of inquiry extends such an analysis to children's perceptions of parental emotions or affective reactions, not just the events per se. What does it mean to the child that he or she feels responsible for a complex emotional state in the parent? What emotion does this evoke in the child? What does it imply for the child's understanding of not only what causes an emotion to occur in the first place, but what makes an affect go away? What do I do to make mommy happy when she is mad? How does this particular "set" influence the child's own affective state? What is the child's understanding of what makes his or her own emotions come and go, and how does this change with development? These are types of questions that must ultimately be addressed in pursuing the interaction between a child's developing understanding of his or her emotions and the emotions of the significant others in one's life.

Practical Implications for Intervention

The preceding discussion has pointed to certain implications that a child's level of emotional understanding holds for everyday life. Another practical question is paramount: Can we intervene to alter the child's level of emotional understanding, to foster shifts toward ontogenetically higher levels of functioning? Here we address the same issue faced by neo-Piagetians who have attempted to influence the child's rate of movement through the basic cognitive–developmental stages, as well as those who have attempted to promote higher levels of moral judgment from the perspective of Kohlberg's stage model.

My own efforts to bring about conceptual change have to date been confined to the play-therapy room where I have worked with children for whom problems in emotional understanding appear particularly salient. Let me return to the case of K, where these intervention attempts began. Recall that K's major presenting problem involved her school learning difficulties. When we began treatment she had just entered the first grade. Within a few weeks, she structured our sessions around a classroom scenario in which she was the teacher and I was a pupil, a *dumb* pupil. For weeks, I was chronically assigned the role of the dummy, the child who could not learn, who did poorly in all of the basic first-grade skills, who incurred the wrath of the teacher, and who was ridiculed by classroom peers. I interpreted this continuing saga as K's projection of her own feelings of stupidity onto me; it seemed that she felt totally incompetent, stupid, and basically dumb in every area, a view that was unrealistic given that she was a relatively bright little girl who could perform quite competently in some areas. (For a fuller account of those processes underlying play that led to my making such an interpretation, see the original article, Harter, 1977.)

My first attempt at intervention came well into the first year of treatment after my repeated attempts to talk to K directly about her feelings had failed. The breakthrough occurred during a typical command performance, during which I was being chastised by the teacher for not paying attention to the lesson and for doing poorly on my math. I finally donned a look of extreme frustration and raised my hand. (Failure to do so in this particular classroom setting was tantamount to a criminal offense!) I began with an urgent plea: "Teacher, teacher, I just *can't* concentrate on my math, I can't think, there is something that's bothering me, and I want to tell you about how I am feeling." I was given an authoritative scowl tinged with a mild look of disgust and was informed that if I did not do my math immediately I would be sent to the principal's office and would have to stay after school. I persisted, in the same vein. Finally I asked if I could come up to the blackboard and try to draw something that might help to explain how I was feeling. Hands on her hips, tapping the toe of one foot (in a characterization that would have well won her an Oscar) she sternly retorted: "All right, but make it quick, we have *work* to do!"

So I went up to the blackboard and began to draw a circle, explaining that the circle was kind of like me. Then I drew a line down the middle of the circle, putting an S on the left and a D on the right (see Fig. 6.6). My explanation was as follows:

This is sort of a picture of me and the way I feel. The circle is kind of like all of me, and it feels like there are two parts. There's this part that feels pretty dumb a lot of the time over here, the part with the D, like when I can't do my math. D is for

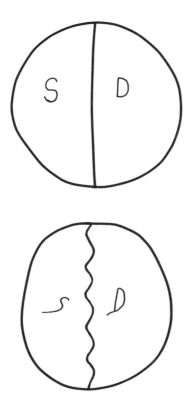

FIG. 6.6.   Top: My original drawing depicting the smart part and the dumb part. Bottom: K's reproduction of the drawing.

dumb. But I don't always feel dumb. Because there is also a *smart* part, here with the S. I feel smart when I can figure out other things, like the things I do right in my workbook. So it's not like I feel all dumb all the time. There's a dumb part and a smart part. Well, I just wanted you to know how I felt because it might help you to understand me a little better and why I do some of the things I do.

Because she perceived that my speech was over, she gruffly informed me to return to my seat and put my head down on my desk, and as I did so rather dejectedly, she quickly and deftly erased my drawing from the blackboard. (At that point I thought to myself: "Well, as a therapist, I have only one part, and it's all dumb!") It was with considerable effort that I resumed my attempts at my math lesson. About 10 minutes later in the session, the class was beckoned from their seats with the following call from the teacher: "Class, I want you all to come up to the blackboard, I have something to say to you. I want to explain to you how this pupil feels." She pointed to me. Trying to keep my jaw from dropping and to convince my unbelieving ears that this was not simply a therapeutic reverie, I watched and listened to the following. First she reproduced my drawing, with a slight change in the center line, depicted in Fig. 6.6 (I must confess that I prefer her center line to mine, as it implies more of an integration or infusion of the two areas.) She then proceeded with great fervor, to explain to our imaginary class how:

> This is her, this circle, and this is the smart part and this is the dumb part; sometimes she feels dumb when she can't do her work, and sometimes she feels smart, when she can do her work. She feels both. Alright, class, go back to your seats.

In a very small voice, which was all I could muster at the time, I thanked the teacher for explaining to the other kids how I felt, as it was very important that both she and they understand. I indicated how much better I felt after I had a chance to explain it to her, because I was not sure she completely understood before now. Then the school bell rang, heralding a wonderful day of new learning.

During the ensuing weeks, I decided not to initiate the drawing myself but to see what K would do with it, if anything. She did a great deal. Over the next several weeks, the drawing spontaneously appeared on numerous occasions. Sometimes it was accompanied by an explanation, other times it was not. Sometimes it became the basis for a lesson. For example, she would reproduce the drawing, and then as we went through our math problems she would put pluses on the smart side for correct answers and minuses on the dumb side for errors.

In terms of K's *actual* school situation, there were ongoing changes. She switched schools due to a family move, and in her new school she was assigned to an exceptionally good remedial program to help her in the scholastic areas in which she seemed to be having the greatest difficulty. She began to blossom as a function of this special help and, in a word, was becoming "smarter."

Concomitant with this change in her school situation, her drawings began to undergo some interesting changes. After an initial series that resembled the original drawing, she ultimately produced the two drawings depicted in Fig. 6.7. The second one occurred 3 weeks after the first. Two things seem noteworthy about her alterations. First, there are more smart areas than dumb, and second, the smart areas are more central, with the smaller dumb areas placed on the periphery. I am tempted to interpret this as a symbol of her changing self-concept, related to her actual school progress. That is, realistically she was becoming smarter, and the size, number, and centrality of this component in her drawings seems to communicate this symbolically, at the level of graphic metaphor.

K could not articulate the basis for these changes in her drawings, just as she could not yet directly discuss with me how this symbolization depicted her *own* feelings. However, it was clear that this had become a very compelling means of

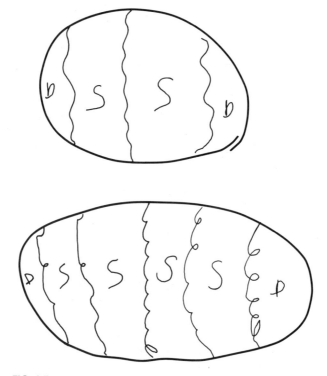

FIG. 6.7.   K's subsequent modifications of the smart–dumb drawing.

expression for her. It became a ritual. My own interpretation is that it provided a very concrete depiction of the powerful but conflicted feelings she was experiencing. It seemed to help her think about the simultaneous existence of two seemingly contradictory feelings, namely the feeling that one can be dumb *and* smart at the same time. It also provided a concrete visualizable symbol to which we could attach real experiences. That is, we could literally "chalk up" the correct answers in the smart area of the drawing and erroneous answers in the dumb area. It somehow allowed her to relate more directly to the conflicting emotional concepts and feelings that she had previously responded to in an all-or-none fashion, acknowledging only one affective pole on the smart–dumb dimension.

In the course of our continuing sessions, I attempted to cast other conflicting feelings into a similar graphic mold. These are described in the initial paper (Harter, 1977) and I will not go into detail here. However, one aspect of these subsequent efforts is particularly noteworthy in light of certain distinctions I raised earlier in this chapter. The first conflict I addressed through the drawing technique would fall into the domain of attribute of one's personality, smart and dumb, as distinguished from the realm of emotion labels. The second type of conflict I attempted to introduce through this technique was clearly within the realm of emotions, namely K's feelings about her grandmother. Although K could only admit to feelings of sadness, I introduced a new drawing that depicted sad on the right and happy on the left. I wrote the words "sad" and "happy" and drew a crying face on the word "sad" and a smiling face under the word "happy." K's own "reproduction" of this drawing the following week was extremely interesting. She did not adopt my emotion labels as such, but wrote in the words "good" and "bad," placing the smiling face under "good," and the sad crying face, complete with tears, under the word "bad." In retrospect, her response is intriguing given our subsequent normative–developmental findings on the earliest levels of emotional understanding. There we found that the very first emotion labels to be employed by our youngest subjects were "good" and "bad." Within these two categories, more precise designations became differentiated with development. It would seem, in the case of K, that a similar phenomenon was occurring. Whereas I introduced the designations of "happy" and "sad," her first attempts in therapy to label her feelings were cast into the good–bad dichotomy. It was only later in treatment that she came to label the good feelings as "happy" and the bad feelings as including both "mad" and "sad." Although one must be cautious in generalizing from a single case, nevertheless my clinical observations of K are consistent with an emerging developmental picture of children's understanding of emotions. They also suggest that in our therapeutic attempts with young children who are beginning to deal with emotion labels, we may wish to model or introduce the normative–developmental sequence that begins with the basic acknowledgment of good feelings and bad feelings.

The attempt to alter those progressions that have definite cognitive–developmental underpinnings must be addressed within the context of the mutability of such structures. As the field has witnessed in the domain of conservation, as well as moral judgment, only those subjects who appear to be in "transition" from one stage to the next are significantly influenced by our manipulations. How one defines "in transition" is often rather tautological in that those children who were responsive to our intervention efforts are often, after the fact, considered to be transitional. Nevertheless, the general concept of "developmental readiness" would seem applicable to the realm of emotional understanding, though there we know even less about what markers signal the potential for shifting to a more advanced level. Thus, in both our normative–developmental research on children's emotional understanding and our observations in naturalistic settings we should address ourselves to this question. Indeed, the problem of specifying the "transition rules" governing the ontogenetic shift to a new stage lies at the heart of our developmental inquiry in any behavioral sphere.

Our final note about the particular procedure that evolved in my work with K, the drawing technique I employed: There is nothing magical nor psychologically sacred about a circle with a line down the middle of it symbolically denoting two feelings! In the case of K, this seemed appropriate given her penchant for blackboard drawings within the context of our classroom scenario. Other materials or formats may be more appropriate in other situations, with other children. For example, with a 9-year-old client who spent many therapy hours producing crayon drawings of her family, I introduced comic-strip "bubbles" over their heads, writing in dialogues or monologues that depicted the underlying conflict I perceived her to be experiencing. With a boy client who refused to do anything related to drawing activities, but preferred to work with clay, I began to put several faces on the clay head of the character I was molding, in an attempt to concretize the fact that one could have more than one emotional reaction. More recently I have felt the need to devise techniques for communicating the *magnitude* of each feeling, along with the possible blending or blurring of affects. Certain clinical models suggest, for example, that depression is a combination of sadness and anger, where the phenomenological experience of depression may be qualitatively quite different from a situation in which the discrete feelings of both sadness and anger are both acknowledged. Can we help our clients envisage these types of affective experience?

Thus, while the drawing technique described may have been appropriate for the case of K, given her particular difficulties and her own expressive style, the technique should not be isomorphically equated with its intent or purpose. Too often in our efforts at both research and intervention, the technique designed to *reflect* a process becomes reified as the very process itself. The conservation task *"becomes"* reversibility, rather than one procedure for tapping one aspect of functioning in the repertoire of the concrete-operational child.

Thus I would caution those of us working directly with children to appreciate the intent of the techniques described. The fundamental assumption underlying the introduction of such a procedure is that the child is experiencing an underlying conflict to which he or she does not have conscious access. From observational material that you can specify, you advance hypotheses concerning the particular emotions that define this conflict, emotions that the child cannot directly verbalize. Although the child may not be able to verbalize the components of the conflict, other behaviors may lead you to believe that he or she is experiencing one side of the conflict to the exclusion of the other (e.g., "I feel all dumb"). Alternatively, there may be evidence for your interpretation that the child is vacillating from one pole to the other, most typically seen in the love–hate dichotomy. In certain cases, the child may have verbal access to one feeling in a pair (or perhaps in a broader emotional network) but conscious access to that one feeling only. Or in the case of vacillation, at any given point in time the child may be able to verbalize only one of the emotions in the pair, but may express the opposite feeling at another point in time. Thus the focus of any technique should be to stimulate the cognitive process by which both feelings can be acknowledged, to *introduce* conflicts, as it were, in one sense, but to rob it of its conflictual overtones or undercurrents in another sense. The goal would be the acknowledgment of two apparently contradictory feelings or self-attributions, without the phenomenological experience that these two feelings are necessarily in opposition. The basis in reality for their coexistence, namely evidence from the life history of the particular client, must necessarily be mustered and presented in such a manner as to permit and perpetuate the conscious acknowledgment of these feelings, and the perception that they can ultimately become compatible.

Admittedly, this is only a very general analysis and we have much to learn about how best to intervene in the emotional lives of children. Such efforts should be guided by our normative–developmental investigations. Without such a perspective, our interventions may be misguided and/or premature. For this reason my colleagues and I have turned our major attention to the empirical investigation of the developmental progression that defines emotional understanding. We, as adult researchers, have our own ontogenetic journey ahead of us in charting this terrain.

Once again, I would like to express my intellectual indebtedness to Jim Connell and Chris Miner for their stimulating and extensive collaborative input during every phase of this research. And begrudgingly, I feel compelled to acknowledge the prior insight of J. M. Barrie, the author of *Peter Pan,* who wrote the following back in 1911:

> Tinkerbell was not all bad; or, rather, she was all bad just now, but on the other hand, sometimes she was all good. Fairies have to be one thing or the other, because being so small they unfortunately have room for only one feeling at a time. They are, however, allowed to change, only it must be a complete change. At present Tinkerbell was full of jealousy toward Wendy [pp. 60–61].

I must admit that upon discovering this quote, an occurrence that happened after we were well into this research, I experienced two emotions of opposite valence directed toward the same target: Part of me was very excited at the obvious convergence; but another part was mildly annoyed at having been so deftly "scooped"!

ACKNOWLEDGMENT

This research was supported by Research Grant HD-09613 from National Institute of Child Health and Human Development, N.I.C H.D., U.S.P.H.S.

REFERENCES

Axline, V. *Play therapy.* New York: Ballantine Books, 1947.
Barrie, J. M. *Peter Pan: The story of Peter and Wendy.* New York: Grossett & Dunlap, 1911.

Borke, H. Interpersonal perception of young children. *Developmental Psychology,* 1971, *5,* 263–269.

Chandler, M. J., & Greenspan, S. Erzatz egocentrism: A reply to H. Borke. *Developmental Psychology,* 1972, *7,* 104–106.

Erikson, E. H. *Childhood and society.* New York: Norton, 1950.

Erikson, E. H. *Identity, youth, and crisis.* New York: Norton, 1968.

Fischer, K. W. A theory of cognitive development: The control and construction of a hierarchy of skills. *Psychological Review,* 1980, *87,* 477–531.

Fischer, K. *Understanding understanding: Piaget, learning, and cognitive development,* in press.

Flavell, J. H. *The developmental psychology of Jean Piaget.* New York: Van Nostrand, 1963.

Flavell, J. H. *The development of role-taking skills in children.* New York: Wiley, 1968.

Freud, A. *Normality and pathology in childhood.* New York: International Universities Press, 1965.

Harter, S. Mental age, IQ, and motivational factors in the discrimination learning set performance of normal and retarded children. *Journal of Experimental Child Psychology,* 1967, *5,* 123–141.

Harter, S. A cognitive–developmental approach to children's expression of conflicting feelings and a technique to facilitate such expression in play therapy. *Journal of Consulting and Clinical Psychology,* 1977, *45,* 417–432.

Harter, S. Effectance motivation reconsidered: Toward a developmental model. *Human Development,* 1978, *21,* 34–64.

Harter, S. The perceived competence scale for children. *Child Development,* 1982, *53,* 87–97.

Harter, S., Miner, C., & Connell, J. P. *The development of children's understanding of multiple emotions.* Paper presented at the Biennial conference of the Society for Research in Child Development, San Francisco, March 1979.

Hoffman, M. Developmental synthesis of affect and cognition and its implications for altruistic motivation. *Developmental Psychology,* 1975, *11,* 607–622.

Kohlberg, L. Stage and sequence: The cognitive–developmental approach to socialization. In D. A. Goslin (Ed.), *Handbook of socialization theory and research.* Chicago: Rand McNally, 1969.

Mischel, W. Toward a cognitive social learning theory reconceptualization of personality. *Psychological Review,* 1973, 252–283.

Moustakas, C. E. *Psychotherapy with children.* New York: Ballantine Books, 1959.

Piaget, J. *The origins of intelligence.* New York: Norton, 1952.

Piaget, J. *Six psychological studies.* New York: Random House, 1967.

Piaget, J., & Inhelder, B. *The growth of logical thinking.* New York: Basic Books, 1958.

Selman, R. The relation of role-taking ability to the development of moral judgment in children. *Child Development,* 1971, *42,* 79–91.

Selman, R. The development of social cognitive understanding: A guide to educational and clinical practice. In T. Lickona (Ed.), *Morality: Theory, research and social issues.* New York, Holt, Rinehart, & Winston, 1976.

Werner, H. *Comparative psychology of mental development.* New York: Science Editions, 1948.

7

Notes on the Cognitive–Developmental Approach to the Study of Social Cognition in Children

Herbert Zimiles
Bank Street College of Education

In reviewing Susan Harter's very interesting and evolving program of research, several issues arose. My first concern is a familiar one. How can one take seriously what adults, let alone children, say on request about their emotional lives? It is a realm that is too personal, too conflict laden, and too abstract for people, especially children, to deal with effectively when they are asked direct questions by anyone, especially a strange adult. I am not saying that no child is capable of giving very revealing and theoretically significant information in this sphere—but rather that I have doubts about the validity of an aggregate of data obtained by systematically questioning a sample of children along these lines. It is not without interest to learn how children respond to such tasks even if they are not answering the question fully or meaningfully. Data bearing on developmental changes in how children deal with their confusion or express their ignorance are sometimes quite revealing, but in such cases we need to recognize their responses for what they are.

When Susan Harter cited the initial problem that prompted her to begin the line of research she has described, I was surprised by the premise of the early work—the idea that children's ambivalence about expressing a particular emotion is related to their conceptual inability to think in terms of the possibility of harboring several emotions at once. We are accustomed to thinking that cognitive immaturity may play a role in the etiology of psychopathology. For example, cognitive immaturity may lead to a misperception of events—a misperception that brings about an exaggeration of the dangers associated with a particular situation—or it may produce a distorted view of the consequences associated with behaving in a particular way. But Susan Harter introduces a new idea when she suggests that, in some instances, children's emotional problems derive from an inhibition of response stemming from a failure to understand that it is logically appropriate to give the response in question.

I remain tied to a more dynamic explanation of such failures to make an adaptive response. It is fear of the consequences of particular response patterns rather than cognitively immature notions about their appropriateness that creates the problem. I believe that the difficulty that children were observed to have in acknowledging contradictory feelings had more to do with the fact that they regarded it as dangerous to have such feelings, and not that it was illogical or cognitively inappropriate for them to do so. The problem with the children was not how to master cognitively the concept of harboring love and hate at the same time, but how to allow themselves to express and feel forbidden emotions.

How children describe the way in which it is possible for them to have two different emotional reactions at the same time (i.e., whether they think of them as occurring simultaneously or in sequence) would seem to be an accident of the moment in dealing with a difficult abstract question. If there are age-related differences in the way in which children respond to the question, it is probable that they reflect differences in the resources children bring to dealing with a difficult question rather than differences in the way children actually conceptualize this realm. We need to know more about the reliability of such data and the impact of changes in the phrasing of the question before we begin to take seriously the idea that there are clear developmental differences in conceptual content. On the other hand, my guess is that children's ideas about their stable personality attributes, as opposed to their ways of experiencing emotion, are better grounded and may well be found to be related to particular developmental trends.

In one sense, Susan Harter's work can be viewed as extending the current work in metacognition to emotion. But I do not see where the path of metacognition research and now, in effect, metaemotion, is leading to. I am still waiting for the dividends from the current investment in metacognition to appear; they are not yet in sight. I lack the faith in children's degree of awareness, ability to communicate, and willingness to reveal the inner workings of their minds, especially when such information is specifically requested and asked for in abstract terms.

Susan Harter's cognitive–developmental treatment of her study creates the impression that we are dealing with another facet of conceptual development that can be fitted into a stage framework. The title makes it sound as though we are dealing with a close relative of multiplicative reasoning, as though we almost know where on the conceptual shelf we should catalogue these new phonomena. It almost seems like a formula—a formula that I, for one, am not interested in seeing followed.

I am not convinced that most cognitive phenomena fit neatly into a small number of differentiated categories that correspond in one way or another to the Piagetian stages—unless they are forced. The false image of order that we sometimes encounter in the research literature stems mainly from replication studies that use a single method of assessment. As soon as an investigator introduces alternative ways of assessing the same aspect of conceptual functioning, as soon as multiple measures are added, the results become less orderly. It is not unlike personality research, where the use of multiple measures of assessment identifies major conceptual and measurement problems which go unnoticed when a single assessment procedure is used.

In general, Piagetian research, together with the stage theory with which it is associated, has tended to exaggerate the discrete and compartmentalized quality of conceptual functioning. It seems more accurate to describe cognitive development as entailing a process of continuous differentiation interwoven with increasingly complex levels of integration, as Heinz Werner and numerous others have described it. At the same time, there are notable landmarks and changing patterns of acceleration of growth that are captured by stage theories. Stage theory seems useful for describing changes in the salience of particular criteria for defining concepts and ordering events. It misses the mark, however, when it leads us to making absolute pronouncements about how children can and cannot perform conceptually at different age levels. It seems more accurate to speak of the contextual factors that influence the availability of a particular concept at different ages than to speak in terms of its presence or absence.

As matters now stand, our ways of defining stages and describing patterns of increasing differentiation and integration are tied to but a handful of experimental paradigms. As we haggle over the time of onset or proper sequence of a particular set of behaviors, its research literature mounts and helps to divert us from the variety and complexity of cognitive development that need to be taken into account. The sheer volume of literature that accumulates in relation to a given attribute tends to exaggerate its importance. Additional distortion is introduced when we begin to reify the theoretical constructs used to explain the mass of findings. We have been drawn into an excessive concern with identifying conceptual atoms or elements instead of focusing on a developmental analysis of integrative functioning in children.

Susan Harter's work, as well as most of the other presentations at this conference, fit under the rubric of social cognition. As she has characterized the field, it deals with the general conceptual strategy and the cognitive skills that are involved in behavior in the socioaffective realm. However, instead of thinking of the phenomena of social cognition merely as still another sphere whose cognitive underpinnings and mediation need to be described and understood, it would seem more appropriate for them to be regarded as special—as occasions for evoking highly motivated cognition. When viewed from this perspective, the phenomena of social cognition are seen as pivotal in shaping the development of conceptual functioning.

The child's interaction with other people whom s/he regards as essential for his or her well-being activates profoundly important information processing and ordering. Especially in the young child, the need to understand and predict behavior may take on life-and-death proportions. The child is impelled to the cognitive mastery of social events. They become occasions for the formation of basic cognitive constructs—schemata of the permanent object, perceptual constancy, the principles of transitivity, conservation, classification and seriation, and others. The child's earliest perception—of the mother—becomes the basis for object permanence and constancy. At later ages, the child's relation to peers—the regularities in behavior of significant persons, the ability he or she develops to understand and predict their likes and dislikes, judgments, and preferences—are times when the child is especially motivated to learn. The need to control and predict one's social environment—to "figure out" behavior, defend, befriend, etc.—is a primary impetus to conceptual functioning. In the case of many people, most of their intellectual energy is invested in maintaining and/or manipulating social relationships.

In short, the significance to the cognitive psychologist of phenomena associated with interpersonal relations lies in the fact that they constitute an arena in which particular schema are learned, overlearned, and refined. Social cognition provides access to the origins of many aspects of conceptual functioning and helps to identify impediments to learning and sources of distortion. If we are interested in testing the limits of a child's conceptual functioning, it would be advisable to study a child's social-cognitive behavior.

Laboratory studies using emotionally neutral tasks may afford better control over the relevant variables, but they do not provide the setting and the circumstances that are most likely to evoke the child's most deliberate and practiced efforts to process information, order events, and deal with problems. If one believes that conceptual functioning can only be studied contextually, it would seem fundamental to include the interpersonal context among those conditions under which conceptual functioning is studied. For the sake of simplicity, experimental control, and convenience, the study of cognitive development has been largely confined to children's understanding of inanimate subject matter and emotionally neutral events. We have been slow to acknowledge that the child's cognitive mastery of the outer world entails tasks and problems of relating to other people. We have, for the most part, avoided dealing with the social nature of cognitive content because it tends to be more complex and more heavily overladen with subjective experience. On the other hand, it is precisely the social aspect of cognitive content that is likely to render it more salient and compelling.

At the same time, it should be mentioned that the social-emotional life of a child shapes other attributes that influence the effectiveness of cognitive functioning, although they are not part of what might be termed a child's cognitive apparatus. Such attributes as patterns of curiosity, attentiveness to detail, the tendency to ask questions, the tendency to seek and to expect to find solutions to problems, habits of attentiveness and orderliness, and the ability to persevere in working at a task, undergird cognitive functioning, but are themselves not part of the information-processing system. They may be thought of as the substratum of cognitive functioning, the behavior systems that mediate effective cognition. Because they have a decisive effect on cognitive competence, I have attempted to capture their ancillary function by naming them "cognitive dispositions" (Zimiles, 1972). All these dispositions have important affective components and are shaped by the child's social and emotional experience. It is in some ways meaningful to speak of a kind of cognitive personality, a configuration of cognitive strengths and weaknesses, skills, and styles that are acquired, in large measure, in the course of relating to significant others.

Susan Harter's work, and also the main theme of this volume, call attention to one of the most important but elusive issues in psychology—the nature of cognitive–affective interaction. However, I think that the way in which problems of social cognition are defined deals with the least interesting aspect of cognitive–affective interaction. I am more interested in how emotion gives direction to, fuels, and also inhibits and distorts the development of thought than in how conceptual functioning supports and mediates social-emotional behavior (see Zimiles, 1981).

My own efforts to probe aspects of this exceedingly difficult area have not produced very conclusive findings. I once tried to show that a person's spelling ability is associated with and determined by conflict over the demands of authority (Zimiles & Konstadt, 1962). In effect, I asked whether failure to learn to spell represented a disguised (and displaced) unwillingness to accept rules. We developed a scale purporting to measure resistance to authority's demands and examined its relation to spelling ability.

At another time, in the course of studying conservation of number, I decided to look at the relation between conservation ability and tolerance for delay of gratification using Mischel's experimental paradigm (Zimiles, 1967). Because a child's performance on a conservation task seemed to be governed by the ability to withstand the impact of an immediate stimulus, I wondered whether the child's ability to postpone gratification—to resist the appeal of an immediate reward in order to secure an even greater reward later on—represented a similar dynamic, and an important forerunner to conceptual functioning.

The ways in which emotion influences our appetite or aversion to a particular sphere of knowledge, as well as our styles of information processing and retaining, seem infinitely varied and complex, and no less interesting and important. Because we are tied to a tradition of experimental research, and the affective states of individuals are not amenable to experimental manipulation and, indeed, are frequently not even at the level of the subject's awareness, we have largely avoided studying such problems. For example, a basic distinction between levels of knowing and understanding that psychotherapists tend to regard as axiomatic has hardly been examined by cognitive psychologists. Clinicians distinguish between mere intellectual learning and understanding, and apprehending something viscerally and emotionally as though there were two different cognitive systems. They suggest that in order for a message to get through, it needs to be activated and transmitted emotionally. It seems important for cognitive psychologists to explore and amplify what clinicians mean by this distinction—one more way in which emotion and thought appear to be connected.

REFERENCES

Zimiles, H. *Cognitive functioning and tolerance for delay of gratification.* Paper read at the Society for Research in Child Development, New York, March 29–April 1, 1967.

Zimiles, H. An analysis of methodological barriers to cognitive assessment of preschool children. In F. J. Monks, W. W. Hartup, & J. de Wit (Eds.), *Determinants of behavioral development.* New York & London: Academic Press, 1972.

Zimiles, H. *Cognitive–Affective Interaction: A Concept that Exceeds the Researcher's Grasp.* In E. K. Shapiro & E. Weber (Eds.), *Cognitive and affective growth: Developmental interaction.* Hillsdale, N.J.: Lawrence Earlbaum Assoc., 1981.

Zimiles, H., & Konstadt, N. Orthography and authority: A study of cognitive-affective interaction. *Psychological Reports,* 1962, *10,* 623–626.

8 Piaget and the Self Constituted through Relations

James Youniss
Catholic University of America

On several occasions in the past 50 years, social scientists have been offered the opportunity to pursue a model of the human organism that holds promise for synthesizing the individual and social sides of existence. At least three of these occasions have directly involved developmental psychology (Macmurray, 1957, 1961; Piaget, 1932/1965; Sullivan, 1953). The general response of developmental theorists and researchers has been to ignore these opportunities. Throughout this period, developmentalists have clung to a model in which social existence and social functioning have been explained through the organism's individual character. Although that model has appeared in many variations, ranging from socialization to cognitive theories, the variations share in common the assumption that social concepts and behavior emanate from the intrapsychic composition of individuals in a means–end connection.

The general goal of this chapter is to discuss this state of affairs. The discussion begins with a debate in the late nineteenth century. The British biologist, T. H. Huxley, offered the first salvo by presenting an interpretation of Darwin's theory of evolution. Stressing the idea of survival through competition among individuals, Huxley then had to explain how society was possible. He fell back to a position of enlightened self-interest, following Hobbes, in which individuals competed not ruthlessly but within the confines of a social contract. The key to enlightened self-protection was governance, which for Huxley meant subjugation of the individual to authority.

Huxley's antagonist was P. Kropotkin, a Russian-born naturalist who spent his young adult life as a geologist in Siberia. In the latter years of the 19th century, Kropotkin was involved in numerous political experiments throughout Europe. They were attempts to establish communal polities that would be independent from existing national political structures. Known as an anarchist, Kropotkin was jailed by no less than six governments and eventually moved to England for asylum (Woodcock, 1962).

His debate with Huxley was printed in a book, *Mutual Aid* (1902), in which he offered a counterinterpretation of Darwin's work. Specifically, he said that a species' survival depended not on competition among individuals but on their cooperation. He culled from Darwin numerous examples and added to them his own observations of life from the harsh environment of Siberia as well as citations from societal history in Europe. His main point was that living organisms are interdependent by nature. To survive, they must afford one another mutual assistance. This basic fact of existence was part of the organism and, in itself, was a form of governance that insured societal cohesion.

The corollary argument was that government through external authority created interest groups and therefore induced competition. In instances of rule by the majority, the minority was expected to give up its viewpoint and to adopt the "common" will. Kropotkin's contrast was a common will rendered into a consensus through public discussion and dialogue. The result would be a synthesis of views arrived at with all sides being heard and contributing, with each side asserting a position and modifying it. In this manner, society's cohesion would be insured not by coercion or domination from a faction but through the principle of cooperation.

Individuality in Developmental Psychology

As was noted in the foregoing, Kropotkin's position was labeled *anarchism*. In the 20th century, this term has come to imply chaos in the absence of formal government. The underlying assumption to this meaning is that individuals left to themselves will each go in their own direction to enhance personal gain. It is almost unimaginable that society would endure without strong government that states and enforces laws to guide the behavior of individuals. The fact of competition would no doubt take over and the strong would eventually dominate the weak. Instability would ensue, with fluctuations in strength, formation of new coalitions, and changes in personal whims.

It is not hard to find the equivalent of this view in modern developmental psychology. With a loosening of terms and a switch in characters, one can see the model of individualism set forth rather clearly. The assumption that persons are self-contained entities, with their own interests as primary, is the basis of most psychological theories (Sampson, 1977). In developmental psychology, this premise is articulated in descriptions of infants and young children. Among other things, they are said to be "narcissistic," "idiosyncratic," "egocentric," and "impulsive." In general, they are known to be extremely poor candidates for social functioning because they appear to operate from purely interoceptive grounds. If they are nothing else, infants and young children are blatant individualists.

It follows that the need for governance that will harness individuality is essential. Were this need left unattended, the result would no doubt be anarchism and chaos. An image of this result is had in Golding's (1955) popular book, *Lord of the Flies*. Aware of the need, however, developmental theorists have turned directly to the study of means by which governance checks individualism and makes social life possible.

Although theorists differ as to the particular means, they agree on its general form. Children come to learn that there are interests besides their own. They learn that to get things done for themselves, they must make concessions to the reality of others. They learn, for example, that achievement of personal goals sometimes can be met better by giving in momentarily to another's interests than by demanding immediate satisfaction. If they do not learn these things, children are seen as "abnormal," "immature," "impulse ridden," or, in the extreme, "autistic." In each case, that sort of child would be understood to require special help if further development were to occur.

Of the many means suggested, the one most in favor by modern theorists is governance by the self mediated through the guidance of social elders. The general term for this mechanism is internalization, the idea being that adults first state rules to govern behavior, after which children ultimately adopt these rules for themselves. Initially these rules are known to society's members and exist outside the child. Adults act as agents for society by transmitting rules through selective reinforcement, modeling, love withdrawal, and direct instruction. What is at first external becomes internal when children use these rules to govern their behavior in situations where adults are not present. The result is individualism modified by social convention, or simply, a merging of outer with inner authority in the self.

Cognition and Development

The foregoing description is formally known through theories of socialization. Until the 1960s, socialization was the predominant position to which most theorists devoted their attention. Since then, a new version of the socially governed self has emerged. It received its impetus from the criticism that socialization theories unduly treated children as passive and noncreative creatures. The criticism became important when evidence became available that children did more than record reality that passed before them. For example, studies of language acquisition showed that children created grammars they had not heard, abstracted rules from sketchy samples of speech, and transformed sentences according to a structural system they had not been taught but apparently constructed from slim evidence.

The idea of the active cognizing child was quickly brought to bear on the study of social development. Skipping over the specific details, one can see in retrospect the general impact. Instead of having adults teach children about development, theorists said that children discovered what adults knew about society through their own cognitive activity. A key mechanism, which represents this general trend in theory, is found in the process of role taking. It assumes that when two people meet, each brings an individual viewpoint to the situation. Individuality refers to motives, emotions, thoughts, or general perspectives. With focus on one of these persons, either of two results is possible. The individual may either ignore the other person's perspective or try to understand it. The former implies a nonsocial result because the two persons remain individualistic or apart in perspectives, whereas the latter implies a truly social sharing in which the one's perspective is connected with the other.

The interesting point for developmental studies comes from the possibility that role taking evolves in a cognitive progression as a means for enabling social development. Again, theorists differ as to the specifics, but they agree upon the general picture. Essentially it is this. Younger children are individualistic in the sense that they hold to their own singular perspectives. They are egocentric rather than social. Gradually they learn that other persons may have perspectives different from their own and discover strategies by which they may take perspectives of others (Flavell, 1974; Shantz, 1975). The shift from an egocentric posture enables the same result as socialization mechanisms. Ideas that first existed outside the child in other persons are brought into the child's own, inner world. Once brought in, these ideas put checks on rank individuality. What then was originally individualistically personal becomes social.

Piaget As A Transitional Figure

In the 1960s when theorists were seeking to shift emphasis from socialization, directed by others, to inner-directed cognition, a general call was made upon Piaget's early writings. The apparent interest was in finding potential leads for the yet to be charted exploration. Cognition had been relatively ignored by socialization theorists, whereas Piaget had devoted several years to its study. Feffer (1970), Flavell, Botkin, Fry, Wright, & Jarvis (1968), and others, did much to show how Piaget's work might be usefully applied to the new task of bringing cognition into the study of social development.

One of the first constructs to receive attention was egocentrism. Most theorists already held to the proposition that children were asocial and the several descriptive terms then in use, such as *idiosyncratic*, were understood to be in need of explication. Egocentrism seemed to supply a quick solution because it referred to a natural condition within the child that impeded social functioning. Infants and young children were said to be egocentric in the sense of being able to take only a single perspective on events. For example, should they enter a situation with a particular motivation, this motive dominated their behavior and was attributed by the child to all other persons who happened to be in the same situation.

Egocentricism had other valuable characteristics. It was said to be developmental in nature. Being the original cognitive condition, it waned with age as children gained a wider variety of experiences. Gradually, it was said, egocentrism gave way to decentered thinking in which children learned to balance more than one view simultaneously. This sort of development was illustrated by perspective taking, in which children learned that their own viewpoint was only one of several possible and that these several viewpoints could be coordinated. This phenomenon was exemplified in spatial perspective taking (Piaget & Inhelder, 1956) and was well known in the literature.

Almost immediately, theorists pointed to an analogy with social development. Decentered perspective taking fit with the widely known phenomenon of role taking. The referent was to a process in which one person, the self, mentally took the role or psychological perspective of a second person, the other. Egocentric thinking, by definition, would be a deterrent because it limited children to a single view and biased it toward their own rather than someone else's view. But egocentrism eventually gave way to perspectival coordination and this was seen as the means that enabled children to take the role of others.

For at least a decade, researchers studied this general developmental shift. Hoffman (1970) and Shantz (1975) have summarized many of the major findings. Assuming these carefully written summaries to characterize findings fairly, one can see the overall results as somewhat disappointing. That is, the analogy remained just that, with the constructs never having gained the sort of clarity one would desire. It is no wonder, then, that theorists began to parse the role taking process into simpler units of information gathering and testing. For instance, Flavell (1974) suggested that role taking might be more gainfully studied as a hypothesis-testing, inference-making problem (see also Shantz, 1975). Here was a child, the self, and some other person. The question was: How could the self know what the other was thinking or feeling? Which skills would the self have to employ to make a valid inference? When and how did these skills develop?

It is now evident in retrospect that Piaget's writings served a transitional function for the field. Originally, the search was for a general outline of cognition that had developmental prospects. Next, promising constructs were explored but research failed to yield the degree of clarity theorists needed. Piaget's theory was tried, but found wanting. The field turned to other theories of cognition with quite different constructs from those found in Piaget's writings.

Piaget's 1932 Study of Morality

One of the works most frequently cited when Piaget was brought into the picture was his 1932 study of moral development (Piaget, 1932/1965). This book contained descriptions of egocentrism and perspective taking and it is easy to see why theorists picked these constructs for their new exploration. However, this book also contained several other ideas and gave a more complex interpretation of these constructs than the initial commentators suggested (Youniss, 1979). For example, Piaget described two types of egocentrism. One was the sort of natural state, or limiting condition, to be found in very young infants. This was the egocentrism transferred to the 1960 theories of social cognition. The second, rarely mentioned in these theories, was an egocentrism that resulted from children's efforts to take other persons' perspectives (Piaget, 1932/1965, p. 36).

It might also be noted in passing that perspective taking is addressed in several sections throughout the 1932 study. In almost every instance Piaget describes the process through a failure on parents' parts to understand children's perspectives (see Youniss, 1979). These examples are the reverse of what one would expect were perspective taking a developmental phenomenon, because the failure would not be from adults but from young children. For comparison, the lead example in Piaget's (1962) clarification of egocentrism also refers to a failure in adults, specifically a college instructor lecturing to students.

These examples are worth pursuing. Consider first the sort of egocentrism that results from certain relations. Piaget is clear on the matter. This egocentrism results when an authority figure, an adult, asserts a rule that children are to follow. The rule emanates from the adult's knowledge of society and the implications the adult sees for the child's adherence to it. Piaget asks whether the child can understand the adult's perspective. For example, can the child know that if he or she lies, other persons will find him or her unreliable and therefore not trust or like him or her? The answer is, probably not. But neither can the adult pare away the adult's perspective to get to the child's.

Piaget continues by arguing that in relations with adults, even very young children know that adults understand society and have rules of how it ought to function. They also know that adults want children to share in these rules and will offer approval when children follow them. Therefore, children try to get into the perspective of adults, if only because they derive benefits from doing so. Egocentrism then is not due to ignorance that others have different views. It is not cause in the sense that children are cognitively limited. It results when children attempt to understand adults, try to formulate reasons they think adults hold, but end up with their own versions of what adults know.

This egocentrism is the best children can do. It is the best because the rules that children are asked to take are already constructed in the minds of adults and are communicated unilaterally. They are given out as accomplished ideas that children have had little hand in making. Children are then asked after the fact to construct the same ideas, to move toward and adopt the position that adults already possess and have constructed from quite different experiences.

The 1932 study contains several other ideas that are not evident in contemporary commentaries. Egocentrism, as effect rather than cause, is actually only the surface of a much deeper set of conceptions. For example, Piaget also contends that there are two major interpersonal relations in children's lives, relations with adults and relations with peers. Each relation serves different functions in promoting development. And, of the two, relations with peers are the more central to social maturity and morality in later life. Even more important is Piaget's assumption that social life begins during the child's first year of existence when the child discovers that he or she exists in relations with other persons. From that time on, development proceeds within the confines of relations, and the growth of the individual, or self, is a continuing reconstitution of the self *through* relations (Youniss, 1980).

Piaget's Epistemology

Piaget's professional career has been devoted to exploring the possibilities of a psychological theory of relativity (Furth, 1969). In this approach neither the subject, who knows, nor the object, which is known, have absolute status. Each is conditioned on the other within a continually changing framework. Change occurs through interchanges of actions and reactions. Actions of the subject are like probes equivalent to statements by which the subject says: "I think you, the object, are such and such." When acted upon, objects act back, revealing who and what they are.

Piaget's contribution to the study of knowledge has been to escape the philosophic traps of subjectivity and objectivity. The former makes knowledge a self-satisfying concoction where, for the sake of consistency, the subject creates concepts of objects and reality. This position tends toward error through failure to come to grips with the facts of reality. It puts the subject in control of deciding what reality is and, in the extreme, allows distortion for the sake of maintaining the subject's version of how things ought to be. Objectivity errs at the other end and, in its extreme, denies self-initiated definition, making the subject only a valid recorder of reality. Distortion can occur either through exposure to odd circumstances or through breakdowns in the subject's recording devices. The position of relativity seeks solution to both problems. Its clearest expression is found when both subject and object are given defining powers in their interactions. There is double agency, with the object telling what it is just as forcibly as the subject reveals itself through its actions.

With interactions as the basic reality, the context of knowledge is dynamic. It is also the means to knowledge insofar as subject and object are able to extract orderly relations from their interactions. These relations among actions and reactions color definitions of both agents. They are the medium for knowing and provide the terms by which subject and object attain their forms. This is why, for example, Piaget argues that space, number, and the like, remain open to redefinition throughout development. Numbers are not things to be grasped but are products from relations abstracted from subject–object interactions (Beth & Piaget, 1966). True relations become expressed through numbering operations, which coordinate actions of the subject as well as reactions of objects.

Knowledge of Relations

It appears that Piaget's approach is unique among contemporary psychological theories by its treatment of relations as the topic of knowledge. Relations are primary, with subject and object being their products. For other theorists, these terms are reversed; subject and object are posited and relations come secondarily. In Piaget's scheme, neither subject nor object ever get to know one another with certainty. Together they can work only toward relations that are reliable. Validity is always a relative matter, depending on current relations, which remain open to further redefinition (Inhelder, Sinclair, & Bovet, 1974).

This point no doubt has stymied most attempts to bring Piaget's work into the mainstream of psychological theories. It is like the essential key without which notes may sound similar but actually render a different song. The stumbling block is evident, for example, in the many ways phenomena originally generated by Piaget's position have undergone alteration when considered from the view of more familiar theories. Conservation provides the most telling illustration. Few, if any, of these alternative explanations deal with or care to deal with the phenomenon as a conservation of a subject–object relation. The more common explanation states that number or amount is conceived as constant through physical changes in the object. Within Piaget's framework, the physical changes are said to remain constant; they are understood as but two versions of a single relation. The relation is between number- or amount-making actions, with their products made ostensible in the reactions of cubes, chips, or clay.

There is a tendency among contemporary theorists to credit Piaget with having shown that children are cognitively active and control rather than being controlled by external objects or other persons. This emphasis has clouded the fact that objects and persons are not benign, simply waiting for children to transform them into this or that conception. In order to put relations in clear relief, it is helpful to give these things their proper due in knowledge. It helps even to anthropomorphize their role. Objects are as active as children. They move, change shape, enlarge in size, fall off tables, roll, and otherwise respond when they are contacted. Each reaction is reciprocal to something children do. In the case of conservation, to use an example often cited by Piaget, the child who plays with pebbles in his or her back yard may come to understand number-making operations because the stones react as they do to his or her manipulations. That which remains constant in making a row, then a circle, then a tower, and next two columns is only the relation among these actions from the child and the several reactions of the pebbles.

Social Relations in Piaget's Theory

It is now possible to outline the meaning of relations in the social domain where knowledge is based on interactions between the child and other persons. The questions are: What precisely is knowledge of social relations and how does it arise? The following sketch highlights the general points of the theory.

(a) Children enter the world as actors, seeking order and regularity. This search describes their inherent motivation for knowledge. (b) Children look for order first in their own actions by attempting to find that which is repeatable and reliable in execution of actions. (c) Insofar as actions make contact with other things, or persons, effects of actions are not solely under the control of the child. These things react in reciprocity to the actions exerted upon them and together the action and reaction produce effects that differ from those that would result from either alone. (d) This fact of double agency naturally widens children's focus from action to interaction. Because other agents act in reciprocity to children's actions, children are forced to seek explanations for change and order in the interplay between actors.

The foregoing points can be summarized as follows. Suppose the child intends that an action have a particular outcome or effect. The child then executes the act in accordance with this intention. Suppose also that the act engages another person who adds to the original act with a reaction. The coupling of these actions may have an effect that is different from the child's intention or anticipation in performing the original act. It would be futile to seek order either in the child's or the other person's parts, alone. This is why for Piaget, the child is led to seek a solution in the coupling and arrives at the conclusion that the actions of persons are reciprocally related. This is also why Piaget (1932/1965, 1970) contends that naive egocentrism ends most probably during the child's first year. To maintain an egocentric posture, a child would have to deny the facts of reciprocity made evident through the thousands of interactions experienced in everyday dealings with other persons.

(e) Thereafter, the child's search for order turns to identifying the forms of reciprocal relations that occur in interpersonal interactions. (f) Piaget suggests that there are two such forms. One is a direct and symmetrical reciprocity where one's action is free to match or counter the other's action. The second is a reciprocity of complement where one's action must conform to the dictates set down by the other's action. (g) These two forms describe the basic relations in which people order themselves as actors with respect to other persons, who are also actors. They provide the epistemic unit from which self and other achieve definition. (h) For Piaget, development proceeds as these relations are structured and restructured. They give rise to social and moral conceptions that pertain to the self, other persons, possible relations among persons, and principles of societal functioning, both practical as well as ideal.

The Implications of Piaget's Epistemology

Piaget (1932/1965) has spelled out the consequences of pursuing this general epistemology:

(1) The child is considered to be social from very early in life. The child's knowledge of his or her own actions is not the product of private reflection so much as a construction of order obtained from interactions. This means that the child's knowledge is socialized because the self's actions are understood as reciprocal to the actions of others. Mental abstractions on the child's part are

influenced by and contingent on contributions from other persons. Piaget is clear about this conclusion and sees in it a departure from the more typical view that children's thought is engendered privately. Social cognition does not imply the knowledge of "persons" but knowledge gained through social collaboration with other persons. Its object may be persons but that alone does not make it social.

(2) Different forms of reciprocity give rise to distinct relations and these relations, in turn, are the means to differentiated definitions of self and other. In the context of symmetrical reciprocity, self and other are equals as actors who are free to contribute to interactions with like acts. The two may exchange actions on a one-for-one or tit-for-tat basis. In complementary reciprocity, agency is asymmetrical. One person's actions are determining of the other's. One is in charge and the other is in the position of having to follow suit. The two are not equals.

(3) Piaget suggests that these relations lead to distinct conceptions of social reality. Relations of complementariness foster a view of a society already ordered. Persons in charge of interactions know what this order is; they are authorities and have the right to be teachers. Students, on the other side of this relation, are to learn the order and have to work through their teachers to discover it. Their main task is to conform to the authority who knows order. Practically, the relation works through a system in which authorities assert rules of order, students conform to the rules, and authorities offer approval and rewards in return. The familiar referent for this system is heteronomous morality.

A different conception of society is evolved from relations based on symmetrical reciprocity. Here, two persons have equal roles to play in determining order. One person's rules are as correct as the other person's. Insofar as the two may disagree, they must combine their respective authority and seek order through cooperative effort. Practically the interactive system works through the sharing of ideas, comparison, debate, and discussion. With authority and control shared by both persons, the order of society is viewed as an open matter to be determined continuously by consensus gained through cooperation.

(4) Piaget argues that complementary relations serve children in their development during that period when they are unsure of the workings of society and satisfied with the exchange of approval for conformity. It is appropriate, for example, for young children in their relation to their caretaking parents or teachers. At some point in development, however, children experience cooperative relations and discover their ability to construct order with others. At the moment, the discovery may lead to uncertainty but this risk is countered by the new assurance, which is founded on consensus. For Piaget, this side of reality opens up to children through their relations with peers.

(5) Of the two relations, Piaget sees the latter as coming to serve children in their progress toward more mature views of society. He argues, for instance, that peer relations are continuous with adult moral conceptions and replace the limiting conditions of heteronomous relations. He makes this argument in a series of

contrasts. Relations with adults tend to mystify, whereas peer relations engender mutual understanding. Relations with adults tend to keep persons apart whereas peer relations engender social solidarity. Relations with adults tend to make respect a matter of adhering to external criteria whereas relations with peers allow respect to be mutual in the establishment of consensus criteria. In sum, the seeds of a morality based on justice are planted in relations with peers and bear fruit through the interactive process of cooperation, which is, in itself, open to further development.

Ideological Considerations

With little effort one can see reasons why Piaget's position has not been pursued as a whole. In the first place, it conflicts with the normative assumption that persons are independent entities whose social functioning depends on matching or mismatching intrapsychic compositions. For Piaget, the composition of self is social in its establishment. The self constructs and is constructed through relations with others. Sociality is the starting point and individuation is a later product, which comes from membership that has been experienced in relations. Thus, the idea that social interactions involve a problematic encounter between two selves, each trying to penetrate the other's private state of mind, simply does not fit the Piagetian epistemology (Sampson, 1977; Youniss, 1977, 1978a, 1978b).

Secondly, it is obvious that Piaget's attribution of positive social development to peer relations conflicts with a strong cultural bias. The bias can be parsed into two propositions: (1) adults in general and parents in particular are thought to be the necessary agents for transmitting societally preserving rules to the next generation. Piaget appears to minimize this function of adults, restricting it to early childhood and short-term impact; (2) when adults hold the script to society's preservation, peers have only two alternatives in their function. Either they can support adult-based instruction, in the sense of reinforcement, or they can undermine this instruction by encouraging one another to take deviant paths in thinking. Piaget, in contrast, tries to show how peers add positive dimensions to children's social development, and he seems to argue that elements such as mutual understanding and social solidarity are unlikely products of children's relations with adults.

These are ideological matters of some weight and can be shown to have little to do with Piaget's theory per se or evidence on its behalf. Rather, the position it represents does not mesh with prevailing assumptions in social science and, for this reason, the theory has been relatively ignored. Support for this speculation comes from the general avoidance of other theories that express the same viewpoints.

Sullivan (1953) has argued as forcefully as Piaget that the course of social development is not the piece-by-piece composition of the individual but ontogenetic history of interpersonal relations (p. 30). He also holds that children's relations with parents are restricted in outcome, whereas relations with peers, especially friends, contain the immediate origins of the psychiatrically adjusted self (p. 245). The benefits of friendship are, as Piaget sees them also, the results of symmetrical reciprocity and cooperation. These are the means for judging one's own worth by the standards used to judge another's, cooperation being the process by which mutually applicable standards are achieved through consensus (p. 246).

Another, but slightly different case, is found in the work of Macmurray (1961). He has traced the philosophic history of relational theory through the battle between the subjectivists and objectivists (Macmurray, 1957). He has spelled out the solution for a self constituted in interpersonal relationship. And, like Sullivan and Piaget, he attributed social maturity and advance morality to relations based on symmetrical reciprocity. The status of Macmurray's work testifies to its ideological eccentricity. There has been hardly any reference to it by developmental theorists, even those who study morality and its connections with sociality.

Sampson (1977) has already commented on the disparity between relational theory and theories built upon the inviolate individual self. It may be useful here to point to the comparable disparity regarding peers. Lasch (1977) and Bronfenbrenner (1970) may be regarded as spokemen for the prevailing position. They reiterate that adults know the mechanisms for achieving social cohesion. Adults have the responsibility to pass them on to children. Were they not to do so, society would be a mere conglomeration of individuals, each seeking personal gain. Lasch and Bronfenbrenner see in modern society a breaking down of transmission mechanisms as families dissemble and institutions divide persons into isolated groups of age-mate associations.

The specter in this societal analysis rears in the form of peer relations. The rationale is that peers will encourage each other to act out impulses in the pursuit of immediate gratification. The question is who will teach children to be sensitive toward others and to respect others' rights. The prospect is Golding's primitive rule by strength, which is nothing but chaos among self-willed individuals. Should one think this depiction to be hyperbole, it is noted that the same view is expressed by the National Panel on Social Policy for Children (1976), which, it might be added, suggests that children who show strong loyalty to peers rather than adults, tend to be poorly adjusted, to lack achievement motives, and are candidates for neurotic symptoms.

Importantly, Piaget and Sullivan view the prospects almost in reverse. The need for interpersonal sensitivity is engendered by friendship. Mutual respect is a natural product of symmetrical reciprocity. The experience of maintaining a friendship over time is the grounds for opening oneself honestly to assets and defects and learning to live with them realistically in oneself and others about whom one cares. Friendship and not relations with adults is the basis for these achievements and the grounds for social cohesion, first interpersonally and later on a societal scale (Youniss, 1980).

Reciprocity's Development

In one form or another, the Piaget–Sullivan–Macmurray viewpoint has been around for several centuries in Western thought. It has sometimes been called romantic idealism in honor of Rousseau and discarded as an unfounded paean to the goodness of childhood. Were this in fact the case, there would be little value in the position for developmental psychology. What distinguishes this position from its idealistic forerunners is the predication of relations on forms of reciprocity, which ties relations to the empirical facts of interaction. Moreover, the stated consequences of relations become, not assertions about children or adults, but logical outcomes of reciprocity. The detailed argument of this position has already been given in Youniss (1980). For the present, a summary is offered to highlight the main points.

Symmetrical Reciprocity.   There is nothing good nor bad in symmetrical reciprocity. It refers only to a form of exchange with two characteristics. First, one actor's initiatives are contingent on another's reactions and vice versa. Second, in this contingency, one person is free to contribute to interactions with acts just like those with which the other has or will contribute next (Hinde, 1976). It follows that two persons in such a relation may act on a one-for-one basis. When, for instance, one child gives another candy, the recipient is then free to return the gift by offering something he or she possesses in return. The likely result of such an exchange is a drawing together of the two participants in continuing positive exchanges.

But it also follows that when one child offends another, for example, by hitting or insulting him or her verbally, the recipient is free to return the offense in kind. The likely consequence of exchanges of offense–retaliation is a pushing apart of the parties. The freedom and right to retaliate simply passes back and forth between them and it is difficult to imagine that the resulting series of negative exchanges would induce social cohesion.

Consider a third case when one child expresses an opinion about some event or person: for instance, rules for a game or who should be captain. According to symmetrical reciprocity, the other child is free to express his or her opinion. The first may again express his or her opinion and the second his or hers, and so on. The likely result is neither positive nor negative but a stalemate. An impasse is reached because neither party has the unilateral right to impose an opinion to which the other must adhere. Were one to try to do so, the other would be free to do the same.

All three results are likely outcomes of symmetrical reciprocity: positive, negative, and stalemate. For this reason, it must be argued that symmetrical reciprocity in itself does not make for social cohesion. If solidarity, mutual respect, and the like, arise from peer relations, they cannot be the outcomes of reciprocity per se. According to Piaget and Sullivan, these products actually come from cooperation so the question must be: How does cooperation stem from symmetrical reciprocity?

Data obtained in our previous research (Youniss, 1980) provide an answer. Children of about 6 to 8 years, the youngest age level we studied, understood all three uses of reciprocity. They described positive and negative exchanges as well as the reaching of stalemate in their descriptions of interactions between peers or friends. For example, when asked to describe how two peers might become friends, children said that the parties might play together, share material possessions, or exchange visits to one another's homes. When asked to describe how two friends might come not to like each other any more, children said that they might insult one another, fight, or otherwise exchange negative actions.

From these and other data, a conclusion was reached that peer relations for children near the beginning school age are ephemeral. These relations come into and go out of existence as interactions change from positive to negative exchanges. For example, a friendship exists when positive symmetrical reciprocity is being practiced. It changes to a nonfriendship when negative exchanges occur. Children of this age seem to lack a concept of an enduring bond that is constituted by a principle and tolerates different types of exchanges that can be transformed for the sake of preserving the relation. For instance, several children said that after fighting, friends would meet the next day and "Just play." When asked if someone had to make up or do something special, they said, "No," "Just forget about it," or "Be nice to each other."

Cooperative Reciprocity.   Children could live in the world described in the foregoing and in fact appear to do so. But it is not an interpersonally reliable world nor one in which outcomes are efficiently worked toward. While symmetrical reciprocity is a rule, either peer is free also not to reciprocate and, of course, stalemate is a likely occurence. For a lead as to what a more reliable world might be, results from older children, roughtly ages 9 to 14 years, are now considered.

To give the conclusion first, these subjects construct a reliable scheme by converting the literal practice of reciprocity into a principle that guides interactions with selected peers who cooperate in this principle. These selected persons are friends who are distinguished from peers in general by their voluntary agreement to participate in the new practice. This shift is central to the theory as it differentiates assertions about the "natural" cooperativeness of children from the position that cooperation is an option and must be earned.

Evidence comes from diverse studies that concurrently point to the same transition. One example was obtained from accounts of interactions of unkindness. Younger children had invariably described unkindness through aggressive

and harmful acts committed by one peer against another. Older children sometimes did the same but more frequently they described unkindness through acts of
omission. A typical account began with one friend being described with a definite need; for instance, ''My friend was not doing well in math and was trying to
study for a test.'' Given the need, unkindness ensued when the other friend failed
to help; for example, ''He asked me to study with him but I said I was too busy.''

How can an act of omission be construed as unkind? Given the typical classroom familiar to children of this age, there must be at any time several needs
distributed among students. No one child could possibly attend to all of them. It
is doubtful that children think of themselves as living in a constant condition of
unkindness. On the other hand, acts of omission would be unkind if there were
an obligation to assist. From children's descriptions, this obligation appears
evident with respect to friends who selectively agree to help whenever one or the
other expresses a need.

A second line of evidence pointed to the shift from literal reciprocity by a
lifting of two restrictions. In literal reciprocity, younger children exchanged like
acts in immediate time sequence. In older children's descriptions of friendship
both limitations were lifted. First, quite often the exchange was between acts that
only the friends knew were equivalent. For example, the smarter friend could
help with homework assignments, whereas the more socially sophisticated friend
could help the good student get along better with classmates. In the second place,
the obligation to reciprocate applied generally forward in time over the anticipated course of the friendship. When asked what they would do after a friend had
helped them in some way, older children said they would reciprocate when and if
the appropriate occasion arose at some later date.

A third line of evidence appeared in statements of principle, which applied to
questions about conflict and conflict resolution within friendship. Among other
things, conflicts themselves were described as violations of principle, for instance, exclusion of a friend from participation in some activity. Further, several
children said the way to resolve conflict was to articulate the principle that was
violated and to promise to adhere to it in the future. Many of these statements
stressed the theme that friends were to treat each other as deserving of equal
respect.

A fourth piece of evidence occurred in most of the studies through a recognition that friends were, in fact, distinct individuals with different needs, talents,
emotions, assets, and deficits. Responses to these differences were typically
overt signs of the merging of strengths with weaknesses. Although younger
children appeared to believe in literal equality, older children acknowledged that
friends were not necessarily equals. They were, however, deserving of *equal
treatment*. For example, children admitted that a friend in a weakened emotional
state, such as anger or depression, could not be made psychologically whole all
at once. Appropriate responses indicating the right to equal treatment included
''sympathy,'' ''empathy,'' ''just listening,'' or ''being with them.''

Procedures of Cooperation.   Cooperation is a general construct that requires fleshing out if it is to be more than an assumed characteristic of children's relations. Fortunately, in their descriptions of ways to make and keep friendships or in correcting the relation gone awry, older children offered a long list of procedures by which friends put the principle of cooperation into practice. These included: discussion about disagreements, the joint making of plans, conceding to the logic of another's argument, seeking and offering advice, self-revealment for purposes of comparison, keeping trust, taking turns, willingness to submit opinion to debate, and taking responsibility for one another's actions.

These and other procedures exemplify the means by which the principle to cooperate in reciprocity is brought to life in friendship. They represent a sharp break from younger children's naive and literal practices, which seem to be ad hoc and lacking in future orientation as well as mutual interest. Older children, in distinction, seem to have identified common interest with personal goals, so much so that the outcomes of procedures can hardly be distinguished as benefits to the relation or to the individuals. They are almost one and the same. Most notably, the individuals in these procedures could at any moment be imagined as going in private directions and being better off as a result. But they did not. Instead they stayed within difficult situations to assist one another, with the consequence being only enhancement of solidarity in their relation.

Summary.   The foregoing data may be taken to represent a development course covering the period from beginning school age through early adolescence. At its start, young children practice symmetrical reciprocity concretely with immediate exchange of like acts between peers. The very practice yields uncertainty through its production of positive and negative results as well as impasse. After about 9 years of age, peer relations take a new turn. Symmetrical reciprocity is converted to a principle of cooperative usage, selectively and mutually agreed upon by friends. The task that then lies ahead is formidable because friends must devise interactive procedures whereby the principle is enacted (Youniss, 1980; Youniss & Volpe, 1978).

The Products of Reciprocity

The developmental course of relations based on symmetrical reciprocity helps to allay the tinge of idealism that might be brought into a discussion of peer relations. Cooperation may rightfully be seen as the solution to a realistic problem. Symmetrical reciprocity does not inherently engender positive social relationship. The principle of cooperative usage is achieved through a struggle and, once glimpsed, needs to be worked out through specific procedures. A similar argument is now made concerning the products of reciprocity that have been postulated by Piaget, Sullivan, and others.

As postulated, the characteristics of peer relations may appear to be exaggerations of the "good impulse" nature grants to childhood. Seen within the present context, these characteristics become logical outcomes that follow from the procedures in which cooperation is embodied. Consider the characteristic of *mutual understanding*. Piaget defines it as the other's understanding of the self in the same terms by which self understands self. How might this arise from friendship?

Recall that in symmetrical reciprocity, one party is free to act like the other in contributing to interactions. In children's accounts of friendship, this idea was represented by expressions of ideas or opinions. First one friend set forth an opinion, then the other friend offered an opinion about something. According to principle of equal treatment, diverse opinions indicate freedom of expression. The same principle, however, adds a demand that each opinion be listened to and not simply be negated by one's own idea. The dual requirement of presentation and listening provides the prerequisite base for mutual understanding between persons.

It is worth noting here that a contrasting case occurred in children's accounts of interactions with parents. They described a unilateral process in which parents were allowed to state opinions and children were allowed to listen. The reverse was less true. Although children said that they expressed opinions different from their parents', they acknowledged that parents often viewed this as "talking back," which was defined as a violation and source of conflict. They also said that parents would, upon hearing an opinion different from their own, explain or otherwise convince children to adopt the parents' position.

The most convincing evidence for mutual understanding was obtained in children's accounts of best friends. Among other things, children said that friends reveal themselves to each other, an obvious but essential step toward being understood. Moreover, children said that friends talked out these revealments, compared private feelings, and decided together how to act with them. Lastly, children, in particular the young adolescents, believed that their friends understood them better than their parents, teachers, or siblings.

Mutual respect is another characteristic that can be documented as a product of procedures used in friendship. When reading Piaget, one may be struck by his continual reference to respect "for procedure," almost as if it were impersonal. The potential obtuseness of these remarks can be cut through by the realization that cooperation must be jointly constructed and is not a given. Friends must evolve those procedures that make cooperation workable. They then become the means for keeping the friendship alive.

A quick review of these procedures shows how respect may emanate from them. Each requires the participation of both friends. In making them work, either friend can do only so much. That friend makes his or her contribution, for example, by stating a current emotional problem, and then must wait for the other friends to carry the procedure further. Because the next step cannot be coerced, the other friend who enacts his or her part is voluntarily picking up where the first left off. The other is, in fact, submitting the self to the procedure rather than going off in a personal direction, which, of course, he or she is free to do. In this sense, respect for the procedures, which have been jointly constructed, is an attestation to respect for the person who initiates that procedure. Simultaneously, it implies respect for self as a mutual adherent.

Comparable arguments can be made on behalf of characteristics such as solidarity, intimacy, standards of worth, and the like. In each case, the same general point is made that characteristics attributed to children's relations of friendship can be understood to follow from procedures of interaction. They are derivatives that must be constructed in the same way that procedures are results of a joint enterprise.

Maintaining Friendship

The last link in removing idealism from the Piagetian position is found in children's accounts of actual interactions in friendship. Again the evidence comes from concurrent findings across studies. Children's understanding of relations of friendship was found to be clear in principle as well as realistic in practice. As shown previously, children articulated the procedures of cooperation and the guiding rule of equal treatment. At the same time, however, they also admitted that friends do not always act as they should or could. Indeed, they admitted that the task of maintaining friendship over time required tolerance of failures to live up to expectations.

One piece of evidence concerned the ease with which children were able to generate instances of conflict between friends. Many of these instances involved violations of principle. Several of these violations were of the sort that one of the friends put self-interest over some mutual benefit. This occurred most frequently when the friends were known to be in differential conditions. Instead of acting to reduce the disparity, the friend who was better off ignored the plight of the friend in trouble.

This set of results must be seen in conjunction with another set. It is one thing to admit conflict, but quite another matter to know what to do about it. To summarize, older children understood that violations of friendship were acts that could be corrected. They spelled out specific means by which rifts in relations could be repaired. Additionally, they argued that violations were to be expected, did not necessarily lead to the relation's termination, and required work on both persons' parts to be reestablishing of the relation.

Another piece of evidence came from descriptions of types of friendship and the peculiar dynamics that apply to each. Perhaps the most interesting case appeared when friends were not and knew that they were not equals in important respects. For example, one friend might be popular whereas the other was shy and had few social opportunities. Conflicts that occurred in this context were peculiarly resolved. It made little difference which of the two friends was responsible for an offense. In either case of cause, the friend in the one-down position had to take the initiative in bringing about repair. Children seemed to reason that the one-up friend did not need the other friend, whereas the one-down friend would suffer from the loss of relation. The burden of repair was therefore more imminently feared by the latter, whose anxiety would lead to ameliorating action.

Implied in these data is a sort of dialectic between realistic happenings in and knowledge of the possibilities within friendship. The principles upon which friendship is based would, if lived out, lead to social union where interactions work for mutual benefit. Factually, children do not consistently live up to principle. The dilemma is handled by a conception of friendship as an enduring relation that may have high and low points, moments of distance and intimacy, and yield pleasure as well as pain. The solution is not to eliminate the negative side; such a goal would be artificial and unrealistic. The solution is, instead, to work out procedures that can enhance the positive moments and transform momentary breaks in relation through remediating actions.

From these and other results (Youniss, 1980), it may be seen that friendship contains the elements for two sides of social existence. One side is the possibility of union where the friends work with and for one another. The other side is the loss of union that follows when one friend pursues personal gain at the expense of and disregard for the relationship. It seems appropriate to conclude this section of the discussion with a flat denial that childhood or reciprocity are in themselves conditions for social unity. Rather, they lead to an understanding of social cohesion, are the context for generating procedures to achieve it, and expose children to the fruits of mutual existence, which depend upon cooperating equals.

Reciprocity of Complement

The dominant themes in developmental theories regarding parents' relations with children have had constant and variables parts. One constant part has been that parents serve as the link between society and children. Another constancy has been that parental influences, made in early childhood, are long lasting. For example, they have been suggested as the source of personality characteristics in the mature organism. The major variable parts concern mechanisms by which parents influence children. For several decades, the literature has been lively with argument about such mechanisms as reinforcement or modeling and about differential effects of child-rearing styles. With regard to the latter, much research has been designed to determine how personality characteristics are fostered through such techniques as punishment or induction.

These themes may be seen as representative of a major ideology. In our society, parents are authority figures who pass on society's wisdom to their offspring. At the same time, authority itself may be divided into two camps. For some, authority represents a condition to be avoided as it might demand blind obedience and stymie change. It might be said that promotion of enlightened techniques of rearing emanate from this position, as encouragement is given to parents to teach in a democratic fashion rather than by means of harsh pronouncement. For others, authority is an essential condition for self-discipline. Adults provide the means for control, which might not otherwise be discovered by children without external intervention.

It is not easy to weave Piaget's epistemology into this mixture. First of all, the position accepts parental authority as a given; in this regard it minimizes the hypothesized effects of enlightened rearing techniques. Secondly, the position considers parental authority to play essential roles in young children's socialization. But it does not hold that the content transmitted during early childhood accounts for personality in later adulthood. And third, the position holds that much of what may be learned during childhood is modified or transformed subsequently through new learning that occurs within relations of cooperation.

The key to this position is found in the argument that parent–child relations are developmental in nature. This removes the fixedness often associated with discussions of the topic. There is not *a* parent–child relation but a sequential development in which the relation is reconstructed into new forms by children and by parents. This development occurs while there is simultaneous development in peer relations. At present there is no way to tell how these two courses interact and affect one another. Piaget suggests that friendship influences parental relations and some of our findings support this idea, in particular for early adolescence (Youniss, 1980). For the present, however, the central question concerns the proposition that parent–child relations may be conceived as following a developmental course from infancy through early adolescence.

Structure.   Piaget describes the structure of parent–child relations, roughly for the period of 3 to 11 years, with the term *unilateral constraint*. The referent is to an exchange system in which parents propose courses of action, children conform to them, and, in return, parents offer signs of approval and acceptance. The system is equally expressed through the exchange of disobedience, or nonconformity for disapproval, or punishment. Either type of exchange emphasizes that children's parts in interactions are built around and complementary to adults' parts. This is to ackknowledge that parents hold directive rights and have the final say in judging children's behavior.

Before one rejects this view out of hand, the fuller argument ought to be heard. The context for this relation is both personal and cultural. Personally, parents are knowledgeable adults who have experience with society. Additionally, they can be assumed to have positive intentions toward children, being concerned with their immediate and longer-term welfare. Culturally, this intentional attitude is reinforced by our society in the idea that parents are responsible for the well-being of their offspring. These contextual factors clearly place parents in the position of authority.

Infants, of course, have no idea of this perception. For practical purposes, they may be considered as independent agents whose actions may have only self-reference. However, at some time early in development, the picture changes at the instigation of parents. With the children's welfare in mind, parents begin to set up the exchange system that seems to persist at least through childhood. It starts when parents apply contingencies to children's actions through acceptance of some actions and rejection of others. Here, Piaget does not refer to specific content so much as to the structure of interactions that may be abstracted from social episodes. The content may pertain to habits of nutrition or sanitation, rules of social etiquette, and moral prescriptions. What is important is that parents believe that there are better ways of acting and that they exert editing rights in attempts to communicate these ways to their offspring.

Piaget argues that the thousands of instances of such interactions are bound to result in children's conceptions of the general exchange system. The system becomes articulated through exchanges of conformity for adults' approval and nonconformity for disapproval. The unilaterality of this system does not imply passivity on children's parts. They are active collaborators in its construction and continued practice. The referent is to the controlling person, who is the experienced and benevolent parent. Constraint refers to the parents' perception of society and the child's eventual place in it. It does not imply that parents are coercive or demanding of blind obedience. Parents wish to have their children be members of society and membership requires adherence to certain rules for behavior.

Egocentrism as a Product.   For ideological reasons, psychologists have handled parental authority with caution. With few exceptions (Baumrind, 1968; Damon, 1977; Gadlin, 1978), theorists have dressed parental authority in other clothes by suggesting that parents can communicate their ideas to children through the creation of an empathic bond. This provides a means for getting children to believe what parents believe through self-acceptance (internalization) instead of harsh insistence or demand (Hoffman, 1970). Piaget (1932/1965), and Sullivan (1953) as well, doubt that such empathy can be achieved in early childhood and consider it an illusion on parents' part.

They ask whether parent and young child could achieve mutual understanding as empathy and internalization imply. As we have already seen in friendship, the elements for it are dependent on processes of openness, give-and-take, free discussion, mutual revealment, and consensus. If this analysis is correct, then mutual understanding within the parent–young child relation is an unlikely prospect. Each of the preconditions is missing. Consider the matter of openness as one example. The question is: Can parents enter interactions with children honestly looking for social order through dialogue? To say yes, requires that parents be willing to give up their ideas in light of counterpresentations. Although parents can undoubtedly do so in some instances, it is unlikely that they can in most matters. These matters include health, psychological well-being, social acceptance, and the like, and are expressed through instances such as when to sleep, when to wash one's hands, how to speak to visitors, what to wear to school, and with whom not to associate. By what wisdom do children gain convincingness, better than or equal to parents on such matters?

Both Piaget and Sullivan add an insight to this question that bears repeating. They assume that children are primarily concerned with the here and now. For example, a child may want to wear his favorite jeans, T-shirt, and sneakers to an impending visit from Aunt Mary. The motive is simply comfortableness and familiarity. Parents, on the other hand, frequently think of current events from a much broader perspective that includes their own past and the child's future. What the child wears for Aunt Mary's visit may have to do with their past relations with her as well as their desire to have her think well of them and to like their child. Their communication to the child may consist of telling him to wear his nice clothes and may even include statements of other reasons. But the real question is just how much of the parental viewpoint can be communicated and just how much the child can comprehend.

It is precisely the thousands of such communications to which children are a party that leads Piaget to the conclusion that complementary reciprocity deters mutual understanding. Again, as with symmetrical reciprocity, it may help to drop the terms parent and child; one might even substitute them for peers. It makes no difference as long as the exchange is predicated on complement. Both persons can be well intentioned and still the likely product is two quite different viewpoints. That is, the child will no doubt wear the clothes suggested by the parents and receive approval for it. But the reasons held by both will probably remain disparate just as they were at the start of the episode.

Perhaps the use of the idea of egocentrism as a product cannot be clarified at this time, given its traditional meaning of cause. Fortunately, Piaget (1970) has suggested a revised term *sociocentrism* (p. 729), which conveys the idea better. It emphasizes that children want to understand adults' views. But centering, or misunderstood distortion, occurs because these views cannot be mutually understood. The reason is that the views have not been cooperatively constructed. Thus, parent and child may think that they have communicated and share an idea even though both remain locked into the views they originally held (see also Piaget, 1932/1965, p. 36).

Development.   The structure of complementariness is probably constructed early in infancy and evident within the first 2 years of existence. It is central in children's realization that their actions are not independent but reciprocal and dependent on the actions of other persons. Continued existence within this structure is probably based on two elements. First, it is a fair system insofar as approval and privileges follow from conformity and obedience. In general, children perceive it as legitimate (Damon, 1977) and say that failure to provide approval upon conformity is "unfair" (Youniss, 1980). Second, insofar as adults are perceived as knowing society and the way it is ordered, children's attempts at understanding adults engenders a sense of mastery and privileged entrance into the way things are ordered (Piaget, 1932/1965; Sullivan, 1953).

Just how long this structure retains its stability is not known. Piaget and Sullivan speculate that it begins to quake when children discover the possibility of mutual understanding through cooperating construction with friends. They attribute to friendship the impetus for a transformation in the parent–child relation and suggest that children, at around adolescence, begin to bring symmetrical procedures to it. Whether or not this speculation is correct, it is evident from common observation that the complementariness of earlier childhood loses its appropriateness during adolescence and beyond. The degree to which this relation can be transformed remains an important issue for research. Following Piaget's epistemology, however, the point is that in normal circumstances, the parent–adolescent relation is based on a new structure and founded on new uses of reciprocity. Consequently, the products of the structure, such as the revised definition of self, cannot be the same as they were during earlier childhood. This entails that new characteristics of the personality are likely to be engendered by the new relation and that these characteristics may be more continuous with the personality of the adult than those that emanated from and were appropriate to earlier childhood.

Models of Social Development

The dominant models of psychological theorists have followed either of two general ideologies. One has been the identification of growth with acquisition and internalization of adults' views, with the adults serving as the transmitters. The other has been to put growth in children's own cognitive capacities and skills, in which case, adult's ideas are achieved through a self-initiated process. In either model, the child begins existence as an asocial individual. Next this individuality takes on social texture either through external intervention or self-generated entrance into others' perspectives. Lastly, individuality reemerges in a new and enlightened form. In one instance the individual has internalized society and no longer depends on monitoring agents. In the other instance, the individual becomes autonomous and acts on his or her own under the guidance of self-made principles grounded in prior social knowledge (see Goslin, 1969, for versions of each of these models).

The relational position sketched in this chapter offers a third option. Individuality is checked early in development through the realization of one's relational membership. The fact of reciprocity in interpersonal interactions is the grounds for this insight. Thereafter, the organism's individuality undergoes numerous changes. The basis of definition of self is interpersonal relation in which the self is a member. As relations are developed through collaboration or cooperation with others, new definitions of self become possible and are constructed to meet the terms of these relations. The organism never loses individuality but, at the same time, individuality is a product of relations, past, present, and possible.

Specifically, the mechanism of development cannot be arbitrarily divided into self- and other-generated processes. If one assumes the self to be the constructing agent, as in Piaget's epistemology, one also has to admit that the other person participates directly in the process of construction. Were this not the case, knowledge would not be social except in the trivial sense that the self focused on a person or society as object. The object does not in itself determine the domain of knowledge; the process of interaction and the resulting relation do. If one assumes with socialization theorists, as in Piaget's epistemology, that others influence the self's ideas, one has also to agree that the self radically modifies the other's idea both by interacting with other and by reconstructing it for self along with the other.

Perhaps the major blockage to this perspective is the simultaneity of individuality and sociality. Theorists have tended to want to find the completed self and stable individual at some point in development. This individual is then free to act independently or autonomously in new situations. Moreover, theorists have looked for the causal social experience that led up to that creation of the self. The present relational position suggests a modification of this search. One's stable individuality relies on membership in relations, and relations can be developed, therefore, providing the means for revisions of the self.

It is possible that theorists have focused too closely either on the gain in independence from parents or the step to autonomy from convention of some group. Relational theory may help to open the focus to another fact. As individuals leave dependency on family or achieve autonomy from familiar traditions, they enter new relations that are as demanding of sociality as those they left behind. These obvious relations involve new settings of work, family, and community and include specific membership in relations of boss to worker, fellow workers, husband to wife, parent to child, spouse to in-laws, neighbor to neighbor, and citizen to state.

There are not a priori reasons for arguing that the self constituted in childhood through the child–parent relation is or has to be the self that will be reconstituted in these new relations. Without question, these new relations put demands on the self that were neither appropriate for nor anticipated in prior relations. For example, the intimacy required in childhood relations with one's parents seems to be distinct from the intimacy apropos one's relation to a spouse in marriage. The former is based on a covenant, the latter is voluntary; the former functions through complementariness, the latter holds the possibility for full cooperation.

These examples are only means to stress that individuals retain relational membership with rights and obligations throughout life. The search for the moment when the individual becomes an independent self, becoming *the* product of social existence, seems misdirected. Entrance into new relations enables the transformation of the self, with the products being a series of selves through the discovery of new relational possibilities. This view answers few questions but suggests new lines of research. At present, we know little about the continuity of self across relations. We know next to nothing about the development of relations or the dynamics involved in maintaining them or transposing individuals in them.

One purpose in reviewing this epistemological approach is to encourage pursuit of such questions. Although it is possible to ask them without adopting this relational framework, some may find it useful for at least moving away from those models that have yet to generate these questions and ideologies that have constrained alternate approaches.

Ideology

The Huxley–Kropotkin debate need not be restaged to see its relevance to modern social science. Huxley's competitive individual is alive in many psychological theories today. This is true especially in developmental theories in which younger children are shown to possess rational skills for processing environmental information and schematizing it in the head. This child may be the incipient adult who earns a place in society through merit, merit in this case being the cognitive competence to make rational decisions (Steinfels, 1979).

On the other side, one of the most popular movements in contempory society has been toward the fostering of inner consciousness with its supposed byproduct of interpersonal sensitivity. In one of its more apparent variants, this view endorses a social community where everyone attains acceptance by right and no one is regarded with conditions. Although such a view seems impossible within a relational perspective, where self and other are definitely mutually limiting, it may be taken as the expression of a need to counter unmitigated individualism that threatens to dissemble society into competing elements.

The present epistemology holds promise for integrating useful parts of both sides. It allows social consensus without denying individuality. And it permits individuality on the grounds that relational existence is its constituting condition.

Admittedly, there is a bias in the present perspective. Emphasis is given to social cohesion and the mechanisms engendered through cooperation. This bias, found in Piaget, Sullivan, Macmurray, and others, is consciously adopted by the author. It is intended, in part, as a response to the present cultural context in which modern liberal democracy seeks to redefine its moral bases (Lowi, 1969; Steinfels, 1979). By popular definition, democracy necessitates individual expression of will and readiness to subject self to the majority. When either requirement is weakened, decision making passes to selected groups who then may demand adherence to their position. It is sometimes stated that the guard against such a result is moral principle or a sense of justice.

To the extent that developmental psychology pertains to such weighty matters, it is important that morality be understood through its development and not just as a completed set of philosophic propositions. In this regard, developmental theorists have tended to study morality as general rules for action or universal concepts. What is missing is research on morality as it applies to interpersonal relations, the society to which most people are attached and committed (Philibert, 1979). This morality, with "m" rather than "M," is already evident in preadolescents who understand the fairness of exchanges with adults and the principle of equal treatment between friends (Youniss, 1980).

Ignoring this interpersonal world, theorists are liable to involve themselves in such questions as the disparity between Moral judgment and action, or how a complete Moral system that will check individualism can be achieved through education. The judgment–action question seems secondary in a relational context where the stakes are the preservation or loss of relationship with which one's self is identified. Knowledge of the relation cannot be meaningfully disjoined from actions it controls or actions that lead to it. Establishing, keeping, correcting, intensifying, and terminating relations are the real social business of existence and cannot be separated from interpersonal transactions.

The question of a Moral comprehensive system may be difficult to address by skipping from the abstractions attained in childhood to the abstractions that pertain to society at large (Macmurray, 1961). The real possibility is that the individual's relation to the whole of society is not determining of everyday interpersonal interactions. The task, of course, is to identify the latter and then to try to trace its development from personal life to the impersonal commonweal.

In conclusion, the break from individuals as distinct entities to selves constituted in relations requires awareness of ideological assumptions as much as attention to contemporary theories and data. The position based on the propositions that there is no self outside of relations (Piaget, 1932/1965) and that the self is constituted through relations (Macmurray, 1961) provides a fresh insight into development whose fuller outline is unknown but promising (Youniss, 1980).

REFERENCES

Baumrind, D. Authoritarian *vs.* authoritative control. *Adolescence,* 1968, *3,* 255–272.

Beth, E. N., & Piaget, J. *Mathematical epistemology and psychology.* Dordrecht, Holland: D. Reidel, 1966.

Bronfenbrenner, U. *Two worlds of childhood: US and USSR.* New York: Basic Books, 1970.

Damon, W. *The social world of the child.* San Francisco: Jossey–Bass, 1977.

Feffer, M. Developmental analysis of interpersonal behavior. *Psychological Review.* 1970, *77,* 197–214.

Flavell, J. H. The development of inferences about others. In T. Mischel (Ed.), *Understanding other persons.* N. J.: Rowman & Littlefield, 1974.

Flavell, J. H., Botkin, P. T., Fry, C. L., Wright, J. W., & Jarvis, P. E. *The development of role-taking and communication skills in children.* New York: Wiley, 1968.

Furth, H. G. *Piaget and knowledge.* Englewood Cliffs, N.J.: Prentice–Hall, 1969.

Gadlin, H. Child discipline and the pursuit of self. In H. W. Reese & L. P. Lipsitt (Eds.), *Advances in child development and behavior* (Vol. 12). New York: Academic Press, 1978.

Golding, W. *Lord of the flies.* New York: Coward-McCann, 1955.

Goslin, D. A. (Ed.). *Handbook of socialization theory and research.* Chicago: Rand McNally, 1969.

Hinde, R. A. On describing relationships. *Journal of Child Psychology and Psychiatry,* 1976, *17,* 1–19.

Hoffman, M. L. Moral development. In P. H. Mussen (Ed.), *Carmichael's manual of child psychology* (Vol. II). New York: Wiley, 1970.

Inhelder, B., Sinclair, H., & Bovet, M. *Learning and the development of cognition.* Cambridge, Mass.: Harvard University Press, 1974.

Kropotkin, P. *Mutual aid.* London: Sargent, 1902.

Lasch, C. *Haven in a heartless world.* New York: Basic Books, 1977.

Lowi, T. S. *The end of liberalism.* New York: Norton, 1969.

Macmurray, J. *The self as agent.* London: Farber & Farber, 1957.

Macmurray, J. *Persons in relation.* London: Farber & Farber, 1961.

Philibert, P. H. Conscience: Developmental perspectives from Rogers to Kohlborg. *Horizons,* 1979, 1–25.

Piaget, J. *The moral judgment of the child.* New York: The Free Press, 1965. (Originally published, 1932.)

Piaget, J. *Egocentrism comments.* Boston: MIT Press, 1962.

Piaget, J. Piaget's theory. In P. H. Mussen (Ed.), *Carmichael's manual of child psychology* (Vol. 1). New York: Wiley, 1970.

Piaget, J., & Inhelder, B. *The child's conception of space.* New York: Norton, 1956.

Sampson, E. D. Psychology and the American ideal. *Journal of Personality and Social Psychology,* 1977, *35,* 767–782.

Shantz, C. U. The development of social cognition. In E. M. Heatherington (Ed.), *Review of child development research* (Vol. 5). Chicago: University of Chicago Press, 1975.

Steinfels, P. *The neoconservatives.* New York: Simon and Schuster, 1979.

Sullivan, H. S. *The interpersonal theory of psychiatry.* New York: Norton, 1953.

Toward a National Policy for Children and Families. Washington, D.C.: National Academy of Sciences, 1976.

Woodcock, G., *Anarchism.* New York: Meridian, 1962.

Youniss, J. Socialization and social knowledge. In R. Silbereisen (Ed.), *Soziale Kognition.* Berlin: Technische Universitat Berlin, 1977.

Youniss, J. Dialectical theory and Piaget on social knowledge. *Human Development,* 1978, *21,* 234–247. (a)

Youniss, J. The nature of social development. In H. McGurk (Ed.), *Issues in childhood social development.* London: Methuen, 1978. (b)

Youniss, J. A revised interpretation of Piaget (1932). In I. E. Sigel (Ed.), *Piagetian theory and research: New directions and applications.* Hillsdale, N.J.: Lawrence Erlbaum Associates, 1979.

Youniss, J. *Parents and peers in social development.* Chicago: University of Chicago Press, 1980.

Youniss, J., & Volpe, J. A relational analysis of friendship. In W. Damon (Ed.), *Social cognition.* San Francisco: Jossey–Bass, 1978.

9

Piaget, Play, and Cognition, Revisited

Brian Sutton-Smith
University of Pennsylvania

The 1970s have already witnessed the publication of over 20 research-oriented books on the meaning of play. One has to include the prior 50 years to arrive at an equivalent number of works, even with a fairly liberal definition of research and social science. The three major influences in this novel play research appear to be Bateson (1956, 1972), Berlyne (1960), and Piaget (1962). Bateson speaks to play at the cultural level and in largely communication-theoretical terms. Berlyne focuses on play, along with humor and art, in terms of revised forms of stimulus–response theorizing. And Piaget discusses infant and early childhood play in terms of his own theory of cognition.

In this chapter I consider Piaget's (the pre-1960 Piaget's) contribution to the current state of the art although, as it turns out, Berlyne and Bateson are included. I add also that I am more concerned with how to theorize about play than I am with how to theorize about Piaget. I begin by acknowledging the very important stimulus and encouragement that Piaget's *Play, Dreams and Imitation in Childhood* (1962) had for me. I had begun my own studies of children's play and games in the late 1940s and in those days found little encouragement for such esoteric concerns except among pre-1930 psychological studies (Lehman & Witty, 1927/1976) and among folklorists (Gomme, 1894/1964). To read Piaget was to receive the sudden gift that one's intuition about the primary importance of play and games to children and therefore to the study of childhood was not a totally deviant and trivial obsession. I feel sure that some others felt the same sense of relief, and that even those who didn't care for the subject matter were subsequently prepared to consider that this least serious matter might indeed be quite serious after all. Almost 30 years after Piaget's book one now has the pleasure of seeing that there are even some systematic social scientists who find

229

the subject matter the most serious one that they care about. What Piaget did at one stroke for psychology is what Huizinga (1944/1949) had done 10 years earlier for history. He suddenly made the subject of play a critical aspect of a major theory of human culture. It was no longer possible to be a concerned student of child development, or at least of cognitive development, without tackling this aspect of the Piagetian theory.

Not unnaturally, however, after the first flush of salvation, troubles began to arise. Obviously my commitment to play was in the first place emotional and in the second place scientific. For me it was a metaphor of a kind of living and a kind of distancing from conventional behavior. And persons under the sway of such unreason do not like to see their loved ones trifled with lightly.

So I worried over what I liked and disliked in Piaget, typified perhaps by his brave contention: "In reality, the child has no imagination, and what we ascribe to him as such is no more than a lack of coherence [1962, p. 131]." In a visiting year at Clark University (1962–1963), and with much stimulation from Joe Glick and Bernard Kaplan, I came to believe that there were three major interrelated problems with the Piagetian play theory. These were described in my article of 1966. I repeat each of these objections now, and my talk is a kind of retrospect on the status of each problem and what we have learned about it from the subsequent literature. More particularly I want to look this time at what support I can find for Piaget's side of the case. The problems that I cited were: (1) that despite their apparent equipotentiality in his theory of intelligence, Piaget had contrived an asymmetry or imbalance between the contributions to be made to cognition by imitation and play—imitation was the star performer and play was its aborted partner; (2) that this inequality was brought about by Piaget's focus on directed or rational or convergent, rather than undirected or imaginative or divergent cognitive operations; (3) that it was also a result of presupposing play to be a predominantly infantile state of development, a not uncommon assumption in the workethic ideology of Western culture.

The Asymmetry of Imitation and Play in Cognitive Activity

In Piaget's view of intelligence there are *states* and *transformations*. The first register themselves in the mind through a figural component derived from perception, imitation, and imagery. The second, the transformations, are the cognitive components of mind that derive from the subject's own actions. Play is of this latter kind, and occurs when there is a primacy of such subjectivity and no attempt to submit the transformation to the criterion of objective fact. Play is pure assimilation just as imitation is pure accommodation. In symbolic activity, the figurative aspects of intelligence (imitation, etc.) are converted into interiorized imitations and as such become available for the transformations of cognitive activity (or play). Such interiorized imitations (or language or images) are the essential bases of the signifiers used in all symbolic activity. Play, on the other hand, which provides us with an extreme illustration of how transformations of these signifiers can operate, does not appear to be able to contribute equivalently its own kind of transformations to serious cognitive activity. We have no problem knowing how the imitation-derived signifiers get used, but we are at a loss to discover in Piaget's writings how the play-derived transformations get used. In fact, we are led to understand that they cannot be used to constitute rational thought processes, because they are by nature subjective, *distorting, confusing,* and *deforming* (to use some of Piaget's own signifiers).

Apparently our view that there is some imbalance between the adaptive cognitive contributions of imitation and play is not entirely solipsistic. Recently others have taken it up also. Thus, Brian Vandenberg (1979) writes:

Piaget has stated subsequent to his exchange with Sutton-Smith, that development proceeds through the progressive equilibration of assimilation and accommodation which can be expressed in terms of centration and decentration . . . play is centration since assimilation predominates and is corrected through the decentering action of imitation, where accommodation dominates. Imitation serves as the "decenter" because it moves thought away from the idiosyncratic perspectives of play toward the externally valid reality; play can only egocentrically distort while imitation can decenter. . . . Consequently, the cutting edge of development is imitation, from which new and accurate images of reality are generated. Play serves a kind of cognitive holding function which facilitates the assimilation of new images, but itself does not create new directions in thought [p. 4].

Greta Fein (1978) comments on the paradox that Vygotsky and Piaget pursue opposite and reversible paths in their conceptions of play. She says:

For Vygotsky the press for symbolic play is emotional, for Piaget it is intellectual. And yet, in developing their positions, these theorists switch sides. What for Vygotsky is created by unrealizable wishes becomes an occasion for the organization of meaning in language and thought. What for Piaget is created by the functioning of intelligence becomes a medium for the expression of personal concerns [p. 5].

And Ken Rubin (Rubin & Pepler, in press) says:

Our second criticism of the Piagetian position stems from an apparent inconsistency vis-à-vis the causes of the decline of egocentric thought and conversely the onset of social thought in childhood. . . . Piaget (1932) feels strongly that peer interaction and peer conflict serve to decrease egocentric thinking and to increase accommodation (and thus compromise) in young children. On the other hand, *play,* during which much peer interaction takes place, is seen as pure assimilation or as the most characteristic reflection of egocentric thought. As a result one may come away with the opinion, following a reading of Piaget's position concerning play, that such

> activity is not particularly conducive to the onset of socialized thought. We, of
> course, beg to differ from Piaget. It is our belief that the Piagetian definition of play
> as pure assimilation is unreasonably restrictive [p. 17].

Given this consensus across several current play researchers and realizing that
it could easily be a false consensus (Youniss, 1979), what then can be said on
behalf of Piaget's view that "the essential property of play . . . (is) . . . the
deformation and subordination of reality to the desires of the self"? What can be
said on behalf of his view that it serves to preserve ego continuity and to
consolidate prior adaptive operations during the infantile period when the child
lacks more realistic adaptive operations?

First, these are the kind of descriptions that for many years have been used in
child play therapy. They are descriptions likely to be true of children sufficiently
overwhelmed by conflict and anxiety that such play as they can attempt is very
much of a defensive and wish-fulfilling exercise. Second, in a quite different and
clearly more "structural" emphasis, Piaget's view also receives corroboration in
some descriptions of animal play. Thus Loizos (1967), discussing animal motor
patterns, describes them as involving situations where: (1) the sequence may be
reordered; (2) the individual movements making up the sequence may become
exaggerated; (3) certain movements within the sequence may be repeated more
than they would normally be; (4) the sequence may be broken off altogether by
the introduction of irrelevant activities and resumed later—fragmentation; (5)
movements may be both exaggerated and repeated; (6) individual movements
within the sequence may never be completed and this incomplete element may be
repeated many times.

Now this sounds like the sort of egocentric, fragmentary, unaccomodated
activity that Piaget is talking about. It is true that some animal investigators
(Bruner, Jolly, & Sylva, 1976; Reynolds, 1976) see these "fragmented" behaviors as more likely to occur in species where greater flexibility is needed, which
is not at all what Piaget has in mind, but still we do have at least some com-
parability at the descriptive level. Third, another direction in which we can take
the inquiry is into the *exploration* literature, which although it has been more
influenced by Berlyne than by Piaget, has established a distinction between
exploration and play that has some parallel with Piaget's distinction between
imitation and play. If we think of a continuum between accommodative and
assimilative activity, whereas play represents the extreme of assimilation and
imitation the extreme of accommodation, exploration is presumably at a point
from imitation in the direction of the center of such a continuum. It is closer to
imitation than it is to play. And in the extensive experimental literature on the
relationships of exploration and play, exploration has very clearly been found to
have the priority as an adaptive response. Within exploration there have been
those most interested in responses to novelty, complexity, etc., responses that
have come to be known as *specific exploration* (or curiosity), and there have
been those more interested in responses that are activated more by boredom and

habituation, which have come to be known as *diversive exploration*. Hutt (1979) has taken this distinction and rephrased it as a difference between investigation and play. Hers is very important evidence that suggests that the imbalance that Piaget has depicted in his description of imitation and play may indeed truly represent the state of nature. Hutt has further shown that in exploratory activity, as in problem solving, the heart rate is quite regular, whereas in play it is most variable. She notes (1979): "The child's behavior was video-recorded by one camera, while its heart rate was telemetred and the paper tracer recorded by another camera. The two pictures were then superimposed to give a composite picture of behavior with accompanying heart rate changes [p. 185]." This description has a parallel with the research of Dansky and Silverman (1973, 1975), who found that in their play condition, as compared with their work condition, attention was wandering and peripheral. In Hutt's study, the condition that most approaches what the heart rate is like in play was, significantly enough, looking out the window.

To this point then we have brought together three kinds of research—therapeutic, animal, and child experimental—all of which can be read to give considerable support to Piaget's notion that play does not contribute as importantly to cognition as does imitation or exploration. This body of research shows that exploration has priority over play, has more persistence than play, and seems to be more clearly related to learning.

Against this direction of thought, we can only raise the possibility that the apparent prepotence of exploration may be in part a product of the strange situations made use of in these studies. There is evidence in both the animal literature (Suomi, 1979) and the child literature (Ellis, 1979) that when children are in a setting with which they are already familiar, the introduction of a novel object can lead to its immediate assimilation into playful themes without anything more than the most perfunctory moment of investigatory attention. Novel settings and novel people do give a predominance to exploration, but in more normative situations exploration does not have that priority at all. When children are in command of their circumstances and familiar with peers, play is the most characteristic and enduring of their responses. Normally, play is not secondary, but is primary in their activity. It is the kind of response that they prefer. Still, even if this is so and even if its tenacity and endurance creates a mystery for us, this is still not yet to gainsay Piaget's point that its cognitive role is illustrative and consolidatory rather than constitutive. One may enjoy play without learning much from it—though we are left with the anomaly cited earlier that these "distortions" of children or "fragments" of animals are accounted by some as the very ground of their learned flexibility, a point to which we return later.

The Disjunction of Directed and Undirected Thinking

We come now then to my second, parallel problem with Piaget, which is the relatively inferior role he gives to undirected thinking, as represented here by play, as compared with directed thinking, as represented here by imitation, exploration, etc. As we have seen there is some evidence that he is on reasonable empirical grounds for making such a disjunction. According to his viewpoint, play is not, cognitively speaking, a particularly productive phenomenon.

If that is the case, however, what are we to make of what has now become a considerable body of research in which some forms of play, usually sociodramatic or make-believe, have been shown to be correlated (perhaps causally) with innumerable cognitive outcomes. We are referring to the work of Dansky and Silverman (1973); Feitelson and Ross (1973); Fink (1976); Lieberman (1977); Lovinger (1974); Rosen (1974); Saltz, Dixon, and Johnson (1977); Singer (1973); Smilansky (1968); Smith and Syddall (1977); and Sutton-Smith (1968). It is contended by some of these authors that the labile activity of the player increases his or her repertoire of responses and therefore there are more responses available when diverse responses are required on tests of creativity. Or it is empirically demonstrated that having available imaginative associative processes, the individual is more capable of delaying reaction, is less aggressive, has better memory storage capacity, and is more verbally fluent. As Sherrod and Singer (1979) say:

> It is almost impossible to argue other than that make-believe play and cognition facilitate each other. The two must develop in parallel: they form bidirectional not two separate unidirectional systems. . . . (We should not argue) for the influence of imaginative play on cognitive development, because training in fantasy activity necessarily involves training also in cognitive skills such as representation and imagery [p. 9].

One way to bring these kinds of data into line with Piaget's thinking, however, might be to argue that it is not actually the fantasy play itself that contributes to cognitive development, but that rather by being brought together by their high motivation for fantasy play, children are forced into various kinds of disequilibrating interaction with others that require them to decenter, take the perspective of the other, develop more adequate vocabulary and consistent thought processes. Smith and Syddall (1977) and Rubin and Pepler (in press) argue, for example, that in the few studies where there is a causal link between experience in a play group and posttest scores there is most typically a tutorial relationship between experimenter and subject that can itself be held accountable for the shift in scores. The work of Matthews (1977) suggests further that in the midst of fantasy play, the peers come into conflicts that lead to readjustments of an accommodative kind. Given that Piaget postulated such conflicts as a source of development, then perhaps these various studies on the linkages between play and creativity only mislead us into thinking that play itself is the formative agent. Rather, it may be that play is only the formative context for the formative event, which is that of social conflict between peers or of children modeling from adults.

Still there are problems with this solution also. First, there are the indications that in *solitary play* both humans (Weir, 1962) and chimpanzees (Dolgin, 1979) do more novel things with words or objects, associating them in a greater variety of combinatory ways, than they do within the social constraints of others present. The findings here are few in number, but at least indicate another interpretation, the one favored by Lieberman, Singer, and others that it is something fundamental to the play experience itself that contributes to cognition—not just the social encounters that occur in the midst of that experience.

What I would like to do now, therefore, is to look more closely at the play experience to see if there might not be another kind of learning involved than that discussed by Hutt. Piaget's account of early play appears a useful vehicle for this discussion. Piaget's account of the sensorimotor play structures of the first year of life accords nicely with his theoretical views. Infants who have been shown in sober exploratory activity developing schemata of sensorimotor response, are shown subsequently to be varying or distorting their own achieved sensorimotor responses in ways that they find particularly amusing. They throw their heads back with laughter, they kick the side of the crib with glee, they blow raspberries on their mothers' cheeks. It is easy to think of these examples as being of great affective value but of little cognitive virtue. They mimic cognition rather than contribute to it.

Piaget's account of the symbolic structures of the second year of life, however, seems to have a different character. There are, for example, a series of four steps in the development of symbolic play:

	0	Where the child detaches his prior actions from their original contexts and displays them somewhere else (pretending to sleep on the rug).
	1A	Next there is the projection of symbolic schemata onto new objects (the toy is put to bed).
IMITATION		
	1B	Next there is the incorporation of imitated acts into play (child sweeps like mother).
	2A	Next one object is identified with another (stones are food).
IDENTIFICATION		
	2B	Finally the child identifies with another (plays mother).

Here in Piaget's account children's symbolic play is used as an illustration of the development of representational competence rather than as a mockery or distortion of it. Piaget does not give us a set of representational stages first, and then a set of play variations second, as he has done for the first year of life, with the various sensorimotor circular reactions and the plays derived from these. One might naively think that in the case of symbolic play, symbolic representation develops through this play activity and the play activity is what constitutes its development. One might think that the development of substitute objects in play (toys, etc.) is a precursor to the development of symbolic thought in general. This is the approach that Vygotsky (1967) has taken. This is the approach also that a number of researchers have taken, in seeking for relationships between Piaget's symbolic series and the child's development of language. If Piaget is correct in general, there should not be any anticipatory relationship between his kinds of play symbolism and kinds of linguistic symbolism. If Vygotsky is right there should be such an anticipatory relationship.

The results to date are mixed. Those who have used either Piaget's five stages in some more or less complex form have certainly found no one-to-one relationship between the two, but they usually have found some relationships. The symbolic play stages are certainly not totally irrelevant to the sequences of language development (Nicolich, 1977), to the contents of language development (Rocissano, 1979), to language comprehension (Fein, 1979), or to productive language beyond the first words (Kavanaugh, 1979). These results intensify the ambiguity of any purely affective or expressive interpretation of the stages of play symbolism as described by Piaget.

But again, of course, we could argue that what has happened here is that Piaget has perhaps underemphasized in his description the "amusing" qualities of these symbolic states. He has become caught up in the symbolic sequence that is illustrated there and has unintentionally made it seem like a cognitive sequence, rather than, as he really intends, only the illustration and distortion of the true cognitive sequence to be found somewhere else. I think it is quite probable that that has in fact occurred and the apparent discrepancies between the description of sensorimotor play and symbolic play are more apparent than real, and that, although the nature of symbolic operations in the second year is not otherwise described in such detail by Piaget, that is more of an oversight than a fundamental change of purpose. Play's symbolic operations are not meant in themselves to change thought processes.[1]

Still, the few allusions we have made to interrelationships with language (and creativity) suggest that there may be more afoot here than Piaget has discovered. Perhaps there is a kind of *learning* going on in play at some more fundamental level than the kind discussed by Hutt (i.e., learning the novel properties of objects). In order to examine this possibility, however, it is necessary to take into

---

[1]Because Piaget very much limits his interpretation of play to the distortion of some original cognitive template, we were led to say in our earlier paper that it was *as if* (and we stress the *as if*) he had bootlegged a copy theory of play. Our reference was to the way he had limited his interpretation of the play phenomenon not to his really having a copy theory, which we carefully precluded. Then as now copy theory is a red herring. The limitations of his interpretation of play, however, are something else.

account the more radical play theory of Gregory Bateson (1956, 1972). In Bateson's cultural interpretation of play, play is not an awkward handmaiden to thought. In Bateson's theory, play is primarily a kind of communication, a phenomenon that has to do with the way we interpret experience, the way we orient ourselves to meaning and to others. Orienting ourselves to meaning is often called *framing* in this kind of discourse. Sometimes it is called *metacommunication* because we are making communications about how we intend to make communications. Making these kinds of communications logically precedes saying what we have to say. People must know with what voice we speak before they hear the speech itself. Are we father, mother, lecturer, pro Piaget or against him?

But let us bring this whole thing to earth by taking an example from Piaget and reinterpreting it in these terms. Piaget's first clear example of one of his children at play in the first year is of T at 2 months. He says (1962):

> At 0.2 (21) T adopted the habit of throwing his head back to look at familiar things from this new position. At 0.2 (23 or 24) he seemed to repeat this movement with ever increasing enjoyment and ever decreasing interest in the external result: he brought his head back to the upright position and threw it back again time after time laughing loudly. In other words, the circular reaction ceased to be "serious" or instructive, if such expressions can be applied to a baby of less than three months, and became a game [p. 91].

Now, as we have said, Piaget is interested here in the repetition of the serious primary circular reaction in the nonserious play. And he suggests the child does this "merely for pleasure accompanied by smiles and even laughter [p. 90]."

I would like to suggest, following Bateson and many others who have been working out the implications of his view over the past 20 years (Geertz, 1976; Goffman, 1974; Handelman, 1974, 1977; Stewart, 1979; Turner, 1974), that the example we have just given is much more complex and much more cognitive than even Piaget describes, and that it may be interpreted to demonstrate a number of characteristics.[2] Most of these characteristics I present here are already familiar in the various theories of play. I do not think, however, that they have been brought together as an account of what might be thought of speculatively at least, as the distinctively structural character of the imaginative and expressive life. Since Eliot Turiel Chapter 2, this volume introduced the polytheism of psychological, social, and moral domains, I now add my own to this growing pantheon. Given the place of sports and the arts in cultural life, this is undoubtedly, in his terms, another system of knowledge. I begin with Bateson's primary point.

---

[2]We are particularly beholden in this analysis to Susan Stewart's recent study of nonsense (1979).

1. Reframing.   This is our first structural characteristic. The fact that the infant smiles shows that he or she discriminates the actions in the last part of this observation as different from the actions in the first part of this observation. All Piaget's examples in the first year of life have the child either smiling or laughing, which makes it a strong possibility that this is the main signal that infants can use to communicate such a reframing of activity. Older children use verbal cues about pretense, and they negotiate the different frames they wish to use, but in the infant's case what is being done here is, according to Bateson, basic categorical work of a communicative kind. (The infant is saying that this is other than proper behavior—not p. but − p.)

Of course, we do not know how the infant can do this, any more than we know how the dog in Bateson's description can know that his playful nip connotes a bite without connoting what a bite connotes. But what we must make clear is that this reframing of the event is of a hierarchically more primary order than the play event itself. It is a kind of communicative accommodation without which the players cannot join terms on their playful assimilation. And as Garvey (1977) and others have shown, there is a constant interpenetration of social play by this kind of accommodative framing activity. Learning how to create frames that will be acceptable to others and promote the assimilations of play is primary stuff in early childhood.

2. Reversals.   Our second characteristic of play comes from the major emphasis in Freudian theory that play involves a shift from the passive to the active. Play involves some kind of capacity for reversal. A primitive mechanism that might mediate this discrimination is the child's very early ability to *negate* the flow of stimulus events by shutting eyes or turning the head away. This turnoff mechanism could give us at least part of the effect. In addition to turning off the circular reaction, however, there is an added switch in direction of intentionality from goals to instrumental behavior, a definition often used as a characterization for play behavior (Miller, 1973). Perhaps this built-in capacity for reversal may also mediate the reframing just mentioned. The concept of reversal or inversion has in recent anthropological literature been used as a way of describing pervasive features of cultural life (Babcock, 1978; Turner, 1974), and it would not be too farfetched, against the background of that literature, to consider play as a microrite of reversal or inversion. Elsewhere we have analyzed children's development through play in terms of a hierarchical series of reversal operations— reversals of control, roles, tactics, rules, identities, and so forth (Sutton-Smith, 1978a). When Piaget says in our example that the infant continued with "ever decreasing interest in the external result," he is certainly implying such an ability to switch direction. Chukovsky (1966) says: "they only know sense, who nonsense know," implying perhaps that one can learn a more flexible approach to routine behavior through "playful" reversals in orientation. "The envisagement of impossibility" would seem to be a kind of learning.

3. Abstraction of Prototypes.   Our third major structural category is derived from Vygotsky's theory of play. In addition to being a reframing (the smile) and a reversal (decreasing interest in the external result), the actions that are played with are also a kind of abstract (Fein, 1971). They are taken out of their original context in these sensorimotor examples, no less than they are in the symbolic examples where the child pretends to sleep in the new situation. It is true the sensorimotor distancing is on a more microlevel and is still in the same physical setting. But the instrumental behavior is clearly detached. As Piaget says: ''he brought his head back to the upright position and threw it back again time after time.'' But we know that he is not doing that to look at the familiar things from a new position. Throwing back the head is detached from that intentionality and therefore from some of the original stimuli.

The compelling importance of thinking of play as a kind of prototypic abstraction is conveyed to us by Vygotsky's (1967) brief example: ''Think of two girls who are sisters playing a game called two girls who are sisters.'' Now obviously they can play bitchy sisters or polite sisters or alternate the both, but they do not play sisters as they are in all their ordinary contextualized behavior. Play cannot proceed without some selection from ordinary behavior. The principles of such selection have never been fully studied, although we are familiar with the notion of play as dealing in caricatures and stereotypes (Sutton-Smith, 1978b). Children's behavioral abstracts, like their toys and like primitive masks (Turner, 1967), appear to deal in the use of salient characteristics for purposes of rapid and vivid information acquisition and usage. In Piaget's examples it seems that a primary characteristic of these early sensorimotor plays is the abstraction for subsequent manipulation of the child's own grosser motor response from the stimulus context.

4. Theme and Variation.   The notion of theme and variation does not derive from any one of the major play theories (except perhaps Berlyne), but it seems to be as fundamental to play as it is to aesthetics. What we see so often is that the child in play focuses on some central act or object and then permutates that action through some of the immediately available contingencies. In all the symbolic levels mentioned in the excerpt from Piaget we have such a central vector (the sleeping action, the toy, the mother), which is brought into variable relationships with surrounding phenomena. The toy doll is first put to bed, is fed, is clothed, is toileted, is put to bed, is clothed, etc. In the sensorimotor example we would suggest that head throwing back is also both repeated and variable behavior. What is implied here is that the theme and variations kind of organization is an infrastructure underlying both those of the sensorimotor and symbolic kinds discussed by Piaget.

Speculating further on the peculiar character of this vectorial–permutative structuring in play, one observes a strange reversal from the child's vaunted egocentricity. Here the centration is objectified as some action or object or toy, external to the child; and the toy is then out there in the world brought into novel relationships with surrounding phenomena. It is as if the child's very ego-centricity is objectified in the acts and objects, thus reversing the typical centrational orientation of subject–object relationships. Furthermore, the vectorial center of action then becomes background for the foregrounded novel variations and novel relationships. The vector is the constant (the stereotype) and the variations are the figures against that ground of action. I have elsewhere shown how most of children's early, 2- to 3-year-old stories have this same character. Thus:

> The monkeys
> They went up sky
> They fall down
> Choochoo train in the sky
> The train fall down in the sky
> I fell down in the sky
> I got on my boat and my legs hurt
> Daddy fall down in the sky

Going up and falling down is the reversible vector. Monkeys, choochoos, train, Daddy, and I are the variations. Here an action is the central vector and characters are the variations. More typically in later stories the characters are the central vectors and actions are the variations (Sutton-Smith, 1981). Even in children's games in mid-childhood, we have a similar kind of organization in what I have called central person games (Sutton-Smith, 1959, 1982).

5. Boundaried Space–Time. We have wandered further than Bateson would to discuss what seem to us to be some essential structural characteristics of play (reversibility, abstracted prototypes, theme and variation). But these, of course, can only occur within the context given by the reframing activity and this becomes even clearer when we discuss other matters that Bateson would take into account, namely the need to indicate clearly for communication purposes the boundaries of the behavior in space and time. At the adult level we have no difficulty with this because of the existence of spaces and times set aside for play in stadia, theaters, and playgrounds. All these physical contexts communicate immediately what is supposed to be afoot when people gather there. In early infant play these boundaries are less explicit to us as adults, apart from those we ourselves impose by creating play centers and the like for children. But there is no reason to believe that even infants do not have a similar need to set boundaries. When they have slipped amusedly into a new frame, they exist in a world of boundless possibility or impossibility unless limits are quickly sketched. How is this achieved? There seem to be a number of techniques for "boundarying" (Herron & Sutton-Smith, 1971):

1. The most basic one is *miniaturization*. Most toys are clearly marked as apart from the proper world by their scaled-down and stereotypically salient features. Their microscale shows clearly what can and cannot be done with them. They are tightly confined. Even in the sensorimotor toys we give infants (rattles, etc.) careful steps are taken to see that the infants cannot hurt themselves, that is, that behavior does not exceed appropriate built-in limits of the toy.

2. *Hyperbolation,* exaggeration, giganticism are also devices used with children's toys, though usually with the large soft toy variety so they can, again, do no harm. Small toys can be made of hard materials. Large toys must usually be made of soft materials, if limits are to be maintained. Clearly this kind of gigantic approach is of secondary importance to miniaturization in the toy world, but as applied to the children's own spontaneous behavior it seems that hyperbolation may well be primary. It is an empirical question as to whether the variations that children introduce into theme and variational play are only variations or are also exaggerations. Sometimes they clearly are the latter, and some have taken the position that such exaggerations are critical to our understanding of play ("galumphing" as Miller, 1973, has called them, borrowing from Lewis Carroll). What seems reasonable is that the more the play shifts from the solitary to the social axis the more necessary might become such exaggerations in order to communicate to others the true/untrue character of the frame in which the player is engaged. By writing the actions large, their separate "boundaryness" is made explicit and decontextualized from the situations with which they might otherwise be confused. In sum, caricature heightens figure–ground relationships, as well as communicates information rapidly, the point made earlier. Stewart (1979), in her study of nonsense, has even suggested that it is only through this kind of exaggeration that we can actually abstract the figure of fun from its ground of sobriety. Which at the very least reminds us that our present distinctions among reframing, reversal, abstraction, theme and variation, boundariedness, miniaturization, and exaggeration are of an intricate structural reality strongly interwoven in human behavior.

As well as space, time itself must also be bounded. Otherwise moving into a new frame might permit of infinite temporal possibilities and impossibilities. The one that we derive from Stewart as particularly useful to us is:

3. *Cyclical repetition.* By repeating the play action children can again boundary time. Instead of being caught in its incessant unidirectional flow, they can bond it to a beginning, a middle, and an ending of their own volition. Their circularity at the sensorimotor level ("He threw his head back again and again") is a microscale of the adult football season. Both repeat and delimit. The fundamental problem of metacommunication is "What is within the frame?" Repetition of cyclic sort makes that abundantly clear. Throughout

childhood, children's primary technique for managing time will be cyclic repetition through turn taking.

6. Modulations of Excitement.   What is not hinted at either in Bateson or in Piaget, but becomes primary in Berlyne's approach to play is the modulation of arousal (1960). In the patterns of play of which we have been speaking, children are not simply varying frames because they must communicate, or categorize flexibly, or because they seek mastery of their circumstances. They are doing it because it is generally the most exciting activity they know. Although the bulk of play theory has to do with the socializing effects of play (or their unsocializing effects), children themselves are there primarily for the pleasure. We should therefore direct our attention to what are the structural characteristics of their excitement, as have several researchers such as Shultz (1979) and Mihayli Csikszentmihalyi (1975, 1979). All we wish to do here is to point to the tempo of excitement in Piaget's example and suggest the presumption of mounting excitement, anticipations, and climaxes. In the first year of life we see clearly the child's increasing temporal control over such tempos, just as the same can be traced in children's games, as climaxes become less episodic and more cumulative (Herron and Sutton-Smith, 1971, p. 298).

7. Conclusion.   What we have done here is suggest a hierarchy of structures that might be involved in the episodes of sensorimotor and symbolic play that Piaget has used for his own discussion. We have borrowed our concepts from the major kinds of play theory as shown in Table 9.1.

TABLE 9.1

Play Theoretical Variables	Class of Psychological Event	Kind of Play Theory
1. Framing	Communication	Bateson
		Geertz
		Goffman
		Handelman
		Schwartzman
2. Reversal	Conative	Freud
		Erikson
3. Abstraction of prototypes	Cognitive	Vygotsky
4. Theme and variations		
5. Boundaried space and time (Miniaturization, hyperbolation, circular repetition)		Stewart
6. Modulation	Affective	Berlyne
		Ellis
		Hutt
		Shultz

In these terms it might be argued that Piaget has paid attention only to lower-level and more content-influenced categories, and perhaps his interpretation of their character is due to this surface nature of his treatment. What appears as undirected thought, pure or distorting assimilation at the content level, is here demonstrated to involve at least two deeper levels of operations (first, framing, and second, categories 2–6). Furthermore, the second of these levels involves variables some of which (like reversibility) are also required in convergent or rational thinking, but others (like abstracted prototypes, theme and variation, and modulation) are the heart of divergent and imaginative thinking and, therefore, of playful and artistic productions. The peculiar syntheses of the imagination and the arts involve bringing central schemata or ideas into unexpected relationships with peripheral events in a manner that preserves the excitement of those relationships in the perceptual medium. Directed thought, on the contrary, seeks to dissociate central ideas from the excitements of mediated and ambiguous relationships. In these terms the dialectic that Piaget introduces between imitation and play does insufficient justice to the autonomous structure of imaginative thought as a distinctive kind of thinking in perceptual media. If there is any truth to these assertions then much is being learned in play, but it is of another kind than that being dealt with by Piaget or by Hutt.

Play as an Infantile State

Piaget has dealt with play most thoroughly at this age level. Most of my comments, therefore, have been directed at the same age level. At first sight one imagines that he is simply persisting with a work-ethic, sociological kind of view within which children's play is what children do, but not what adults do. When Piaget says such play gradually gives way to the adapted and rational thought of the adult, one is inclined to find in this some kind of historical fault. That is, that he is persisting with the view that children's work is their play, that what children do cannot be very important anyway, etc. However, perhaps there is more to his view than mere historical lag. Perhaps what is at fault here is the definition of the concept of play itself.

Pure Assimilation as Reverie

If instead of using the word *play* when discussing Piaget we used the word *reverie*, much of what he says would fall into place. Reverie is that kind of semiautomatic, purely assimilative process that takes over our minds at in-between times and places and within which we make no conscious decisions. We do not frame it, and whatever goes on in it is beyond our autonomous actions. Now this kind of thing is certainly a dreamlike set of "distortions" of conscious life. It is also possible that children have more of it because they may have more need to subordinate reality to wishful thinking. On the other hand, given that the same phenomenon invades our adult lives incessantly as we drive our cars to and from work, as we sit bored in faculty meetings or lectures, then perhaps children do not have more of it. Or perhaps they do not have more of it than those adults who spend most of their lives in the power of others. Reverie may be more a function of being unempowered than of being a child.

If we surrender reverie to Piaget, then what of the mass of human play where the child alone or with others chooses to pick up his blocks or her jump rope? Here it seems that we have another kind of domain, a more autonomous one and one subject to the various phenomena already dealt with—reframing, reversals, and so on. Presumably this domain is easily invaded by reverie, hence perhaps Corinne Hutt's variable heart rates, but unless we are to ignore the communication theory of Bateson or the arousal theory of Berlyne, this domain does not seem to correspond sufficiently to Piaget's account. In hindsight, we might suspect that if Piaget had studied his infants' play in a social context of the mother and infant, then these other variables might have been more in the forefront of Piaget's thinking. Instead he generally studied the infant: (1) in a solitary situation; and (2) as if his own presence as investigator did not make any difference. Now although solitary play is an important form, all our other evidence on mother–infant relationships would lead us to suspect that the original forms of any kind of infant behavior are very strongly affected by the social relationships with the early nurturers. One would wonder if Piaget's babies would have laughed as much in the examples he gives if they had not known *he* was there. One wonders also whether Mrs. Piaget played the usually complex games of tickling, turn taking in noise making, contests with hair pulling and fingers in mouths, choral rhythmic activity with jiggling and singing together, the cumulatively exciting games of "Peekaboo!" and "This Little Piggy," all of which are often the social inheritance in the homes of children of parents of advanced intellectual or economic status (Sutton-Smith, 1979). One even wonders if the circular reactions of the accommodative sort may not themselves even have been modeled by these complex interactions between mother and child. Certainly the secondary circular reactions in which the child at about 4 months notices an effect produced outside himself or herself (as in making the mobile rattle) have long been produced by the solicitous mother imitating the infant in the first 2 months of life. The infant with the high interactant mother has secondary circular reactions from her much earlier than they are recorded in the solitary behavior of Piaget's precocious infants.

In sum, it is difficult not to conclude that by considering exclusively the kind of play engaged in by babies when alone, Piaget has been predisposed to a view of play that is more suitable for the most solitary kind, namely reverie.

Culture as Played

If we follow Piaget's own principles of genetic epistemology, however, we might seek to illuminate the earlier states of play by an examination of the end state. In short, we might expect that the study of games or sports as played by adults (not adult logic) might tell us most about the meaning of infants' play. Even more appropriately, we might expect that an examination of the role of play cross-culturally would be illuminating.

Although there is certainly no consensus on what that meaning is (Schwartzman, 1979), there is considerable agreement that the play of adults does not stand outside their culture, but is functionally related to it. More collaborative cultures have more collaborative kinds of games, more competitive cultures have more competitive kinds of games. As cultures change, the domain of play seems to be one of the most open culture areas in which such changes first render themselves. As anthropologist Keesing (1960) says: "Recreation, by and large is a behavioral zone which is very much an open system. It is strongly marked by fictional premises, by elective variation, by novelty, by risk taking, by relative freedom from demanding goal orientations and strong sanctions. [p. 130]"

Not that one would for a moment want to oversimplify the very considerable diversity of usage being documented in current studies of play, particularly as expressed in the annual meetings of The Association for the Anthropological Study of Play (Lancy & Tindall, 1976; Salter, 1978; Stevens, 1977). In some cases the cultural play seems to be an inversion of the larger cultural system, a message as to the dangerous affective life that underlies it and that should not be tampered with if stability is to be maintained. At least this is how Geertz (1976) sees the Balinese cock fight, and how Turner (1976) describes much tribal ritual. However, in some interpretations, play is the mirror of cultural life rather than its inversion. In others the play area is the domain of instability and conflict, and in yet others it is in contrast, the domain or "communitas" and unity as compared with disequilibriums of war and economics. Clearly, the cultural relationships of play are variable, just as are the adult–child relationships about play. In some circumstances the play of children is deprecated and they are beaten if they play; in others they are not called adults until they give up play; in yet others play is encouraged. What we have in common is that the play enters always into some systemic pattern of social relationships and mythic beliefs. It does not stand aside as a nonentity and unimportant part of the cultural whole. It is for these reasons that some interpreters of culture see each cultural reality as a product of both ordinary affairs and play. Play is that interpretation of the total cultural structure that provides an underlying sense of its overall reality.

Given this kind of interpretation of Bateson and Geertz and others, then the child's play must in due course integrate the child into the larger cultural patterns of behavior and belief. It cannot only be a subordination of reality to personal wishes, although that may be one of its aspects—reverie—as we have seen. The social play of the child and even most of his solitary play must be instead a gradual integration of the child into the constructed reality of his larger culture. If reality is what the culture invents, as many now opine (Goffman, 1974), then play if it is successful is an integration of the player into the cultural reality, though perhaps in his own variant terms. It unites him into the system of interpretation that is that kind of cultural reality. It does this by reinforcing the kinds of framing that it approves, and by sustaining in one way or another those mechanisms of reversal, abstract stereotyping, theme and variation, and bound-arying, that we have discussed.

Perhaps Piaget has missed this kind of interpretation by assuming a too 19th-century dualism of what is real and what is not, and by ignoring the role of play in culture in his discussion of play in infancy.

Conclusion

We have said that Piaget makes an imbalance between play and imitation, between rational and imaginative thought, and between infant and adult play. On behalf of Piaget's views we have suggested that evidence from play therapy, from the animal literature, and from the exploratory literature could be advanced to suggest that play merely distorts cognitive activity but does not contribute to it in a substantive way. Further, it could be argued following Piaget that where play seems to have made a contribution to thought, this may actually have been a contribution arising from the social context within which the play took place. It was suggested finally that if we view Piaget's description of "pure assimilation" as a form of reverie alone, then there is very little to argue with in the case that he presents.

On the other hand, there are other research literatures that seem to imply that for some other kinds of play at least, more active constitutive relations might be found with thought and adaptation. In the animal literatures there seem to be relationships between play and flexibility. In the child literature there are rela-tionships between play and creativity, between play and language, between play and problem solving. In the anthropological literatures there are relationships between kinds of play and cultural world views. So we are ourselves prompted to a view of play that sees infant play in the light of adult play, which highlights the communicational character of play as a form of framing, the conative character of play as a form of reversal of ordinary cultural intentions, the affective charac-ter of play as a kind of modulation, and the cognitive character of play as focusing on the abstraction of prototypes, the permutation of themes and varia-tions, and the boundaring of space and time. We see play in these terms as a distinctive domain of knowledge with its own kind of structure and its own function—which is the management of reality through ludic techniques that all cultures seem to find indispensible to their sense of the life that is worth living.

But still in all fairness, when we say these latter things we have clearly switched epistemological premises on Piaget. His views have to do largely with solitary individuals and cognitive processes within the head. Despite a bow to the critical importance of social interchange in development, his work is within the individualistic philosophical and psychological tradition, perhaps within the real-istic and rationalist one. Most of the important criticisms advanced here, on the other hand, derive from the more sociological constructive tradition, in particular from communication theory. What has been said here, therefore, is not so much to critique Piaget for whom play was not, after all, a major concern, but to lay down a foundation for thinking about play more comprehensively. I would finish by reiterating my own personal debt to Piaget for making what had been for me a slightly cranky personal concern into one that I can now regard as of central importance to developmental psychology.

REFERENCES

Babcock, B. A. *The reversible world.* Ithaca, N.Y.: Cornell University Press, 1978.

Bateson, G. The message, 'This is play'. In B. Schaffner (Ed.), *Group processes: Transactions of the second conference.* Josiah Macy Foundation, 1956.

Bateson, G. *Steps to an ecology of mind.* New York: Ballantine, 1972.

Berlyne, D. E. *Conflict, arousal and curiosity.* New York: McGraw–Hill, 1960.

Bruner, J. S., Jolly, A., & Sylva, K. *Play: Its role in development and evolution.* Harmondsworth, Eng.: Penguin Books, 1976.

Chukovsky, K. *From two to five.* Berkeley, Calif.: University of California Press, 1966.

Csikszentmihalyi, M. *Beyond boredom and anxiety.* San Francisco: Jossey–Bass, 1975.

Csikszentmihalyi, M. The concept of flow. In B. Sutton-Smith (Ed.), *Play and learning.* New York: Gardner Press, 1979.

Dansky, J. L., & Silverman, I. W. Effects of play on associative fluency in preschool children. *Developmental Psychology, 1973, 9,* 38–43.

Dansky, J. L., & Silverman, I. W. Play: A general facilitator of associative fluency. *Developmental Psychology, 1975, 11,* 104.

deKoven, B. *The well-played game.* New York: Anchor, 1978.

Dolgin, K. G. *The importance of playing alone: Differences in manipulative play under social and solitary conditions.* Paper presented to the Association for the Anthropological Study of Play, Annual Meeting, Henniker, N.H., 1979.

Ellis, M. J. Functional complexity and activity levels. In B. Sutton-Smith (Ed.), *Play and learning.* New York: Gardner Press, 1979.

Fagan, R. M. Exercise, play and physical training in animals. In P. P. G. Bateson & P. H. Klopfer (Eds.), *Perspectives in ethology* (Vol. 2). New York: Plenum Press, 1976. (a)

Fagan, R. M. Modelling: How and why it works. In J. S. Bruner, A. Jolly, & K. Sylva (Eds.), *Play: Its role in development and evolution.* Harmondsworth, Eng.: Penguin, 1976. (b)

Fagan, R. M. Selection for optimal age: Dependent schedules of play behaviour. *American Naturalist, 1977, 111,* 395–414.

Fein, G. A transformational analysis of pretending. *Developmental Psychology, 1971, 4,* 203–210.

Fein, G. *Piaget, Vygotsky and the relationship between language and symbolic play: Echoes from the nursery.* Paper presented to the American Psychological Association, Toronto, Canada, 1978.

Fein, G. Play with actions and objects. In B. Sutton-Smith (Ed.), *Play and learning.* New York: Gardner Press, 1979.

Feitelson, D., & Ross, G. S. The neglected factor play. *Human Development, 1973, 16,* 202–223.

Fink, R. S. Role of imaginitive play in cognitive development. *Psychological Reports, 1976, 39,* 895–906.

Garvey, C. *Play.* Cambridge, Mass.: Harvard University Press, 1977.

Garvey, C. Communicative controls in social play. In B. Sutton-Smith (Ed.), *Play and learning.* New York: Gardner Press, 1979.

Geertz, C. Deep play: A description of the Balinese cockfight. In J. S. Bruner, A. Jolly, & K. Sylva (Eds.), *Play: Its role in development and evolution.* Harmondswoth, Eng.: Penguin, 1976.

Goffman, E. *Frame analysis.* Cambridge, Mass.: Harvard University Press, 1974.

Gomme, A. B. *Traditional games.* New York: Dover, 1964. (Originally published, 1894.)

Handelman, D. A note on play. *American Anthropologist,* 1974, *76,* 66–69.

Handelman, D. Play and ritual, complementary frames of communication. In Chapman & Foot (Eds.), *It's a funny thing.* London: Pergamon, 1977.

Hays, D., & Ross, H. First social games. In B. Sutton-Smith (Ed.), *Play and learning.* New York: Gardner Press, 1979.

Herron, R. E., & Sutton-Smith, B. (Eds.). *Child's play.* New York: Wiley, 1971.

Huizinga, J. *Homo ludens: A study of the play element in culture.* London: Routledge & Kegan Paul, 1949. (Originally published, 1944.)

Hutt, C. Exploration and play in children. In R. E. Herron & B. Sutton-Smith (Eds.), *Child's play.* New York: John Wiley and Sons, 1971.

Hutt, C. Exploration and play. In B. Sutton-Smith (Ed.), *Play and learning.* New York: Gardner Press, 1979.

Kavanaugh, R. D. *Relationships between cognition and language in infancy.* Paper presented to the Ninth Piaget Symposium, Phila., Pa., 1979.

Keesing, F. M. Recreative behavior and cultural change. In A. F. C. Wallace (Ed.), *Men and cultures.* Philadelphia, Pa.: University of Pennsylvania Press, 1960.

Lancy, D. F., & Tindall, B. A. *The anthropological study of play.* New York: Leisure Press, 1976.

Lehman, H. C., & Witty, P. A. *The psychology of play activities.* New York: Arno Press, 1976. (Originally published, 1927.)

Lieberman, J. N. Playfulness and divergent thinking: An investigation of their relationship at the kindergarten level. *Journal of Genetic Psychology,* 1965, *107,* 219–224.

Lieberman, J. N. *Playfulness.* New York: Academic Press, 1977.

Loizos, C. Play behaviour in higher primates: A review. In D. Morris (Ed.), *Primate ethology.* London: Weidenfeld and Nicholson, 1967.

Lovinger, S. L. Sociodramatic play and language development in pre-school disadvantaged children. *Psychology in the Schools,* 1974, *9,* 313–320.

Matthews, W. S. *Sex role perception, portrayal and preference in the fantasy play of young children.* Paper presented to the Society for Research in Child Development, New Orleans, La., 1977.

Miller, S. Ends, means and galumphing: Some leitmotifs of play. *American Anthropologist,* 1973, *75,* 87–98.

Nicolich, L. M. Beyond sensorimotor intelligence: Assessment of symbolic maturity through analysis of pretend play. *Merrill–Palmer Quarterly,* 1977, *23,* 89–99.

Piaget, J. *Play, dreams and imitation in childhood.* New York: W. W. Norton, 1962.

Reynolds, P. C. Play, language and human evolution. In J. S. Bruner, A. Jolly, & K. Sylva (Eds.), *Play: Its role in development and evolution.* Harmondsworth, Eng.: Penguin, 1976.

Rocissano, L. H. *Early play and its developing relation to language.* Unpublished doctoral dissertation, Columbia University, Teachers College, 1979.

Rosen, C. E. The effects of sociodramatic play on the problem solving behavior among culturally disadvantaged pre-school children. *Child Development,* 1974, *43,* 920–927.

Rubin, K., & Pepler, J. The relationship of child's play to social–cognitive growth and development. In H. Foot, J. Smith, & T. Chapman (Eds.), *Friendship and childhood relationships.* London: Wiley, in press.

Salter, M. *Play: Anthropological perspectives.* New York: Leisure Press, 1978.

Saltz, E., Dixon, D., & Johnson, J. Training disadvantaged preschoolers on various fantasy activities: Effects on cognitive functioning and impulse control. *Child Development,* 1977, *48,* 367–380.

Schwartzman, H. *Transformations: The anthropology of children's play.* New York: Plenum, 1978.

Schwartzman, H. The sociocultural context of play. In B. Sutton-Smith (Ed.), *Play and learning.* New York: Gardner Press, 1979.

Sherrod, L., & Singer, J. L. The development of make-believe play. In J. H. Goldstein (Ed.), *Sports, games and play.* Hillsdale, N.J.: Lawrence Erlbaum Associates, 1979.

Shultz, T. R. Play as arousal modulation. In B. Sutton-Smith (Ed.), *Play and learning.* New York: Gardner Press, 1979.

Singer, J. L. *The child's world of make believe.* New York: Academic Press, 1973.

Singer, J., & Singer, D. The character and training of imagination. In B. Sutton-Smith (Ed.), *Play and learning.* New York: Gardner Press, 1979.

Smilansky, S. *The effects of sociodramatic play on disadvantaged pre-school children.* New York: Wiley, 1968.

Smith, P. K., & Syddall, S. Play tutoring and non-play tutoring in pre-school groups. *Bulletin of the British Psychological Society, 1977, 31,* 74.

Stevens, P. *Studies in the anthropology of play.* New York: Leisure Press, 1977.

Stewart, S. *Nonsense: Aspects of intertextuality in folklore and literature.* Unpublished doctoral dissertation, University of Pennsylvania, 1979.

Suomi, S. J. *Social play in Rhesus monkeys.* Paper presented to the Center for Early Education and Development, Round Table Conference, University of Minnesota, May 1979.

Sutton-Smith, B. *The games of New Zealand children.* Berkeley, Calif.: University of California Press, 1959.

Sutton-Smith, B. Piaget on play: A critique. *Psychological Review, 1966, 73,* 111–112.

Sutton-Smith, B. The role of play in cognitive development. *Young Children, 1967, 6,* 361–370.

Sutton-Smith, B. Novel responses to toys. *Merrill–Palmer Quarterly, 1968, 14,* 151–158.

Sutton-Smith, B. *Die dialektik des spiele.* Schorndorf: Verlag Karl Hoffman, 1978. (a)

Sutton-Smith, B. Initial education as caricature. *Keystone Folklore, 1978, 22,* 37–52. (b)

Sutton-Smith, B. Play as metaperformance. In B. Sutton-Smith (Ed.), *Play and learning.* New York: Gardner Press, 1979.

Sutton-Smith, B. *The folkstores of children.* Philadelphia, Pa.: University of Pennsylvania Press, 1981.

Sutton-Smith, B. *A history of children's play.* Philadelphia, Pa.: University of Pennsylvania Press, 1982.

Sylva, K. Play and learning. In B. Tizard and D. Harvey (Eds.), *The biology of play.* London: SIMP/Heinemann, 1977.

Turner, V. W. *The forest of symbols.* Ithaca, N.Y.: Cornell University Press, 1967.

Turner, V. W. Liminal to liminoid, in play, flow and ritual: An essay in comparative symbology. *Rice University Studies, 1974, 60,* 53–92.

Vandenberg, B. *Play: Dormant issues and new directions.* Paper presented to the Center for Early Education and Development, Round Table Conference. University of Minnesota, May 1979.

Vygotsky, L. S. Play and its role in the mental development of the child. *Soviet Psychology, 1967, 5,* 6–18.

Weir, R. *Language in the crib.* The Hague: Mouton, 1962.

Youniss, J. Dialectical theory and Piaget in social knowledge. *Human Development, 1979, 21,* 234–237.

10 Sutton-Smith, Play, and Maybe Piaget

George Forman
University of Massachusetts at Amherst

Sutton-Smith has brought us forward since 1966 by making some interesting relations between current research and Piaget's theory of play. Of course, whether data strengthen or weaken a theory depends on one's interpretation of that theory. And we all know how difficult it is to interpret Piaget. Let me offer my interpretation of Piaget in reference to Sutton-Smith's main points, not to protect some form of Genevan orthodoxy, but rather to see how far outside this useful theory we really have to go to inform the new research.

As I understand Sutton-Smith's first point, he feels that Piaget has not given play a strong, constitutive role in adaptive cognition. Imitation serves the cutting edge in Piaget's theory. We are left with the feeling that play is distorting and subjective without a hint regarding the details of how play has positive value for directed and adaptive thought. We are given many more hints regarding the transformation of imitation into equilibrated thinking.

Upon rereading the relevant sections of *Play, Dreams, and Imitation* (Piaget, 1962), I also found the vagueness to which Sutton-Smith refers. The descriptions there of ''pure assimilation'' sound like an autistic perseveration, characteristic of infants and young children, eventually outgrown as egocentrism is shocked back into reality by the demands of an external perturbation. But somehow this picture of play did not fit my understanding of Piaget's constructivism, nor for that matter his general theory of equilibration. Play must have a constitutive role if the perturbation from outside is ever to be interpreted as a perturbation. The child needs the assimilatory schemes to compute the press of the external event. So, if play is primarily assimilation, then play should develop the assimilatory schemes to the point that they are capable of being shocked in the first place. In other words, *you gotta play around or you won't get shocked.*

Perhaps the problem here is a failure to recall that neither play nor imitation can be pure assimilation or pure accommodation, respectively. If we look at both play and imitation not as types of behavior, but rather as relative portions of assimilation and accommodation across a continuum, then the alleged imbalance between play and imitation disappears. Imitation and play are equally important for adaptive thought in Piaget's equilibration theory. Imitation is no more the cutting edge than is play. Each pulls the other back on task. Play pulls imitation away from a mindless empiricism and imitation pulls play away from an object-less idealism. Pure imitation would be just as dumb as pure assimilation.

Now what I have done here is expand the term *play* to include all those cases to the left of intelligence proper where assimilation predominates over accommodation. Although Sutton-Smith might accept this expansion, he still may feel that Piaget has not given us much detail regarding the transformation of assimilatory schemes into adaptive intelligence. But I think Piaget has begun to meet this criticism in his new works, particularly *The Development of Thought* (1977). Here is a quote from that book:

> Since assimilation and accommodation constitute two poles, and not two distinct behaviors, it is clear that the new assimilation plays the *constructive* role (extension of the scheme field, introduction of new articulations, etc.) and the new accommodation plays the *compensatory* role (new adjustments in reciprocity, inversions of the object's unforseen characteristics, etc.) [p. 39].

It is to Piaget's credit that he has endeavored in this book to spell out the details of the et cetera of constructive play and compensatory imitation.

Not all researchers accept this elegant balance between play and imitation, as Sutton-Smith points out by citing the work of Corinne Hutt. Hutt's work suggests that symbolic play is outside the scope of equilibration, that symbolic play is antithetical to learning. Unlike Sutton-Smith, I feel that this would be bad news to Piaget, not good news. But perhaps Hutt's work does not support this conclusion anyway. Hutt's work at most supports a more narrow conclusion, to wit, exploratory play contributes to learning the physical properties of an object, symbolic play does not. (Sutton-Smith also noted this difference). Yet this says nothing about the meaning of those physical properties. The child may learn nothing new about the toy itself when he or she treats it as a pretend truck, but he or she does integrate those properties learned into a scheme of personal meanings and interesting functions. To relegate this type of assimilation to the dark corners of nonlearning seems overly stringent. This is Sutton-Smith's point, but I propose that it is Piaget's point as well. Perhaps the disagreement hangs on the edge of the word "constitutive" as opposed to an illustrative or consolidatory role of play in cognition. I am not sure that these are useful distinctions, but then I would have to hear more about them.

To summarize my reaction to Brian's first point, the imbalance between imitation and play could not have been Piaget's intent if we are to take his constructivism seriously. However, within an empirical epistemology, where adaptive thought results from a corrected vision of external reality, it is reasonable to give imitation a superior role. But within a constructivistic epistemology something like play, that is distorting and subjective, can give rise to intelligent behavior. This brings us to Brian's second point, the alleged disjunction in Piaget's theory between undirected and directed thought.

Although play may be highly subjective and distorting, it is not at all undirected. It simply is directed within self. The assimilatory processes are self-regulated by laws endogenous to any organic system from the amoeba to Einstein. Although these processes, in a sense, do distort and deform the world qua world, they are essential to the construction of a reality that we can understand. Distortions of this variety are not entrophic, but move toward greater coherence. In other words, *the distortions clear things up.*

I find this thrust in the suggestions that Sutton-Smith made about the deep structure of play, the regulations, reframing, reversals, and abstractions. These are all operations that occur when assimilation is ascendant. The same thrust is found in Piaget's reflexive abstraction, construction of negations, and coordinations in his general equilibration theory and in recent work on assimilation strategies by Inhelder, Sinclair, and Karmiloff-Smith. Parenthetically I have some misgivings about Hutt's research approach. She has done some tidy work in separating the characteristics that distinguish exploratory play from symbolic play, but this taxonomic approach harks back to a psychometric approach to mental faculties. What we desperately need is an integration of these taxonomic elements into a dynamic scheme of interaction and transformation, a scheme to which Piaget's equilibration theory is committed.

The corollary point regarding the ostensible imbalance in Piaget's theory in favor of rational thought over imaginative thought can be answered in the same way. It has certainly been said that Piaget's "obsession" with Western science has biased him against the arts and more intuitive forms of thinking. But it is perhaps our own obsession with empirism that makes us split the rational from the intuitive mind. In a constructivistic epistemology, art and science are inextricable, and rationality takes a great deal of imagination. Useful constructions of reality depend on the internal regulations that we commonly call intuitions. There is a method to the madness of our subjective distortions of the world. So, by observing ourselves at play, we externalize and make opaque the constructive processes of our mind so that we might better understand the limits of our understanding. This awareness of self is most intelligent, though it depends on play.

My last several comments also address Brian's third point regarding the relevance or irrelevance of Piaget for the study of adult play. If one accepts the substitution of the word "reverie" for Piaget's term "play," then Brian is probably right. One would have to go outside of Piaget's theory to generate interesting questions for research in adult play. However, I think the term "reverie" is too dormant and nonconstructive for what I assume Piaget to mean by ascendant assimilation. The young adolescent, a debutant in formal operations, spinning off permutations of utopian societies, captures better what Piaget means by adult play, or at least it certainly qualifies as a point some distance to the left of adaptive thought proper.

In regard to the social context of play, I agree with Brian that Piaget gives short shrift to any fundamental difference between social objects and inanimate objects. Yet Piaget maintains that his interest in biological systems determines his lack of interest in cultures per se and the process of acquiring nonuniversal norms. And it's no fair criticizing a biologist for not being an anthropologist. But has Piaget ignored the uniqueness of the social object within Piaget's own enterprise of research on time, space, and causality? A ball can roll behind a chair, but mommie or daddy can pop up, smile, and synchronize intricate motions in tandem with the child. And only people walk through the child's visual field making a sequence of moves that the child can duplicate and extend. Of course the child can mock the tolling church bell, but what unique aspects of the Kantian concepts can children construct through their interactions with objects that not only can locomote, but also can jump, go boo, and tickle. Here is a productive area of research that Brian has rightly suggested we should pursue, an area that some of those who prepared chapters here have already begun. In general it was Sutton-Smith's review of the new uses of play research that I found most interesting.

REFERENCES

Piaget, J. *Play, Dreams, and Imitation*. New York: W. W. Norton & Company, 1962.
Piaget, J. *The Development of Thought, Equilibration of Cognitive Structures*. New York: The Viking Press, 1977.

Author Index

Numbers in *italics* indicate pages with complete bibliographic information.

Subject Index